LILY A

MW00584131

DIRTY
LAUNDRY

The crimes a country
tried to hide.

ISBN: 978-0-6455241-0-9 (Paperback)
          978-1-922532-79-4 (eBook)

 A catalogue record for this book is available from the National Library of Australia

Cover Design: Ocean Reeve Publishing
Design and Typeset: Ocean Reeve Publishing
Printed in Australia

Published by Lily Arthur www.lilyarthur.com

Dedications

Des, who held my hand while I walked through the dark shadows.
My mother, Lily McDonald, for her determination.
My father, Maurice McDonald, for his courage.

Acknowledgements

Inspired by:

Dian Wellfare, Linda Bryant, Elizabeth Edwards, Wendy Jacobs.

Grateful to:

Steve Benko, Senator Rachel Siewert, Senator Claire Moore, Dr Geoffrey Rickarby.

To those fearless mothers, fathers and adopted children who stood with us at Origins SPSA Inc and my Aboriginal 'family' with whom I shared a common cause for justice.

Disclaimer

This publication may contain references to Aboriginal people who may be deceased. Although this is a true and personal account of my journey, some of the names of the characters have been changed to protect their privacy. More information can be accessed on www.originsnsw.com.

About the Author

Born in the debris of a bombed-out East End of London, Lily McDonald was brought to Australia in 1959 by her parents, Maurice and Lily, looking for a brighter future. The 'promised land' brought nothing but failure for her father, Maurice, who returned to England and left his wife Lily and their nine children in a foreign country, penniless and alone.

The story follows the life of the author who, at eleven, became a state ward and was later forcibly incarcerated in a Magdalene laundry in Brisbane for the 'crime' of being pregnant.

Her firstborn was taken from her in the labour ward and adopted out, and she struggled for decades, longing for her lost child and the whereabouts of her son's father, Steve.

Her journey found her seeking and finding her lost child against impossible odds, reuniting with her lost love, and fighting to bring those who destroyed the lives of many women and their children to justice. In this time, she went from an ordinary housewife to a student, and then to become an activist through an organisation seeking the truth about a time in history; a history that saw an estimated 150,000 mothers lose their newborns to illegal adoption practices.

The book is over thirty years in writing and sees the author eventually find an 'ending' where there may never be one, or maybe the reader will.

This is one woman's story, and yet it is the story of many more.

Contents

Chapter 1

The voice of my psychiatrist is speaking slowly, softly, drifting, floating. He repeats, 'You are going down a long set of stairs, lower and lower and lower, slowly descending into the depths of darkness—one step, two steps; you are drifting back into the past. What do you see?'

'I see a little girl in a brown overcoat with a velvet collar,' a voice is saying. I then realise the voice is my own.

Slowly, I can see that girl descending the stairs—it is me. I am drifting again. Awake!

Why is a fifty-year-old regressing into the darkness of her past? What has driven me to seek hypnotherapy to find out long-lost memories of my youth?

My memory is clouded by a fog that has descended to block out all the earliest years of my life. I need to find answers to questions that have plagued me for decades.

I was born in Hackney, the East End of London on 19 March 1950, so one could say that I was a 'Cockney', something that makes me quite proud in a strange sort of a way.

My family history takes me back to the East End of London, where my mother's family settled. My great-grandfather many times removed, Solomon Solomons, originated from Russia, and his wife, Hinda, from Poland in the 1750s. That may have explained my mother's appearance. Short in stature, her dark brown hair framed her sharp facial features and olive skin. Her deep-set eyes and prominent nose certainly did not match the Celtic appearance of us children; all of us took after my father's side.

Looking back over the generations, the Solomons lived close to one another and, looking at the historical data, mostly married into their community.

My mother's name was also Lily. She was the daughter of a Jewish newsagent and, like her ancestors, the Solomons, she spent all her life in the east end of London.

Mum was eleven when she evacuated to Norfolk during the Second World War and spent four years with Mr and Mrs Fox, an old couple who were forced to take in children from the city to protect them from the severe bombing of the East End.

Her stories of being unwanted and forced to sit out in a barn in the cold until an evening meal was served before bed made us feel glad that at least we were with our own family.

Throughout her life, Mum was very superstitious and suspicious of anyone she met until she found out if they had any ulterior motives. Her eyes would narrow, and her fixed stare meant that if we pursued anything that annoyed her, we would 'cop it' with a clout across the ear, or she would tap us on the head. She was more frightening than my father in a much quieter way. We children learned at a young age never to cross knives or put up an umbrella under the roof. We threw salt over our shoulder if we spilled it.

My father, Maurice, was born and bred near Tipperary in Ireland, a good Catholic—when it suited him. In 1939, at the age of eighteen, he enlisted in the Royal Irish Rifles Regiment at the outbreak of the Second World War.

Still a boy, one could hardly imagine that at that tender age, he was sent to Italy, France, and North Africa to fight a war that was not his own.

God only knows what he saw in the line of battle; maybe that is why he was driven to drink.

The death of his older beloved brother Tom in Italy left scars in his mind that he could never erase. From what Dad told us children, he deserted his regiment and went to the frontline to see his brother shortly before he died; that episode cost Dad time in the army prison.

My father had been out of the army a short time when he met my mother; she was just seventeen, and he was twenty-seven. It was a quick relationship, and before long, they married in the local registry office in Hackney.

Maurice had a roguish look about him; taller than my mother by at least a foot, his curly brown hair and his broad Irish accent charmed not only my mother but the most rigid of nuns when he needed the contents of the poor box. It consisted mostly of pennies, but his charming ways were more of an incentive to keep in favour with the nuns, who were predominantly Irish.

To ensure the ongoing charity, we were sent to mass every Sunday at the church behind our Catholic school. This was not only to keep my grandmother happy but also to make sure we could fall on the grace of the church when times were hard.

I was one of seven children. My six siblings ranged from my older sister Janet (we called her Jenny) born in 1949—a year before me—followed by our only brother Tom in 1951, and then sisters Bridget, Kathleen, Maureen, and May, each born a year apart after we moved a short distance from Hackney to Russia Lane in Bethnal Green, in 1951.

My mother was very reserved in her affection for her children, not really showing us any sort of pride in our achievements that made us stand out from each other.

Dad, on the other hand, saw us more like his army of workers, getting us to do different jobs for him: any pulling and pushing while he was building houses or fixing his old car, chopping wood, digging gardens, and making us help our mother with the washing and shopping.

We were the ones to be sent out in the winter to look for wood when they couldn't find enough money for coal, scavenging around the bombed-out debris of buildings that still hadn't been cleared from the war.

When Dad was happy, we loved him, and he would do things for us, like taking us out to the movies each time Jeanette McDonald and Nelson Eddy appeared. We were brought up on classical and Irish music. If he thought we were good, he would give us a few pennies for sweets, but his personality could quickly change into a rage that saw us getting a hiding; we always knew when to be quiet or go and hide in the bedroom.

Childhood memories of me are pictured in my mind as a snotty-nosed kid in a weather-beaten overcoat, cold, and nearly always feeling the pinch of hunger in my belly.

We were poor—bloody poor—and that was all there was to it.

Our family lived on Russia Lane, in Quinn's Building, which was one of four blocks of flats that were built during Queen Victoria's time. Each building was depressingly grey and crowded. Our flat was above the Cabin, an off-licence that sold beer and sweets, amid a square of seven-storey high flats.

Our building was crowded with families forced to share with all and sundry: widows, large and small families, and those who hid behind closed doors. It was basically just a place to sleep, with two bedrooms, a small living room, and a kitchen. Places like this were for the people who could not afford better surroundings or were waiting for the council to provide them with another home. There were no modern conveniences, and the only time we had a bath was the rare occasions when we used to go to the local council baths for a decent wash.

Each landing had four flats accessed by a long foreboding concrete staircase that seemed to go straight up to heaven. The smell of cooking, dog and cat piss, along with the clatter and shouting, seemed to find its way to the top floor of the building. The old grey brick building even seemed to shake during the harsh thunderstorms that saw our mother hiding us in the coal cellar.

These were miserable surroundings still scarred by the debris of the bombed-out buildings of the Second World War. It was a depressing life for a poor mother who dragged her pram laden with kids up seven storeys to get to our flat.

My father was no help to her. He was too busy being the loveable Irish rogue who made friends with everyone he encountered.

Hearing him roaring at the top of his voice and singing his Irish songs in the square in the middle of the night was an indication of whether he was in a good mood or likely to fight with my mother after his night out at the pub, which was usually when he got his wages on a Friday night.

The neighbours throwing down empty bottles at him and telling him to shut up made him sing even louder, and to top it off, he woke us up to sing for him when he managed to climb the stairs.

Dire as it was, my memories of Russia Lane had always been a mixture of sad and happy ones. Although the happy ones were few, they take me back to a time where I was entrenched in my surroundings.

The 'Lane' was a few streets away from the Roman Road Markets, which were not as big as the Petticoat Lane Markets in nearby Spit-alfields, but it was the local market where I spent a lot of time just wandering amongst the stalls that sold everything from second-hand clothes to live chickens and eels.

I was fascinated watching the eels slithering around in the flat steel trays, twisting and wrapping themselves around each other and, with each purchase, the 'eel man' chopping off their head and tails and gutting them and cutting them into little pieces.

Christmases were magical. The chicken for our dinner hung on the back of the front door by its legs, still with its head-on, its glassy eyes watching us as we opened the door. Jellies were set on the windowsill, and custard was the treat for special occasions.

We older kids looked forward to the yearly Christmas party at our school: there was a lot of lovely food, much nicer than the daily meal we were given every day, and if we were really lucky, we were invited to the children's hospital party where we received a present. It was also a wonderful time to be around Auntie Masie and Auntie Josie, my father's sisters, who lived near my grandmother Bridget and often gave us a small present.

Altogether, we were quite a big family. We went to school with our cousins and afterwards played at their terrace houses that surrounded the 'square' where we lived. Their families were in a better financial situation than we were, so they received more toys, which gave us even more incentive to play with them.

I loved my father's youngest brother, Uncle Mike, who used to visit nearly every Friday night and give us a two-bob piece to buy some sweets. He was different from Dad—far gentler. His lovely red hair framed his round, happy face that always seemed to be smiling.

We never saw much of my mother's side of the family; she was ostracised by her Jewish family for marrying into 'outsiders'.

Her sister would quietly visit her and tell of the latest happenings of the family. It must have been very lonely for Mum hearing of her brothers and sisters getting married, having family events and not being invited. Still, we had Dad's family, and that was enough for us.

Grandmother Bridget, who I always called 'Nanny', lived in the next block of flats on the bottom floor. I saw her and my Auntie Florrie after school each day. We would sit on her bed, and she would tell me stories about her life as a child in Ireland and the places she had been. Auntie Florrie was my grandmother's second child. She had medical problems; I was never quite sure what they were, but Florrie lived with my grandmother and took care of her, a spinster who never married or had children.

A teapot was always on the stove, kept hot for the string of visitors that would visit Nanny every day.

Nanny was my hero: a real Irish woman with the remnants of her red hair, a rosy complexion, short and dumpy, and a fiery temper that went along with it, yet she was always good for a cuddle, something my mother never did for me.

Looking at photos of my grandmother, it was quite obvious where I came from. I looked like a younger version of her, graced with a long frock sitting between her brother Patrick and my grandfather John.

Nanny married Granddad John in the late 1800s at the age of sixteen, which was quite common for young Irish girls from Tipperary. He was in his thirties at the time and a soldier. He spent most of his time peacekeeping overseas. In those days, wives could accompany their husbands to far off places such as India.

A sepia photo told a lot of stories of a young girl from Thurles, Tipperary, and the adventure of being a military wife.

My path in life was to be revealed as similar as one could get to my grandmother's.

A hidden scandal in 1910 saw Nanny accused by her husband for the crime of 'immorality', and she was convicted at the Old Bailey. She spent twelve months in jail doing hard labour.

The result of her 'crime'—a scorned child of love—was to unknowingly visit me decades later.

Yet despite her colourful past, she commanded respect within her family, and none of her children would give her cheek, or there would be no one to borrow a shilling from if the coin-operated electricity meter shut off.

Although life in the square was hard, we all seemed to be happy. We knew nearly all the people who lived around us, and from a young age, I ran errands for all the people that lived in my block.

Ada, the old woman across the landing, would send me down to the off-licence. 'Ask for a pint-and-a-half of brown ale and three pence worth of nut-brown tobacco snuff,' she'd say. She always smelt of the snuff, and I thought it was no wonder that she was so small and bent over, her dirty grey hair covered in a dirty old scarf.

As soon as I brought back the small, rusted tin, she would take a pinch and sniff it, and then she would sneeze into a brown-stained rag pinned to her apron. Only then would she give me a penny, and I'd run off happily to the Cabin and buy myself a sweet.

Mr Green, in the landing below us, also used to get me to run to the shop on a Friday night for a packet of Murray Mints and a bottle of Tizer, a raspberry fizzy drink that tasted like creaming soda. His wife was dying in hospital, and he used to let me come into his flat and ride on his grown-up daughter's rocking horse.

I felt quite sorry for him even though I was only about eight years old because he would tell me that he was very lonely, and it would be nice if I sat on his lap, and he'd bounce me up and down. I didn't see much wrong with it, but my mother told me not to go to his flat again. I didn't realise till later what he was doing it for.

My best friend was an Irish girl by the name of Bridget Shields; she had the loveliest long red hair that hung down in long tight curls. I envied her beautiful hair—her mother would always plait it nicely with ribbons tied around it. My hair was a mousy brown and was always as straight as sticks.

We had a good friendship as far as kids' friendships go: her sister Katherine was my older sister Jenny's friend. I remember we used to get into all sorts of trouble. Even though we were quite young, we still didn't act it: too much responsibility at looking after the younger siblings made us grow up quite quickly.

Even as eight- and nine-year-olds, Jenny and I were wandering off to places without telling Mum and staying out late to play with our friends.

Best friend of all, my sister Jenny, was always there for me.

She was the personification of innocence and beauty, her lovely white skin surrounded by her curly black hair. Named after the beautiful film star Jeanette McDonald, her quiet and graceful nature never pushed her to stand out, and yet she did.

I remember the time we wagged school and went to visit the Tower of London. We didn't get home till late that night; my mother was panic-stricken. 'Where have you been?!' she screamed at us.

When we told her, she was horrified. 'How did you get there? You didn't have any money.' When we told her that we just hopped on a bus and it took us there and back without paying, she gave Jenny and me a good clout around the ears and told us, 'If you do that again, I'll murder you.' Needless to say, we didn't do it again.

I was considered a bit of a tomboy by my father's family. They warned my mother, 'That girl is going to give you what for; you better keep your eyes on her.'

A good little Catholic girl, I loved to sing in mass and got quite spiritual at the smell of incense, thinking that I was clever and brave and nothing was ever going to hurt me. God was going to look after me. I was always a little cheeky but knew when to be respectful.

Little did I know that life was going to teach me lessons that would never be forgotten. Hadn't my father instilled in us his famous last words every time he arrived home drunk? 'Don't bow down to any man: we are descended from kings.'

Of course, we believed every word he said—and why wouldn't we? Children of the slums had to have something to make them feel worthwhile.

I was nearly nine years old when my father came home and told my mother that he had met his cousin Jacky down the pub. Dad hadn't seen Jacky since he was arrested five years earlier and put into jail for breaking and entering. It seems that he and Dad had climbed over a fence when they were both drunk one night and were caught urinating at the back of a factory.

It appears that Jacky had suggested to the copper that they could 'do away with him and nobody would be any the wiser'. Dad spent three months in jail for that episode.

My mother had a hard time trying to feed the children she was left to look after, so Jacky's name was not the topic of polite conversation in our house. 'What did that bastard have to say?' Mum asked in her usual direct way.

Dad went on to tell her about Jacky getting a letter from Johanna, a distant cousin in Australia, who was writing to him to get someone in our family to go to Australia and work for her. It seemed that she had a large number of properties and had no family to help her look after the maintenance of it.

'What has this got to do with us?' Mum asked.

'Well, Jacky doesn't want to go to Australia,' replied Dad. 'I want you to write to her and tell her that we'll go over there. Send her a photo of the kids and tell her I'll work for her; we've got nothing to lose here.'

The letter and a photo were duly sent, and a reply came back from Johanna in a matter of weeks.

Having no children of her own, the photo must have impressed her, as a few weeks later she wrote saying that she was sponsoring us to go to Australia. The agreement was that Dad would work for her maintaining her many houses in Townsville, and we would rent one of them.

The letter arrived from Australia House, the high commission in London, telling Mum and Dad to go for an interview. I was taken along. I suppose it was to give the interviewer the idea that Mum and Dad had good-looking, strong children.

After the interview, the man said to my parents, 'You'll bring a lot to Australia; we need to have families like yours migrating.' Dad turned to him and told him that we were all looking forward to going to a place where we could have a new life with plenty of sunshine and food.

The next couple of months were spent dreaming and talking about the faraway country we were going to be living in. We carefully studied brochures of fruit-laden trees, beautiful beaches, and kangaroos, and the pictures almost became a reality.

Nanny was distraught at the prospect of us leaving her. 'Sure, you'll be going soon, and I'll never see you no more. Who's going to keep me company and sing to me?' she'd cry and blow her nose into her handkerchief.

'Don't worry, Nanny. I'll come back and visit you again.' She gave me a big hug, but I wasn't aware the distance between Bethnal Green and Townsville was a world apart and a six-week voyage on rough and calm seas.

The night before our departure was spent at Auntie Masie's house being scrubbed up in her bathtub. What a treat it was! She had put some bubble bath in the water, and the foam flowed over the tub onto the floor. We were all the centre of attention of our aunties and cousins. If this was what leaving was like, I wished we had left years before.

Just before my ninth birthday, two black cabs came the next day to take us to the train station. Our luggage consisted of three large tin trunks and a couple of suitcases. Not much for nine people to start a new life, looking at it from a grown-up perspective. Mum took some of the younger kids in one cab, and Dad took the rest with him. Nanny Mac, Florrie, and Uncle Mick and his family were there to say goodbye.

Tears flowed like rain as the cab took off down the street. I took one last look at the little group waving and weeping, never dreaming that it would be at least forty years before seeing some of them again.

We arrived at the rail station and caught a steam train down to the docks; this was as exciting as the prospect of the boat trip. The rolling green countryside flew past, each minute seeming like an hour. The clacking of the wheels seemed to say, 'When are we going to arrive? When are we going to arrive?'

We eventually did arrive at Tilbury Dock, and there she was, the SS *Orontes*, the biggest, bluest, and whitest, most beautiful ship I had ever seen—not that I had ever seen one before anyway.

We were then shown to our cabins, and because we had such a large family, we were given two. There were four bunks in each, and I remember Jenny had the top bunk, and I had the bottom.

As the ship moved away from the pier, people were waving and throwing streamers at each other, the last connecting ties breaking as we pulled away from the dock. With the groaning of the horn and the sudden lurch of the ship as the engines forced it away from the landing, relatives wept and waved to loved ones, and then we were gone.

We had no idea of the voyage that lay ahead of us and where we would be stopping. We felt the excitement of strange and wonderful things.

The first week of our six-week voyage was spent with me being sick regardless of the weather. We had gone through the Bay of Biscay, where the sea was very rough, tossing the boat as if it were inside a washing machine. This made me feel even sicker, although not as bad as poor Jenny, who fell out of the top bunk, badly hurting her head.

After the seas became calmer, we were caught up in all the children's activities on the ship. We would go to the children's playroom every day and do all sorts of wonderful things like playing games and dressing up; there were lots of toys to play with.

Two weeks into the voyage, some of the younger ones had picked up a dose of measles, and poor Mum had to go into quarantine with them, leaving Dad to have the time of his life. Jenny and I were told by Dad to look after the remaining kids. It wasn't hard as we were in the playroom for most of the time.

Like little adults, we went to the dining room for our dinner and could even order what we wanted from a menu: food such as melons and fruit and cakes we had never seen before—even the butter was curled up into little round balls!

We passed through the Suez Canal in Egypt and were fascinated by how long it took us. It was wonderful to see the pyramids as I had only seen them in books, and, brightened by the colour of the red and gold sand, they stood out, shining and beckoning us to come closer and climb them. There was a peaceful, surreal feeling as the ship slowly sailed through the narrow channel.

We were excited when Dad took us off the boat at the British colony of Aden (in what is now Yemen) for a walk through the town.

There were noisy, crowded bazaars with beggars lining the streets demanding coins; some of them had amputated limbs and scarred faces. We feared the strangeness around us and hung onto Dad for dear life, knowing that he would protect us; after all, he had spent five years after the war in Palestine and could speak Arabic.

The natives got a shock when they pestered us for money and my father told them to 'piss off' in their own language.

I had my ninth birthday on the boat, and Mum and Dad bought me a leather handbag with a camel on it in Port Said. It had a small mirror inside. To me, it was the best present I had ever been given.

The crew put on a party for all the children, and the ship's captain gave all those who had a birthday through the voyage a brooch of a ship's steering wheel. I felt particularly important when my name was called out, and the captain shook my hand as he gave it to me.

We disembarked again in Colombo, Sri Lanka, and Dad took us into town. While we were there, he had his tattoo coloured. It was fascinating to watch. The men in the tattoo stall gave us a sweet fizzy drink—a taste so strange I have never tasted another drink like it since.

By the time we arrived at Fremantle on 31 March 1959, we were well and truly getting sick of the ship.

On arrival in Sydney, we had been on the ship for nearly six weeks. The passengers on the ship were changing their English money into Australian, and because of Dad's good time on the ship, we didn't have any money to change. That was our welcome to Australia—flat broke, not even enough money to buy a cold drink to ease our thirst upon our arrival at Sydney's Central railway station, where we waited hours for the train to Brisbane.

Fortunately, our train fares had been paid for. It was a long journey, and I don't think any of us had any idea of how far we were going to be travelling. All we wanted to do was stop. The upright seats in the old train meant we had to sit up all night. By the time we arrived in Brisbane, we were all well and truly fatigued.

Aunt Johanna was waiting for us at Brisbane's Central Station. Seeing her in person was a greater surprise than seeing her in the photo we were sent of her and her mother.

She was a commanding woman—tall and large-framed—and her black skin and tight curly hair gave the impression that she was a woman to be respected.

Dad lined us all up, introducing us one at a time: first Jenny, then me, followed by Tommy, Bridget, Kathleen, Maureen, and baby May. Each of us went up one at a time to kiss her and shake her hand.

We were taken to an old army hostel at the inner-city suburb of Kangaroo Point, where we stayed for two weeks until leaving for Townsville. I liked the hostel, even though we had to sleep in long, round, galvanised iron sheds. There was an element of fun—it was almost like camping out.

Back on the train again, and another long, tiring journey, but at least this held the promise of being the last trip, and a home—our home—would be waiting for us at the other end.

The further north we travelled, the more the landscape changed from bush to flat plains—to large plantations of sugarcane, dry rivers, and burnt bushland. This country was certainly a far cry from Russia Lane and the narrow streets of East London.

We arrived in Townsville, and Johanna took us to the house that she had prepared. It was in Wills Street, a couple of streets back from Flinders Street, Townsville's main street. It was a pleasant little white weatherboard house with a tin roof, furnished with an old but serviceable lounge and beds, and the thing that intrigued us most was that each bed had a mesh net tent over it. We could not wait to go to bed that night, having no idea it was there to protect us from the scourge of mosquitos.

It was great living in Wills Street. We had a large backyard and were only a short walk to the beach. Jenny, Tommy, Bridget, and I were enrolled in St Joseph's Catholic school, which was across the street from the beach, and each lunchtime, we were allowed to go for a walk along the sand. The coconut trees, with their large fruits that were too far for us to reach, tempting us. The kids from Bethnal Green had made it to paradise!

We had been living in Wills Street for a few months when Dad proclaimed that he had bought a five-acre block of land just north of Townsville at a place called Black River. The land was used as an old American hospital base during the Second World War and was covered with concrete slabs, which would make it hard, if not impossible, to grow anything useful. God knows what he was going to do with it, but it was cheap.

Dad bought an old house in town, and the idea was to move the house in one piece on the back of a low-loader out to the land and plant it fully erect on a slab so we could just walk into it that night.

The morning of the big move came and Dad went off early to get the house out of town before people started to go to work. Mum and us kids waited and waited and waited.

It must have been somewhere toward ten at night when my father burst in through the door drunk as a lord. 'What the bloody hell have you been up to?' Mum cried. 'I've been waiting here all day packed and ready to go!'

'Shut up!' Dad yelled. 'I've fucking had enough for one day. I had to dismantle the fucking house on the side of the fucking road, 'cos a fucking copper pulled us up for not having a licence to move the fucking thing.'

Mum didn't know what to say. 'What the hell are you talking about?'

Her exasperation at my father's drunken state did little to calm Dad down. 'The fucking house is lying on the side of the road in pieces,' he repeated. 'I'm going to bed.' He staggered into his room.

The next day the story became more understandable; the house had to be dismantled, and Dad and the man he bought it off had to rebuild it again.

Our move out to Black River was postponed for another few weeks while the house was being rebuilt.

All packed up again, and we were assured by Dad that the house was ready to be moved into. Laden with boxes of chicks and baby ducks, we made the long trip in the back of Dad's small utility truck. On approaching the house, all we could see was a square wooden building with an open gap a foot high between the slab and the bottom of the walls; we could see through one side of the house to the other.

This was not what the house looked like when it was bought.

The inside was as bad as the outside. One large room with no interior lining, with two double brass beds he had picked up from the rubbish dump, and an old wood-burning stove standing in the corner.

We children thought it was great. The idea of living in the bush really sounded like fun. We saw wild horses on the way up to the house from the road. This was the sort of thing that the brochures showed: horses, kangaroos, and koala bears. We were going to have the lot.

That night and all through the next day, it rained non-stop, so Dad couldn't work on the house. We were all stuck inside swapping buckets and saucepans around while the holes in the tin roof leaked. It must have been in the middle of the night when Dad awoke us. 'Quick lads, get out of bed. The house is flooding!' Dad would refer to all of us children as 'lads'. I don't know why—I guess it was easier for him to speak to all of us at the same time instead of trying to remember who he was ordering about.

Hastily we jumped up and found ourselves up to our knees in water. 'Dad! Dad!' we were screaming as we tried to hang on to him to save us.

In the light of the kerosene lamps, I could see a couple of our little ducklings managing to float around amongst the chaos.

Tommy and I grabbed them, and Mum and Dad grabbed the younger children, and we waded through the water up the paddock to the next-door neighbour's house.

They were surprised to see a bedraggled flock knocking on their door in the middle of the night. We were taken in and dried off in front of their wooden stove, ducklings and all.

The next day, after the water subsided, we went home to inspect the damage. The beds were all wet, and our clothes were all lying around inside and outside of the house. 'What a bloody mess,' said Mum. 'You kids get out in the yard and find what you can.' Out we went, to look for anything the flood left behind: a shoe here, a dress there, and when we found the dead bodies of our little chicks, we all started to cry.

'Don't worry; we'll buy some more,' Mum said. 'Anyway, you've got two little ducks to look after in the meantime. What are you going to call them?'

We decided on Mary and Donald. By the time Mary and Donald had grown into a duck and drake, we had happily settled into the house in Black River. Dad had made the house more presentable, and the bits and pieces that were either picked up from the rubbish dump or donated to us made us feel quite proud of our bush 'ranch'.

The eerie Min Min lights, fast-moving balls of light that glow in the night sky, told us we were living in a very enchanted place.

*

The first north Queensland summer we endured tested us. Jenny had broken out all over in blisters and boils, and Mum and Tommy were suffering from tropical ulcers. The mosquitoes at night were enough to carry us away. No amount of mosquito spray seemed to give us a decent night's sleep. Little did we know that the spray we were pumping out from the old tin can was to be banned later due to its toxicity and also being a probable carcinogen.

A man Dad befriended from a nearby property told him to gather up dried cow's dung and burn it; from then on, the mosquitoes didn't stand a chance.

The house had no running water and no water tanks. Saturdays were spent down at the riverbank, where us kids, forming a relay, bucketed water up to Dad, who would pour it into forty-four-gallon drums on the back of his utility for us to use through the week.

He decided that this exercise every Saturday was giving him 'the shits', so after a drunken night out with the neighbours debating the positive results of water divining, he decided that he would look for water using a bent coat-hanger and then sink a well.

The coat-hanger performed well, and Dad decided that water lay only a few feet down not far from the house. Day after day, he dug the well, and when he had dug to a depth of about eight feet, he decided that instead of continuing to keep expanding the six-foot-wide well, he would use a post-hole digger to go deeper.

One ten-foot length after another, and he had reached his limit. 'I'm going to buy some dynamite and blow the bloody thing up,' he roared with frustration. The dynamite was bought and the expected 'blowing up' was to be performed on the weekend. Mum and all of us kids went as far away into the scrub as possible.

We waited, and waited, and waited for the big bang and still nothing. A couple of hours had passed, and the scorching heat of the sun was making the smaller ones cry non-stop for a drink, so

Mum told us to wait while she went to see what was happening. A few minutes later, she called out for us to come home.

It seemed that the fuse to the dynamite was not the kind to light with a match, and Dad was trying every way he could to light it but with no success.

'Stupid bastard,' Mum said. 'We've been sitting out in that bloody heat for hours. We're going to have to buy a water tank instead of going through all that bloody trouble again.'

A few weeks later, a second-hand water tank was purchased from a neighbour; all it needed to do was to rain.

A year later, the electricity poles were finally going past our property and we were connected to power. What an event: you'd thought that we had won a million quid!

A stove, a fridge, and—best of all—an electric wireless were bought. No more worrying about running out of batteries for our old radio to hear our favourite programs—we could have *Tarzan* and *Jet Jackson* every night!

Mum had given birth to her eighth child about this time—another girl who was duly named Colleen, our first little Australian with an Irish name.

Dad was starting to hate working for Johanna and decided that he was not going to take orders from her anymore. 'I'm going to get meself a decent job,' he said in his Irish brogue, and after looking around for a while, he found himself a job in a factory in Townsville making cupboards.

With the dreams of having our farm with animals and such, Dad decided to buy a couple of goats. He thought that they would mate, and we could end up having a goat farm.

Each afternoon, Tommy and I had to round up the goats and tie them to a tree so they would not run off into the bush at night.

As soon as they saw us coming, they would take off at top speed and we would chase them until they finally got caught up in the Chinese apple bushes, which were growing all over the land. Dragging them out by the horns with the sharp spikes of the bushes tearing our arms to pieces, we cursed the day that Dad had brought them home.

Cash-strapped, Dad sold the billy goat to a couple of fellows who were working with him at the factory. The two men were sold on Dad's glowing description of how great goat's meat tasted. He cut the throat of the billy goat and had it hanging from a tree while he was skinning and gutting it.

Bluey, our new cattle dog, was sitting and watching the proceedings. As the goat's intestines spilled out of the slit in the middle of its stomach, Dad cut off the gall bladder and said to the men, 'Sure, this is the best part of the animal; if you give it to dogs, it's just like giving them medicine.' Before we knew it, Dad had tossed the thing to the waiting dog, who snapped it up in mid-air.

A couple of minutes later, Bluey let out an almighty howl and started to foam at the mouth. He started to run around and around the outside of the house and then took off like a greyhound in a straight line through the bush. We never saw him again. We were devastated and lived in hope that he would return.

Dad had thrown in the job at the factory and refused to ask Johanna to take him back again to work for her, so things were starting to get desperate. The animals were killed off to feed us.

First went the nanny goat, then her two kids, then the chickens, and then Donald.

The final upset came when we returned home from school one afternoon and asked Mum what we were going to eat for tea, and she answered that we were going to have duck. 'Not Mary!' my brother cried.

This was the end. Our poor duck that had managed to struggle around all her life with a limp from the night of the storm was gone. None of us kids ate tea that night—how could we eat our favourite pet?

As the months passed, it became apparent that the farm at Black River was not going to be the pot of gold at the end of the rainbow. Dad was on the dole by then, and things seemed to be a little better. At least there was the promise of food on the table each night.

The unforgiving heat of the North Queensland summer was ruthless with the younger children's health and did little for Mum and Tommy's tropical ulcers, which were close to the point of gangrene. No doctors were nearby to help, so it had to be treated on a neighbour's advice.

Mum and Dad had saved up a few pounds and decided that they would sell the house and take their chances in Brisbane. Dad planned for us to drive down to Brisbane in the little utility.

He built a wooden canopy frame on the back of the utility and covered it with canvas. Standing back admiring his work, he boasted that it would hold up to 'Noah's Flood'. The truck was packed with eight children, two adults, a tent, a couple of water drums, and whatever clothes we could carry. As the little truck slowly crept out of the driveway, we said goodbye to our little bush ranch.

As we slowly passed the bottle trees and scrub, we sang all the songs that we had sung so many times when awoken by Dad in the middle of the night.

We told each other stories and jokes to take the monotony out of the never-ending miles of lonely road we had travelled for over a week.

It was just a couple of days before Christmas, and the prospect of getting any presents was a long way off. Each night, Dad would put up the tent and we would build a fire, and Mum would try to prepare what she could from the tinned food that we were carrying.

We had camped for the fifth night on the banks of a large river when it started to rain. We were huddled together in the old tent wrapped under blankets when the middle roof of the tent started to groan under the weight of the water and started to drip all over us.

'Come on, lads, get the things packed up; we're going to get moving before the river floods,' Dad yelled.

We quickly threw all we could into the back of the truck and took off to the next town and shelter. We sat in the back of the utility, wet and miserable. The canvas canopy was sagging under the weight of the water and leaked uncontrollably. Each time the canvas bulged down with water, we would push it back up to empty the water out of it.

We drove all through the night into the rain and arrived at Sarina, a rural town near the east coast, south of Mackay. Dad pulled into a caravan park and rented a caravan so we could dry ourselves and our things out for a few days.

After a few days in Sarina, we were back on the road again. We were driving along in the middle of nowhere when the engine of the old truck started to boil. Dad filled it up with water and tried to start it, but with no luck; the old ute had died. We waved down a passing truckie who offered to tow us to the nearest town, about twenty miles down the road.

After inspection of the engine, Dad was told that the truck had a cracked head and that it would cost more money to fix than we had. After explaining to the mechanic our predicament, he agreed to settle for less, provided Dad helped him with the repairs.

The truck was ready to go, and we were off again on the long trek to Brisbane.

We were just approaching Brisbane when the truck ran out of petrol, and there was no money to buy any more. Dad haggled with the owner of a garage, who agreed to give us a tank of petrol using Mum's wedding ring as security until Dad could pay him back.

As we drove into the outskirts of the city, Dad yelled to us, 'Keep an eye out for a church, lads.' This was one of the times he resorted back to being a good Catholic.

'There's one, Dad!' we all yelled in unison. We sat in the truck while Dad went to ask the priest if there was somewhere where we could stay the night or if he could give us a few bobs to buy some food, and we could camp somewhere in a park.

As luck would have it, the man who lived next door to the church had just built a new house, and his old house next door was vacant. He said that we could stay in it rent-free until we found a place to stay and Dad had found a job. That night we all kneeled and thanked God for looking after us and giving us a miracle.

It only took Dad a couple of days to find a job, so the mood of the family was happy; we had a place to live, Dad had a job, and we were enrolled to attend a school up the road.

Things were getting back to normal again. A few weeks later, Dad came home and told us that he had put a deposit on a block of land at a place called Rochedale. It was mostly scrubland with a few houses a few miles from where we were staying.

'What sort of a block of land?' Mum demanded to know.

'Sure, it's a fine piece of land, five acres with a creek and a lot of trees to build with,' Dad replied, satisfied with his purchase.

'I'm sick to fucking death of living in the scrub. I want a decent house to live in with all these bloody kids.' Mum's frustration was showing at Dad's pipedreams of owning his own dream farm.

'Don't worry, I'll build you a house, and it'll be a bloody good one,' replied Dad.

'We'll see,' replied Mum scornfully.

Dad worked through the week in a factory, and on the weekends, he and Tommy would go out to the land and work on the house. 'We're moving in next weekend,' said Dad. 'I want to get away from here as soon as possible. I hate that old man next door wanting to know all of our business.' Again, the truck was packed, we thanked Mr Hickey for the use of his house, and we were off to our new home.

I was eleven, and again we had to leave our school. This was the fifth school we attended since our arrival—we had only started to get settled when it was time to move on. The disruption to my education was to be noticed later. The move to Australia and the first school I attended held me back two classes, so I was always the oldest child in the class.

As we passed our future school—a state school in Rochedale and a far cry from the Catholic schools we had attended—a sort of sigh of relief passed over me. *At least we won't be saying prayers every hour or forced to attend mass.*

Still excited at the prospect of a new home, we drove for about five miles up a dirt road. Out in the middle of nowhere, Dad stopped the truck and said, 'Well lads, we're here.'

He went ahead of us, scrambling through the scrub until we reached a small clearing and there it was: a ten-by-ten-foot tin shed with three walls and a large piece of hessian masquerading as a door.

We were stunned into silence, looking at the miserable shed that was to be our home. I felt like crying.

The inside was as bad as the outside: one large bed comprising of two long tree trunks and two sets of double bed springs thrown on top, an old wood stove in the corner, with an old table finishing off the setting on the dirt floor. That night the mosquitoes again had a feast on us; there was no way of keeping them out.

So, this is the promised land, I thought. *Give me back Russia Lane, my friends, and television any day.*

Rochedale was a nightmare, and to make things worse, the truck broke down and refused to start again, and after each long school day and the long walk home, Dad would get us out to push the truck up and down the small hill on the road to try to get it started. Hot, dry afternoons were spent pushing the dead piece of machinery while Dad would sit in the cabin yelling, 'Push lads! Push!' He eventually gave up trying to resurrect the old ute and bought an old motorbike with a sidecar to get around in.

Each day, we five older children would climb on the old bike— three in the sidecar, one on the back, and one on the petrol tank—

and Dad would give us a ride to school, much to the amusement of the other pupils making fun of us on our arrival.

Weekends were spent building a bigger house further up the hill. Dad had again thrown in his job and worked from morning till night chopping down trees and scrub with just an axe.

The small amount of dole money was spent buying food, and whatever was needed for the building of the new house and, once again, the rubbish tip came in handy for building materials.

Mum was pregnant again with her ninth child and the hard work of dragging water from the creek for washing and drinking was shared by the older children.

Each afternoon we would go down to the small creek and swish the green slime off the water and quickly dip the buckets in to gather up the water before the slime flowed back into the buckets. We would carry them up the hill and fill up the concrete laundry tubs so that Mum could wash our clothes by hand each day.

After realising that we could access more help from our Catholic background, we were eventually moved from the state school at Rochedale and into St Barnard's Catholic School at Mt Gravatt. Dad knew that we would be able to access the mercy of the church when things got tough; a good Irish Catholic was always worthy of a helping hand.

Dad was unemployed, and we were hungry; the nuns at our school were starting to become concerned about our welfare. Dad had approached them a few times for food and the contents of the poor box. Word of this seemed somehow to get around the school, and we were always being pointed out and ridiculed as the 'poor McDonalds'.

The nuns seemed to make the situation worse by making us go to the convent each day to get soup for our lunch.

'What sort of soup did you get today?'

'Are you wearing my old uniform?'

'Is that my old hat?' the kids would scornfully ask. Tommy would get angry and take a swipe at the hecklers, and then he would get into trouble for fighting.

Jenny and I quickly made friends with two sisters: Ursula and her sister Thea. They had a Polish background and, from what we were told, they were not happy in their home, either.

The word of our situation was eventually passed onto the Department of Children's Services, and they sent a welfare officer, Mr Howard, out to the property to inspect our living conditions. As soon as Mr Howard saw how we were living, he told my father that if he did not move us out of that house and into a housing commission house he had arranged for us, he would take all of us into care. We had to move within the week.

Although Mum was glad to accept Mr Howard's offer of a nice house in town, Dad was hostile to the idea. 'I'm not moving off my land,' he declared.

A few days later, a removal truck took our few possessions to Mt Gravatt five miles away and deposited our things at the pale blue weatherboard cottage on the higher side of the street. It looked lovely, and a hedge with flowers at the front made it look very much like a home.

Mum was over the moon that this was going to be our home. It had three bedrooms, a real bathroom, and a large yard for us to play in. The house was not far from our school, so from then on, we could walk to school instead of turning up on Dad's old motorbike.

It was a week before Dad decided that he either had to move into the house or stay out at Rochedale on his own. He turned up at the door with his carry bag and a few clothes and a defeated look on his face. All of us were a bit disappointed at his arrival as we had enjoyed a week of not being yelled at or having to work.

Dad found a job in a factory and things were starting to pick up again. We even became financially stable enough to rent a television set. It was the start of happier days and the promise of a new life to come—or so we thought.

Although we children were happy with our surroundings, Dad was not. He would disappear after he got paid on a Friday, and we would not see him until he showed up on either a Sunday or the police would turn up at the door and tell Mum he was locked up in one of their cells.

Mum was ready to give birth to her ninth child by then, and to make sure that Dad did not spend his wages getting drunk, she would walk the few miles to the factory to meet him and collect his pay. One Friday, he got his pay early and skipped out before Mum arrived.

She was livid by the time she arrived home and told us that, 'If that bastard spent all his pay on booze this time, I'm going to throw him out.'

He arrived home the following Sunday night, a couple of packets of tea under his arm, singing out, 'Come on lads, get up and have a sing-song.' He pulled out his treasured harmonica and commenced playing one of his Irish tunes.

While Mum was yelling to us to get back to bed, Dad was dancing around in a drunken state in the living room. There was a lot of yelling and then the sounds of silence. The next thing we heard was the squeaking of the old brass bed in their bedroom.

'So much for getting rid of him,' Jenny said.

It was then that a plan to run away was hatched. Tommy did not want to be in on it, so it was down to Jenny, me, and Bridget. The following weeks were spent preparing for the night when we would run away and catch a tram to Sydney, nine hundred miles away.

We planned our escape down to the last detail. We had a tent, tins of food, blankets, and our friends Ursula and Thea had stolen money for the great escape. The night of the great escape had come, and we climbed out of the bedroom window after Mum and Dad had gone to sleep.

Running down the road to the partly built house where we had hidden our supplies, I sensed a real feeling of freedom: we were escaping all the unhappy times, and most of all, we were going to Sydney for a better life.

We met up with our friends and then caught a tram to the other side of the city. The conductor kept asking us where we were heading off to. 'We're off to visit our Auntie Mary in Sydney,' we said.

'Well, this tram only goes to the terminus,' the conductor replied.

'What tram do we have to take to go to Sydney then?' I asked.

'You can't get a tram to Sydney; you can only go by train.'

It never occurred to us that roaming around in the middle of the night at the age of eleven would attract attention. I was sitting across the aisle from a young couple who started a conversation with me. They were worried that I was too young to be out at that time of night. After they spoke to me for a while about the worry that my parents would have if they woke up and found me gone, I agreed to accept a lift home with them.

Jenny, Bridget, and our friends stayed on the tram, but I took the coward's way out and went home. I knocked on the window, and Tommy helped pull me back into the house. 'Where are the others?' he asked.

'I don't know; they stayed on the tram,' I replied.

'Bloody hell, they'll be in for it when Dad gets a hold of them.'

'Jesus, I better get back into bed,' I whispered as I headed for the door. I crept back to bed and drifted into a nervous half-sleep, expecting a knock on the window. Worse still, there was a loud pounding on the door. It was the police.

I was pulled out of bed by Dad. He had a tight hold on the top of my arm and was squeezing it for all it was worth.

'Were you in on this?' he asked.

'Yes, Dad,' I replied feebly. After some discussion with the police, we were sent to bed, and the policeman said that he would return the next day with Children's Services to investigate why we had run away.

After the police left, Dad dragged Janet, Bridget, and me out of bed and clouted each of us around the head. 'I'll fucking give you running away!' he yelled. 'When those bastards come tomorrow, you tell them that you did it out of devilment, or you'll have me to deal with,' he threatened.

'Yes, Dad,' we answered, cowering. We knew what Dad was like if he got angry with us, and boy, was he furious. The deadly look in his eyes told us that he meant every word he said.

Mr Howard arrived the next day with the police and questioned us. We said exactly what we were told to say—that we had run away because we wanted to, and no, Dad did not hit us or anything else.

Mr Howard was not entirely convinced and told Dad that they would have to regularly come and see how things were going with us from then on. That made both parents angry at us and we wished that we had not been so bloody stupid. We were going to be 'in for it' all the time instead of now and then.

This was the end of Australia as far as Dad was concerned; no one was going to keep checking up on him to see how he was bringing up his family. It was then decided that he was going to work non-stop and save up the fares for us to return to England.

True to his word, he worked all the overtime he could get, and Mum saved as much as she could.

She had given birth to another daughter named Frances, which then made us eight girls and one boy.

Dad had given up hoping for another son and saw the arrival of the newborn as another ticket to find the money for. How was he expected to save up the fares for eleven people to return home?

Three months after the birth of the baby, Dad came home late one afternoon and announced to all of us that he had bought his ticket on a boat that was leaving the next week for England.

Mum was stunned. 'What the bloody hell do you think we are going to do? How are we going to live? On fresh air?'

'Sure, I'll be saving me money up over there, and me mam will help. It will only take a couple of years at the most to save up enough money to bring you home.'

'Yeah, I bet it will; as soon as you get back with your old mob again, you'll drink all your money and forget all about us,' Mum said, knowing full well that she had lost any argument before it began. When Dad made up his mind, there would be no stopping him.

We could not believe our luck; he was finally going. There would be peace at last. The week could not go quickly enough for us.

He arranged for a photographer to come and take a photo of all of us so that he could have something to remember us. The nine of us smiling like statues and yet disguising our glee knowing that we would not be seeing him for a long time to come.

The day he was leaving, he gave us all a kiss before we left for school and told us to be good for our mother. We rushed home from school that afternoon to see Mum sitting in the living room crying.

'Is Dad gone?' I asked.

'Yes,' she answered, wiping her eyes, trying to look brave.

It was 1962. Just over two years after our arrival to the 'promised land', our father had returned home, leaving our mother and nine children under the age of twelve with no family, no friends, and no money.

We were alone.

Chapter 2

Dad had only been gone a couple of days when we had Mum's English friends, the Bakers, staying with us for the night.

They were doing what was called a 'moonlight flit', selling all their possessions that were on hire purchase and absconding back to England with the proceeds of the sale.

They were leaving for England that week, and on the day of their departure, we awoke to find out that Mum had been admitted to hospital during the night.

'We're sorry we can't stay to look after you,' Mrs Baker apologised. 'I'm sure your Mum will be okay.'

'Don't worry about us. We've looked after the kids before,' Jenny said, reassuring her that we were quite capable. The Bakers left us that afternoon.

'What if Mum dies? We'll be stuck here on our own,' Tommy cried.

Fear took hold of all of us. 'Let's say some prayers for Mum to be okay,' Jenny announced. We all kneeled and prayed for our mother to get well and come home soon to us.

Mum was in the hospital for a week; she had another miscarriage. Jenny went up to the hospital each night, and Mum gave her a little money to buy food each day.

There was no one to turn to, and each day Jenny and I took turns minding the younger children while the others went to school.

No one, not even the nuns, had any idea that nine young children were looking after themselves.

Mum came home to an empty food cupboard and nine hungry children.

Her first chore was to go to the Brisbane City Mission and ask for a food voucher. Her next move was to find a job. A couple of weeks later, she started work in a smallgoods factory and was able to bring home sausages and packets of bacon.

Most of her work was at night, so Jenny and I could look after the younger kids instead of having to take too much time off school during the day.

Mum was able to work for a couple of months, but the strain was too much for her, so she went to Children's Services and put her name down for welfare payments.

The visit to the welfare department resulted in Mr Howard coming back to see us again, and he suggested that we would be better off taken into care. Mum was angry and told him that we did not come from England for her children to end up in a children's home.

He relented and said that we were too nice to end up in such an unhappy situation, so to ensure that we were looked after, we were going to be made wards of the state.

The first thing I noticed about being made a state ward was that we were given a whole new standing in school.

Our raggedy school uniforms were exchanged for new ones, and textbooks and stationery were given to us freely.

The poor McDonalds had risen to a new level of acceptance. The whole school seemed to notice that I had a brand-new pair of shoes, and no more were we intimidated in front of the class for not paying our school fees.

Every second week, Mum would go to the Brisbane City Mission and buy us clothes. Of course, they may have been 'cast-offs' from those better off than us, but they were usually quite good, and we waited eagerly to see what 'treasures' she brought home to us.

Christmas 1961—our first one without our father—was an exciting event, with a box of second-hand toys delivered to us, gift wrapped and all. Even hiding them up the top of the linen cupboard did not stop us from climbing up to take a sneaky look at the loot.

Yes, the world was a new place for us once Dad had gone. Cliff Richard was singing 'Summer Holiday' and Jenny's deepest wish—and mine—was to go and see his film at the Princess Theatre.

Mum couldn't afford to let us go to the pictures, so it was off to try to find enough soft drink bottles to claim the refund.

We walked for miles looking around the parks, the lover's lane lookout at the top of Mt Gravatt and, believe it or not, the cemetery. We managed to collect enough bottles for the tram fare and admission to the pictures for Jenny, Tommy, and myself.

Sitting in the old canvas seats was heaven to us. A tea bun shared between the three of us and Cliff Richard, and the Shadows took us out of our world for a while.

Life was starting to get better as the months went along. We were getting the little things that were important to kids: a bag of sweets, a little bit of pocket money, and an outing now and then.

Our mother had become quite independent and resourceful since Dad left. We had always looked to our father for protection, but it was Mum who was the stronger of the two. Her determination to survive and keep us safe made us do anything we could to help her.

Jenny had turned fourteen and had decided to go looking for her first job. She started working in a processed meat factory and gave every one of her pay packets to Mum.

Mum wanted to move from the house at Mt Gravatt as the neighbours and the welfare were always checking up on us. 'I can't stand those bastards watching every move I make; the sooner we get out of here, the better,' she would say.

I was nearly thirteen, and Dad had been gone for over twelve months. And after saving every spare penny, Mum bought a little house near a mangrove swamp at Lota. It was very cheap; a small fibro house with nothing very attractive about it, but it was just a short walk from the beach, and the prospect of swimming in the sea and days lazing in the sun on the beach brought the 'promised land' dream even closer.

As Jenny and I walked along the beach listening to Ruby and the Romantics singing 'Our Day Will Come' on her little transistor radio, we planned and dreamed about the good times we would have. One day we would even get a flat on our own together and set up a little home that we would call our own.

Mum was happily settled. She was receiving a widow's pension and child endowment payments. Coupled with Jenny's wages, we were doing very well financially, and in the two years since Dad left, there was no husband to drink away our food money, and there was peace in the house and no more worrying about our father.

It was 1963, and I was still in Grade 7 in primary school. I should have been in high school for at least a year, but being held back in lower grades saw me fall behind, and the fact that I was quite short-sighted didn't help as I could not see what was written on the blackboard. I was approaching fourteen, and the urge to leave school and follow my sister to work was driving me mad; the months couldn't go fast enough.

Two months before I turned fourteen, I told Mum that as far as school was concerned, I was finished. She didn't argue but told me that I would have to get a job or the welfare department would be after me.

A few days after my grand announcement of quitting school, I managed to find a job at a boot and shoe factory at inner-city Woolloongabba and spent the next twelve months gluing the sides of boots together before they were sewn up by the machinist.

My weekly pay was the grand total of four pounds, nineteen shillings, and sixpence, which today would be about $147.00.

The house by the sea was not the nirvana that Mum had expected. The roof leaked, and it was not lined inside. Looking up at it, I could see sunlight through the holes made by previous use—it was obvious that the roof was second-hand tin. In the winter, it was cold. In the summer, we cooked, and when it rained, it leaked like a sieve. It was time to move on.

In 1965 Mum found a small house on three and a half acres in Woodridge, a quiet outer suburb of Brisbane, and as soon as we saw it, we knew this was the place we were looking for.

The weatherboard cottage was a bit run-down; it was probably built fifty years before and only had two bedrooms, a small kitchen with a wood stove, and a small lounge room, but it had the potential for improvement. There was a small verandah that Tommy could sleep out on, and Jenny and I could have one of the bedrooms, and the rest of the kids could sleep in the bunks in the dining room.

The house was a good distance from the neighbours, and there was a small creek where we could pump up water to the house for washing. The house had two water tanks and, most importantly, it had electricity. It was about three miles from the train station down a dirt road crossed by three small creeks.

We moved in a few weeks later and the first week, it poured rain; luckily, the roof did not leak. At fifteen, I left the boot factory and started a job the same week as a machinist in a mattress factory called Sleepmaster®. I had used a sewing machine at school and did a bit at home on Mum's old Singer®. I was moving up in the world—or so I thought.

On the first day of the new job, I woke at four in the morning to get ready for work and the walk along the long dark road to the railway station. It was pouring rain. Mum got up to see me off and gave me a torch to see where I was going. Jenny had a week's holiday, and I was terrified to be taking the first long walk on my own.

Struggling along, the rain blinding my eyes, I came to a part in the road where the creek had overflowed and was rushing across in front of me. Pulling up my dress and wading through the rushing water, I took each step warily, fearful of falling off the shoulder of the road and into the deep creek.

It was up to my waist before I reached the other side. There were two more creeks to cross before I was on safe ground again. I arrived on my first day at work soaking wet and freezing cold.

The manager, Mr Rose, told one of the girls in the factory to make me a dress after hearing about my experience and said that if it was raining the next day not to come in. I was made to feel something of a hero for braving the elements to get to work on time for my new job.

I loved my new career, and at fifteen, I was the youngest girl there, and the older women spoiled me. My days were spent sitting at my sewing machine, daydreaming and reading.

Although my job was quite repetitive—just hemming the borders of the mattresses—I did a little sewing when I had breaks for morning tea and lunches: little dresses and knick-knacks for my sisters' dolls.

My mother had started going out with a man, John Johnson, who had a second-hand shop near the railway station. He was a short, fat man in his early forties, dressed immaculately, and despite his very ordinary appearance, he came across as being somewhat successful.

He had spent his former life in the navy and never married. Unbeknown to us, he was also an alcoholic who put on his best behaviour in front of us. We were glad that she was seeing him, as he was giving her gifts like record players and furniture.

It had been over four years since my father left, and Mum needed to have someone to take her out now and then. Giving her luxuries like a record player with countless records made him even more acceptable to us.

However, boyfriends were not on the top of my agenda: I was too busy having fun with Jenny going out to TC's, the disco in Elizabeth Street, or movies on a Saturday night and raceways on a Sunday.

I never thought of myself as still being a child; that vulnerability had gone from me a long time ago, having been responsible for my younger siblings. I was drawn to friendships with the older and wiser. I had become a person who thought that she could survive in the outside world and having a job made me feel quite independent.

This feeling of maturity attracted me to make friends with Neil, who was at least four years older than me; he was a quiet, thoughtful guy. His good-looking features were slightly flawed by the scars of his earlier bout of acne, but his caring and soft internal nature made up for his outward appearance. Jenny and I met him on the train going to work. He struck me as being a little on the rough side: he wore a leather jacket and rode an old Triumph motorbike.

Many happy days were spent riding around on the back of his bike. He tried to teach me how to ride it, but at five foot tall, I was too small to hold it up.

Jenny was going out with Neil's friend, Graham. She adored him, but he broke up with her during one of my on-again, off-again times with Neil.

It was a very casual 'puppy love' affair with Neil. When I wasn't going with him, my friend Rosemary went with him, and funnily, there wasn't any jealousy between us. This went on for about a year.

One week I thought that I was in love with him and the next week he was just my friend. During the times we were going together, he wanted me to have sex with him. I could not bring myself to do it. He promised me that he would stand by me if anything ever happened, but my fear of getting pregnant far outweighed how I felt for him.

The temptation to give in to him crossed my mind many times as we lay close to each other on the nights we spent around the campfires at our 'bush parties', if you could call them that, where some of our friends would sit around drinking beer telling dirty jokes and 'pashing off' with our boyfriends.

I don't know how we drifted apart; I guess we both grew up a little and moved on. However, he did leave me with the love of motorbikes and leather jackets.

My next romance at sixteen was different. Greg was twenty years old, quite mature, tall, and had black hair with a very neat moustache; he was incredibly good looking. He was always joking and spoiled me with chocolates. I thought I would die every time I saw him. He worked at the Brisbane Town Hall and came from a well-off family who owned a block of flats on the Gold Coast. To me, he was a very sophisticated, jacket-wearing smoker—a James Bond type. We would get dressed up and go to concerts on the weekends, and while his mother and father went to the Gold Coast, we slept with each other at his house in Coorparoo.

I was in love or naively thought so.

Seven months together, and I was starting to dream of our wedding day and a future with him. Each day at work, I sat at my sewing machine and daydreamed about him. He filled all my thoughts, and I glowed thinking of our favourite song, 'Bus Stop' by the Hollies, playing over and over in my mind.

We had a routine where I would ring him from a phone box in the middle of the week to say hello and arrange what we were going to do the following weekend. Standing in the phone box at the railway station one day, I wasn't expecting him to tell me that he was breaking it off with me. His reluctant tone told me there was more to his decision than he was saying.

My legs melted with his announcement. I begged him to tell me why, but he answered that I was too young for him. I was shattered. How could I be too young? We had been making love like adults for months. It was then I grew up and felt the pain of my first real heartbreak.

Not only was I shattered by the loss of my first real boyfriend, but I was also unaware that even worse was to come.

Shortly after my break-up with Greg, an unexpected shock threw our family into chaos when John turned up frantically telling my mother that his house caught fire. This saw him spending more time living in our house with Mum and slowly starting to take control of my family.

*

Dad had been gone for nearly five years, and Mum was in the process of divorcing him for desertion. By law, he only had to stay one night under her roof, and the divorce could not be granted, but that was not a concern for us; we had not heard from him for years. He was gone, and another had taken his place.

I arrived home one night to find Mum in a panic.

'What's wrong?' we asked as she was running around checking the windows.

'I don't know if it's true, but John thinks he may have seen your father.'

'He came into his shop looking for me, and John told him he did not know of me. We have to make sure the place is locked up so that bastard can't walk back in again.'

All was quiet that night. Mum had sent the little ones to bed early, and we had the doors locked and bolted.

Around nine o'clock, there was a banging on the door and a voice was calling out, 'Lily, let me in! it's Maurice.' We hid behind the back door, praying that my father wouldn't get in. The banging became louder, and John was standing at the door calling out to Dad to get lost, or he would call the police. We had no phone, and the nearest neighbour was a long way across the paddock.

The banging on the door sounded as though it was being kicked in, and all at once, the door flew open. John rushed to push the door shut, but Dad lunged at him.

'Help me; I've been stabbed!' John yelled to Tommy and me. 'Help me push the door shut!' he screamed as he was trying to force the door back against the weight of my father pushing from the other side.

Tommy, Jenny, and I pushed as hard as we could, managing to force the door shut with dad banging on it, still trying to get in.

'Get my gun!' John yelled to Tommy!

Dad must have heard him say this, and the door slammed shut with our weight against it. Mum was yelling to the younger kids in the back of the house, 'It's okay, go back to bed.'

John grabbed the gun and fired a couple of shots through a crack in the door. Apart from the dogs barking ferociously, there was not a sound.

'Quick!' he yelled to Mum, 'get my car keys and get the kids into the car.' He was bleeding furiously and managed to push us out the door across the dark yard to his car.

We scrambled in while Tommy held the gun, waiting to shoot Dad if he tried to stop us.

John drove a mile up the road to a neighbour who had a phone, and Mum rushed in to ring the ambulance. Half an hour later, the ambulance was on its way to the hospital with John unconscious in the back.

The police came and took Mum and all of us to John's sister who lived in town. We were to wait there until they could find Dad.

There were no trains at that time of night, so Dad's escape had little chance of succeeding.

Another police car with lights flashing pulled up at the front of the house, and one of the officers got out and asked for Mum. I looked in the back and there was my father sitting next to another officer.

'Hello, Dad,' I said through the window to the dishevelled man sitting handcuffed in the back seat.

'Hello,' he answered weakly, his eyes glazed like a madman. 'Which one are you, lad?' he asked.

I was surprised that he did not recognise me; I had always thought that I was his favourite. 'Lily, Dad. Lily!' I answered.

'Have you got a fag there, lad?' he asked. His eyes narrowed on my face, trying to take in my features in the dark.

'Yes, Dad; here's one.' I handed him a packet and told him to keep it.

'Bless you, lad,' he said, stuffing the packet into his shirt pocket.

The first policeman made his way back into the car and told me to stand back. The car drove off with my father in it, and that was the last time I saw him. My last memory of him—a crazed and dangerous man who did not recognise me.

John spent ten days in hospital. The doctors said that he was lucky to be alive as the knife just missed his heart, but he would recover. Mum was frantic, as she would have to move and hide from my father. We would not be safe in our little home again.

After the stabbing, John had become surly and insulting; his true personality was finally being revealed. He could not look at any of us without leering and making some sort of insulting remarks. But Mum, being grateful for being saved by him, stayed silent while he berated us older children.

Dad was held at Boggo Road Gaol until his trial. We never heard anything about it until Jenny had to give evidence against her father. She shook with fright as she lived through the three-day trial. Dad glared at her from the witness box as she gave the details of the night that would result in him being put in jail for ten months for malicious wounding.

John was angry that Dad had not been charged with attempted murder and was not committed for a longer period. This gave them little time to decide what they were going to do now that my father knew where they were living, and so he and Mum were forced to make some decisions on what to do before he was released from jail.

Jenny wasn't the same after the trial. She became introverted and one day announced that she couldn't take the abuse from John any longer and left home to share a house with her friend, Barbara, and her mother. I begged her to take me with her, but she said that there was no room, and her friend's mother only wanted Jenny staying in her house.

The dreams of our little flat were gone. I was alone. My sister— my best friend—had gone. There would be no one for me to confide in and go out with. From then on, it was just me on my own. None of the other kids could fill my older sister's place.

No more would we go dancing at TC's. There would be no more speedway, movies, or skating. No more intimate discussions as we walked the three miles to work each day and back home again. A part of my life had ended.

I felt like Jo out of the movie *Little Women* when she realised that she and her sister and were adults and things would never be the same again.

Chapter 3

It was hard to get used to Jenny not being with me to catch the train home from work. She had left home straight after the court case, and I was feeling quite alone.

Each day as I ambled my way to the station, I would stop at a little shop nearby and buy myself a Coke® or a chocolate bar to eat on the train.

Caught up in my own daydreaming, on a Friday afternoon about four months after Jenny left, a guy caught my attention.

Not overly good-looking, he was a Charles Bronson type. His olive complexion and his black hair gave him a look of familiarity.

He finally introduced himself and said his name was Steve, but it was really Stefan, and he came from Ukraine. Unbeknown to me at the time, my Jewish ancestors originated from Russia; maybe that was why I was attracted to him.

Steve was nineteen but was very mature for his age as he left home at a young age and had to struggle until he ended up living with his brother, Mike.

He was different, not tall like Greg and not as sophisticated, but he cheerfully spoke to everyone who passed by him going to the shop. It made me think that there was something special about this guy.

Having broken up with Greg months earlier and still hurting, I wasn't looking for another boyfriend at that time, but Steve was friendly and outgoing, so we started meeting and talking to each other every afternoon and, eventually, we started to see one another at the weekends.

We would catch a tram down from Coorparoo to Stones Corner and have a milkshake and a hamburger in a cafe that had a jukebox selector in each booth.

Sitting and listening to the music and talking for hours, it was a real Hollywood teenage movie setting, sucking on two straws as we shared the same milkshake, Steve looking into my eyes, smiling while the jukebox played Buddy Holly's 'Heartbeat'. I fell in love.

He told me that he played guitar and that he was trying to get into a band. I thought this was exciting. The Beatles were in full swing at that time and the thought that he might be famous one day made me feel special that he had chosen me to be his girlfriend.

We had been going together for a couple of months when Mum and John decided it was time to move to Sydney. The thought of leaving Steve was more than I wanted to think of, so I told Mum that I did not want to go with her.

I could not stand my future stepfather or 'the old boy' anyway. I had resorted behind his back to calling John this by now. Our mutual contempt for each other was hard to hide. Mum was quite upset, but as I was sixteen and a half and had a job, she agreed to let me stay in Brisbane.

'You make sure you look after yourself,' she said as I packed my solitary suitcase to leave.

Steve had found me a room to rent at Rocklea in the house of a family he knew. They were German and quite friendly.

The room was quite sparse, with a bed, a wardrobe, and a small cupboard to put some of my belongings in. I would come home from work, and the smell of sauerkraut would permeate the air. The best part was I could come and go as I pleased without anyone annoying me, so I was quite happy with the arrangement.

I had been staying there for about three weeks when I started getting a strange feeling of unease. There always seemed to be someone watching me, or so I thought. There was a little peephole in the door looking into the main part of the house, and I would constantly look through to see if there was anyone at my door.

One day I was lying on the bed when I thought I heard a shuffling outside the door. I moved to the side of the door and looked through the hole quickly to see the old father of the family looking through the other side. So, I wasn't imagining things. I told Steve that I was afraid of the old man. As his brother Mike had moved out, he said that I could move into his place: part of an old Queenslander-style house.

Steve's half had a large bedroom with a wooden bed and an old creaking wardrobe in the corner. The kitchen was a long, closed-in verandah area with a small single hotplate stove, sink and cupboards, and a wooden table and chairs up the other end.

It was fairly basic, but it was heaven to me. I would go off to work and rush back to our little home to cook our evening meal. Saturday and Sundays were spent mostly in bed. I would lie beside my sleeping lover and gaze at his handsome face breathing gently, his olive skin and jet-black hair pressed into the whiteness of his pillow.

The hot, lazy days of the Queensland summer came, and Christmas was approaching. Mum and the family were staying on the Gold Coast as they made their way down to Sydney.

Steve and I decided to join them and stayed in the annexe of their caravan. The next few days were almost like a honeymoon as we walked along the beach in the gentle wind-swept heat of the summer nights. I prayed this would last forever.

Mum and John seemed to like him and accepted that we were living together, and after our short break, we went home to the flat and settled back into our own private world.

A couple of weeks later, Steve met Rick, who was in a band and who was looking for a lead guitarist. He would come around, and they would practise each night.

I would sit and watch and listen to them practise each tune over and over, never getting tired of hearing them play and sing. After Rick had gone home, Steve would strum his guitar and sing a little song he said was just for me:

The angels listened in, and they heard me praying.
The angels listened in, and they heard me saying,
'Please send me the whole wide world wrapped up in a little girl.'
My darling and the angels sent you.

Then he would lean over and gently kiss me goodnight.

Steve and Rick and a couple of other guys eventually formed a band and played at a couple of parties. Steve thought it was better if I stayed home because it was not good for the group to be taking around their girlfriends.

After each party, he would come home and tell me of the great time the band had and how much better they were playing with every new number they rehearsed. I was proud of him, dreaming that one day they would all be famous.

It was about this time that I started to feel quite sick each morning. The thought of being pregnant was at the back of my mind. Each morning when I went to work, I would rush out to the toilet to vomit wildly.

It was only a few days before my sickness became apparent to everyone in the factory, and I was called up into the boss's office. Mr Rose was a nice man; he was usually very quiet, and I did not see a lot of him in the two years that I worked at Sleepmaster.

'I've called you up here, Lily, to ask you if you are pregnant. I've been told by Mrs Franks that you have been showing signs of being sick here every morning.'

I thought about what I was going to say and decided that honesty was going to be the best thing so that if I was pregnant, he would understand and possibly tolerate my being sick for a while. I did not want to lose my job; I wasn't ready to give up working at such an early stage of pregnancy.

'I think that I am pregnant, Mr Rose,' I answered.

He frowned at me as though he was about to tell me some bad news. 'I'm sorry, Lily, but I will have to give you a weeks' notice. I can't have you working for us if you are pregnant: you may get hurt or something, and I don't want to be responsible for that.'

I was so upset and embarrassed by being given notice that I just walked out into the factory and did not see all the men in the wire section looking at me. The tears started to flow down my face as I struggled to keep looking brave and unmoved.

I went home and told Steve my bad news. 'Don't worry about it; I'll look after you,' he said, cuddling me. All my fears went, and like a small, wounded child, I felt safe and loved.

It was during that week that Greg, my previous boyfriend, had left a message at the office to contact him. I wondered what he wanted since it was over six months since I had seen him.

It was strange to hear his voice again; I had nearly forgotten what he sounded like. The last time I had spoken to him, he was giving me a thousand excuses of why he thought we should end our six-month relationship. His excuse had been that I was too young for him, but it became apparent to me that he thought he was above me in many ways, so it was intriguing to hear from him out of the blue.

'Lily, can I see you again?' he asked. I told him that I had been going out with Steve for the past months, but it didn't seem to deter him. He pleaded with me; he wanted to explain why he broke up with me. I agreed to meet him that next Friday night outside the town hall.

Steve was really upset when I told him about the arranged meeting. 'Why do you want to see him again?' he asked. 'Do you still love him?'

'No,' I answered. 'But I feel that I needed to see him and show him that I am with someone else, and to be honest, I want him to know what he has lost.'

I don't think Steve understood what I had to do. I was hurt when Greg broke up with me and I felt that I needed to be the one who finished the relationship. I still felt rejected and, deep down, wanted to hurt Greg the way he hurt me.

I thought that I would dress glamorously, just to upset him more. I made myself a strapless gold dress with a wrap and had my hair curled up on top of my head. *Not bad,* I thought as I looked at myself in the mirror.

Steve sat and watched me dress up to meet Greg, still upset at my going on this date.

We met at the arranged time, and I could see that he was surprised by my appearance. I think I must have matured since he last saw me. Maybe it was my pregnancy that gave me a more confident look.

We chatted over a meal and then we went off to see the movie, *Dr Zhivago*. My mind was wandering back to my 'Omar Sharif' waiting patiently at home while I played out my silly game.

After the movie, Greg asked me to go back with him again. 'I'm sorry that I broke off with you, Lily. I realised afterwards how much you meant to me.'

Now was my chance to let him down, I thought. 'I'm sorry, Greg, but I'm going with Steve, and I love him. I think that I am going to have his baby.'

The look of surprise told me that we had reached the end of any further discussion. He kissed me goodbye and wished me well, and I went home—to the home where I belonged.

'How did it go?' Steve asked. 'Are you going to go back to him?'

I put my arms around his neck, 'I love you, and I'll never leave you.' He held my face between his hands and kissed me. Tired and relieved, we went to bed and held each other so tightly we thought nothing, or no one, could tear us apart.

A few days later, Steve's mother came to visit us and brought a photo of Steve as a baby wrapped in a crochet shawl and wearing a bonnet knitted in a traditional Ukrainian pattern. I gazed lovingly at the photo, thinking that this would be how our baby would look.

Later that night, we went out to a friend's party. Steve was playing for drinks only, and his friend said that he could bring me along. We had a couple of drinks and by the time we went home, we were completely exhausted.

'God, I feel hungry,' Steve said. 'I didn't get much to eat at that party.' I was feeling a bit tired but thought that he deserved to have a decent feed after working all day and playing all night at the party, so I peeled some potatoes and put a couple of pork chops under the grill to cook.

We lay down on the bed while the meal was cooking, and before I knew it, I was woken up by the sun shining through the window onto my face.

'Gee, I feel hungry,' Steve said in a dozy mumble.

I went on to say, 'You had tea last night,' then I froze with shock. God, the food was still cooking on the stove! I rushed into the kitchen to be greeted with a frightening sight.

The stove was burnt black, and the pot was no more than a melted piece of metal. The wooden wall was charred right up to the ceiling. I stared in shock. 'We could have been burnt to death!' I was sick with dread. 'What will the landlord say?'

Steve came out and saw the mess. 'I'll fix it,' he said. Even he looked in horror at the thought that we may have been burnt alive. 'I think that someone must be watching over us,' Steve said.

A couple of nights later, Rick came around to practise. I decided that I would go to bed that night instead of sitting up with them; it had been a long day, and I was feeling tired.

Quietly strumming away in the kitchen, I drifted off into sleep.

Before I knew what was happening, I was being shaken awake.

A strange voice was telling me to 'wake up, wake up!' Fear caught me by the throat, and I turned over to see a policeman in his brown uniform bending over me.

'Could you come into the kitchen with me? I want to ask you some questions,' he said. His colleague was standing in the corner with Steve and Rick. I was terrified; they were all looking at me. *What is happening?* My mind was racing to shake off the effects of sleep so I could comprehend what was going on.

The policeman sat me down at the kitchen table and started to interrogate me. 'How old are you? What are you doing here? Where are your parents?' The questions were coming at me from all directions; my mind was spinning around and around.

He then asked me the question that sealed my fate. 'Are you pregnant?' I nodded my head, too scared to lie.

'I'm sorry, Lily, but I will have to take you into custody. If you were a month older, there would be nothing I could do.'

Custody? What did he mean by 'custody'? Where were they going to take me'?

I broke out in a cold sweat; fear was racing through my veins. 'What have I done? Why are they taking me away?' I wanted to scream.

'You had better go and put some clothes on,' the tall policeman directed.

I started to sob. 'Steve, they're going to take me away.' I hung onto his arms crying, hoping the whole thing was a nightmare that I would soon wake up from.

'Don't worry, babe; I'll sort this out. I'll sort this out tomorrow,' Steve said. I quickly dressed in my favourite spotted suit, and before I knew it, I was in a police car driving off into the night.

We arrived at a place I had never seen before, and I was told this was the South Brisbane Watch House and that I was going to be spending the night there.

A fat, grumpy-looking sergeant was sitting behind a high bench. 'What have we got here?' he asked the two policemen. 'We picked this kid up living with a young bloke in Rocklea,' the tall policeman replied.

'How old is she?' asked the sergeant.

'Nearly seventeen,' was the reply.

'Couldn't you take her to stay with anyone?' he asked.

'It was too late.'

'You know you could get hung for bringing her here,' the sergeant said. He leaned over the bar and whispered to the officer, 'I'll put her in a cell, and she can go before the court tomorrow.'

The sergeant looked at me, 'Have you got a belt on or any watches or jewellery?' he asked.

I took off the friendship ring that Steve had given me and a belt that I had my skirt tied up with. My heart was thumping; I could hear it in my ears. My mind was telling me that this was a nightmare that I would soon wake up from. *God, wake me up, please. Please!*

With a bit of a laugh, the sergeant said to me, 'I'm going to put you in the deluxe cell—you get to have sheets on the bed.'

The guard led me up a corridor. Like a zombie, I followed; there was no escape. He opened a steel door with a hatch. 'You'd better go to bed and get some sleep; you've got a long wait ahead of you, and the court won't open until ten o'clock tomorrow.'

I went and sat on the hard bed. The grey blanket scratched my legs. I put my head on my knees and started to cry my heart out.

I had no sleep that night. The yelling of drunks up the corridor, the slamming of the steel doors as they brought in new inmates, and a constant stream of guards looking in through the hatch at me made the night seem a week long.

I was wretched with morning sickness and vomited all night. Shaking, my head pounding, all I could do was dry retch.

Morning came, and they brought me breakfast: a tin plate with porridge, a tin cup of watery tea, and a slice of bread. I felt so sick that I couldn't bring myself to touch it.

The hours passed, and in what seemed to be a lifetime of waiting, I was finally taken to the Children's Court. There was a Justice of the Peace there and the policeman who took me to the watch house.

He read out the details of my arrest to the justice, charging me with being 'exposed to moral danger'.

What the hell was that? I felt that I was watching a play with all the scenes being acted out around me, and any minute I was going to wake up out of this nightmare and I would find myself lying next to Steve.

The Justice broke into my thoughts, then said to me, 'I'm going to commit you into care at Holy Cross until we notify your parents about what is happening.'

I was stunned. 'Where is Holy Cross? How long am I going to be there?' No one was telling me anything; my mind was still trying to comprehend what was going on around me.

'I am going to take you back to the flat to collect some of your things,' the policeman told me.

My heart leapt. I was going to see Steve, and that was all I could think about.

Steve was at the flat when we arrived. We hugged each other briefly, and the police officer was standing nearly on top of me, preventing any escape.

I packed my clothes, crying, shaking, and frightened. 'Take this with you,' said Steve as he pushed a small photo of the two of us into my hand. I put the photo down my bra close to my heart, thinking that while I had it, we would never be separated.

One last tearful embrace, a kiss goodbye, and I was spirited off to Magdalen Asylum in Wooloowin, also called Holy Cross and several other names. The painful goodbye with Steve made me feel sick, and I don't remember much about arriving at the home for unmarried mothers, disabled girls, and infants.

A small, cramped office was my welcome to the austere three-storey building. The greeting nun, Sister Isobel, asked me questions that my mind was trying to unscramble.

Sister Isobel was an intimidating figure, quite tall with an expressionless face. It was obvious she would be the type that would not tolerate nonsense from a brazen child.

Her history of being a missionary in Africa was well applauded, and to be put in charge of delinquent girls was probably seen as a comedown from heroine-like status.

I learned incredibly early this was one nun not to upset.

I was taken upstairs to a long dormitory and shown a bed that was to be mine. The steel gate was shut behind me, and I was alone. My stomach was turning over and over. *I feel sick. I feel sick,* was all I could think.

I was given a straight white shift dress to wear and told to change into it straightaway. Now I was truly a prisoner. I was kept locked up in the dormitory for nearly a week.

I stood at the window most of the day, watching to see what was happening outside in the courtyard. Sometimes the girls would be on the netball court having a game, but most of the time there was no one there. The days were dark and stormy. It was as though even heaven was crying for me.

The other girls spent most of the day working in the laundry adjacent to the asylum. I found out they were wards of the state, and most of them were there because they were uncontrollable.

As I had to go back to court a week later, I was kept isolated from the other girls during the day. It was only at night that I got to meet any of them.

Finally, the court day arrived, and the arresting policeman came and picked me up.

I didn't know what to expect. I thought they might have contacted my mother and she was going to take me home.

My mind was saying, *Please, Mum, be there. Please, Mum, be there,* over and over and over.

I appeared before the same Justice who called the policeman to the bench and asked him if he had been able to contact my parents.

As I looked around the empty court, my heart sank—my mother was nowhere to be seen. The arresting officer said that he had been unable to locate them, and with that, I was committed to Holy Cross indefinitely.

Sister Isobel greeted us at the door. I took one last gaze over my shoulder; this was to be my last look at freedom, for God knew how long. The statue of Jesus in the middle of the garden looking the other way was even mocking me.

'You'd better take off those clothes and put your uniform on,' Sister Isobel directed. 'And from now on, your name will be Leanne,' she muttered as she filled in an index card with my name on it.

'Leanne, Leanne,' my mind trying to confront this new reality, I was not Lily anymore. My name was gone, and from that moment, a new identity was moved into my mind.

Leanne was different from me. Lily was a happy-go-lucky person, she was a tomboy, and she was full of cheek and did not take anything from anyone.

Lily wasn't scared of anything; she'd even ridden a motorbike at fifteen.

Leanne was different. She was quiet, she was frightened, and she did as she was told without uttering a word of defiance.

I spent another couple of days locked up in the dormitory as I couldn't bring myself to stop crying, and the more I cried, the sicker I made myself.

Four days later, I was told to go into the laundry and help the girls there to take my mind off things.

A covered, closed-in verandah led straight into the 'steam room'. At the back of the steam room was the laundry where two men worked feeding the linen into large spinning washing machines.

The washed, hot steamy load was put into cage-like trolleys to be untangled and folded; it was a heavy task to separate sheets that had twisted into knots and had to be forcefully pulled apart.

The steam room had two large round rollers covered in canvas. As they rolled, they ironed out the sheets and linen that were fed into it by two girls on one side and another two on the other side who folded the dried sheets.

There was a large wooden table and benches where the folded laundry was kept and where the girls sat and folded pillowcases and things like handkerchiefs.

In the next room was an ironing room where the 'hospital girls' or unmarried mothers worked. They did the pressing of personal laundry like shirts, dresses, or whatever was sent to be laundered.

The smell of washing soda permeated the air to nearly suffocation levels, and the only distraction was the old radio pumping out all the 'mod' songs of the sixties, the only thing to remind us there was a world outside.

One nun stood guard over us as we worked from eight in the morning until the late afternoon, depending on when the last load of washing was finished. Day in and day out was to be the same scenario of forced labour.

Standing all day on my feet, folding sheets and having a serious dose of nausea made me all the more wretched. I learned from the other girls that if you did not work, you went to a place that was far worse than Holy Cross.

*

It was a few days later when one of the girls told me that she had seen Steve and a girl walking up the driveway. I raced up to the dormitory, my heart beating furiously.

My eyes strained to see, but it was too late; they must have already gone!

Although I was distraught at not catching a glimpse, I was excited, thinking that Steve was still trying to do something outside for me. My sister Jenny must have been with him; maybe she could help get me out as well.

A thousand false hopes went through my mind. It had been a couple of weeks and still no news, then one day, Sister Isobel called me down into the office. 'I have a form for you to fill in,' she said.

It was an application form to marry. My mother's signature was on it, along with the signatures of Steve's parents. My heart was beating like a drum as I signed my name to the form. Steve must have gone down to Sydney to get Mum's and his father's permission. *Oh, God! I'm going to get married,* I thought.

It was like a miracle: one moment of despair and the next complete exhilaration.

I rushed out to the recreation hall where the girls sat of an afternoon and blurted out my good news so fast it took them all by surprise. Now it was only a matter of waiting.

The days passed into weeks. My desperation was building each day. *Will this be the day I'm going to get married? What will happen; will Steve just show up at the door and take me away? Will the priest from Holy Cross marry us?* Questions, questions, questions.

The endless days were filled with fantasies of Steve coming to claim me.

It had been nearly a couple of months since I had signed the forms. Nobody seemed to know anything and each day that passed drew me closer to the realisation that there was to be no wedding for me, no escape, and no rescue.

Not knowing what was going to happen to me and the baby made me terrified during the passing months that brought me closer to the birth of my child.

The monotony of working in the laundry, folding sheets all day and going to school twice a week in the home was a punishment in itself.

Backwards and forwards folding sheets and whispering to each other while we worked gave us little time to gossip; that was to come after work, as no speaking was allowed to distract the never-ending steam roller churning out endless ironed laundry.

I had made very good friends with three Aboriginal girls, two of whom were sisters. Mary, the younger, was a real character: very outgoing and always looking for some fun. She would get very cheeky when the nuns brought boys from the local high school to take dancing lessons with us.

Her sister Jane, on the other hand, was very quiet and kept mostly to herself. Venita, a much taller girl, was also very private and never gave away what she was thinking. We were all a bit different but became very close to each other, like the other girls who formed exclusive small groups to protect each other.

The only bright spot of a never-ending week was a movie on Friday nights and being allowed thirty cents worth of lollies from a little shop the nuns kept in one of the back rooms. On Saturday nights, I was locked away from the world at Holy Cross. It was the saddest part of my week; there were no sheets to fold or television to watch to take my mind off the happy Saturday nights I had spent not so long before.

Sitting around the old wooden radio with some of my friends, we would sit and listen to the latest songs. We would tell each other about other Saturday nights when we were outside enjoying life. Did you ever go here? Did you ever go there? Telling each other of the exciting places we used to frequent. We had heard the same stories repeatedly, and yet it was like hearing them again for the first time. By remembering every happy minute, we were going beyond the walls and transferring ourselves into a place full of music and dancing. We were singing and having fun being what we were: young girls enjoying ourselves and not hurting anyone. We were not bad girls to be locked up and forgotten.

Sandy Posey's voice sang from the radio: 'I've got a boy who is waiting for me, waiting for me to come home, watching the clock all alone.' And there I was, back to reality. *Where is Steve now?* I would wonder. *Is he playing his guitar for someone's party? Is he thinking of me? Is he with another girl who is looking at him the way that I did?*

I could feel my heart sobbing. Then I would think of my baby. The little round ball was growing inside my stomach. I wondered what was going to happen to us. And then the radio would blast out the Beatles, and I was back to the disco again drinking make-believe rum and Coke, shaking my tambourine, and dancing with my sister Jenny.

'Ten o'clock,' said the nun watching us. 'Time to go to bed.'

Up the stairs, into the long dormitory, and the iron gate slams behind us and the key is turned. In the dark, I could cry for all the happy Saturday nights gone and for the lonely ones to come. No one could tell me what was happening to me, how long was I going to be kept at Holy Cross, or what was happening to Steve.

On the rare visit from Jenny, she told me they wouldn't let Steve visit me. I had only been allowed to see her four months after my arrest and never saw her again until two months after that visit.

No one from the Children's Services had come to see me either, and yet they were the ones who were supposed to be responsible for me, and the nuns did not speak to me. It was as if the world had forgotten about me.

My only connection with the outside world was the visits to the hospital.

Each month, I would go to Sister Isobel's office, where an orange maternity smock hung on the back of the office door.

She would make me change into it and pass me a plastic wedding ring to put on my left hand. During each visit to the hospital, I was chaperoned by a different woman who would pick me up on a bus and sit and wait with me while I had my examination. Not a word was said to me as I sat on the hard wooden benches and waited for my name to be called.

The nurse called out, 'Mrs McDonald,' when my turn was due.

The doctors who saw me prodded and poked me, only speaking to let me know that I either needed iron tablets or I had sugar in my urine.

Each visit, I was handed a small bottle of pills to take back to the home with me. It was a waste of time; Sister Isobel took them off me at the door, and I never saw them again.

Weeks passed into months. The monotony of the days was only surpassed by the monotony of the lonely nights.

As soon as the steel gates were locked on us and the lights went out, a quiet hush descended, and then tiptoeing as the girls crept into each other's beds or climbed up into the manhole in the bathroom to smoke. This was the only real escape for some of the girls who were destined to spend years in a place like this.

In one sense, I was lucky; the longest they could keep me in this hell hole was a few months, as I was well on my way to my eighteenth birthday.

Week after week passed with no news, no one to tell me what was happening, no visits from friends, nothing from children's services— just work, school, mass, and endless boredom. My time to give birth was approaching; the closer it came, the more fearful I became. I had nothing for the baby. How I was going to dress and feed it concerned me as the months passed by.

Apart from a crocheted jacket and bonnet that was given to me by one of my workmates, all I had was some talcum powder saved from my monthly allocation from the nuns, which I kept hidden in my footlocker along the verandah.

Shortly before the birth of the baby, I discovered the locker broken into and all my belongings were gone except the bonnet and jacket. All the months of saving the few things I had were lost—now there was nothing.

On the day I went into labour, all of us were hauled out of bed in the early hours of the morning to go to mass. There must have been something special that week, as we had been called out of bed at least three times that week to go to church.

The nun rang her bell as she walked back and forth up the corridor of the dormitory, calling out, 'Come on girls, get out of bed.' It was almost as though the nuns were punishing us as well because they had to attend mass each day.

Even the non-Catholic girls had to attend mass. *Hypocrites*, I thought to myself, *Catholics were not allowed to go to another's religion, and yet these bitches force the Protestant girls to go to theirs.*

I was sitting in the chapel with the other girls who had also been dragged out of bed, when I suddenly felt a strange feeling between my legs. I rubbed myself, and blood appeared on my white shift.

A nun who was standing next to me observed this and motioned me to get up and follow her outside. All the girls were looking at me, wondering why I was leaving the church. She took me up to the office and rang for an ambulance to take me to the hospital.

I was frightened, not knowing what lay ahead of me.

I was taken to the labour ward, where I was dressed in a green hospital gown and examined, with the nurse telling me it would be a long time before I was going to give birth to my baby.

Lying on the hard delivery bed as the hours crept by, watching the hands on the clock go round and round, it seemed the time was going on forever. My baby was not in any hurry to be born.

Nurses came and went, asking me if I had any pains. I told them they were only coming every hour or so. Late in the afternoon, a nurse came along and told me they were going to break my water.

I was terrified because I didn't know what they were talking about. I soon found out. They inserted something into me. I felt a snip and then a rush of liquid running down the bed.

Not long after, the pains started in earnest and became more and more frequent. The hours were passing by, and it was well into the night when the doctor looked at me and said it was time for the delivery.

Turned onto my right side, I had my left leg strapped up in a stirrup at the side of the bed while a nurse pulled my right leg behind me.

The other nurse then leaned on my shoulder, pinning me face down into the bed so I could not move.

I started screaming when the baby was coming. 'Let me lie on my back! Let me lie on my back! You're breaking my back!' My screams went ignored.

Reality was flashing in and out; my head felt like it was getting bigger, then smaller.

The sweet smell of the gas was suffocating me as I tried to push the rubber mask away from my face, but my strength was gone. After what seemed to be forever, I felt something between my legs. It was my baby—no crying, just silence.

The pain was gone. The nurse told me that it was all over the baby was out.

I tried turning over to see my baby, but I couldn't move; the stirrup was still holding me down.

'What did I have?' I pleaded. They eventually told me it was a boy.

Catching a glimpse of a nurse carrying my baby out of the room wrapped up in a green sheet, never seeing his face made my mind frantic. *Where were they taking him? Is there something wrong with him?* A stream of people followed him.

I was freaking out; were all those people in the room while I was giving birth?

They were supposed to give him to me; that's what happens in the movies. Maybe they'll bring him back to me later, I thought, but now I felt sick and hurt.

I passed out, and next thing I knew, I was being spoken to and told to wake up. The doctor told me that because I had been cut to get the baby out, he would have to sew me up. The nightmare continued; the pain of the injection into my insides was enough to make me scream.

I lay there trembling, cold, and in shock while he sewed me up. He was talking to another doctor who was watching him, discussing the stitches he was using, preferring a herringbone type of stitch.

Admiring their handiwork, he investigated every part of me to see if he had sewed up anything he shouldn't have. They never said a word to me. I was just the body on the bed, in shock, in pain, with tears rolling down my face.

I was violated, tortured, and humiliated. No one prepared me for this; no one told me this is what delivering a child entailed—they hadn't even told me how to breathe to help with the labour pains.

I was nothing more than an instrument to deliver a child into the world, scorned and punished.

An injection, and then nothing; my mind swirled into a pit of darkness.

I awoke sometime the following day. The ward was filled with other girls waiting for me to regain consciousness.

'What did you have?' one of them asked.

'A boy,' I replied.

'That's funny,' one said, 'because we've all had girls in here.'

I didn't think much about it at the time, but this would prove to be significant.

My first thought on waking was to contact Steve. I could do it now as there were no locks on the ward to keep me in. I must tell Steve that I have had the baby. My legs could hardly carry me through the corridor down to the main entrance of the hospital. I felt dizzy, confused. The only thing that what going through my mind was, *I have to tell Steve. I have to find Steve.*

The next few days in the hospital were like a bad dream. I asked the nurses if I could see my baby, but they refused. 'You're not allowed to see the baby until Children's Services comes to see you.'

The world around me was huge and frightening. I hid under the bedclothes. I pretended that I was in another place. Little did I realise that the medication I was being given was making me paranoid and drowsy.

Then the incredible happened. I looked up one day, and there was Steve; he had finally found out that I had the baby.

All I could do was hold his hand. I don't remember a word of what was discussed; he was there with me, which was all I knew or cared about.

'Where's the baby?' he asked.

'I haven't seen him yet,' I answered.

'I passed the nursery on the way in here,' Steve said. 'Let's go and have a look.'

Looking into the nursery, there were at least twenty babies.

'Which one is ours?' he asked.

'I think he's that one.' I pointed to a little black-haired baby peeping out from under a bunny rug. My eyesight was so bad I couldn't see properly. *God, why was I so blind?* I cursed myself for being so short-sighted.

Steve left, and I felt so happy. The dreams of being together again with our baby made me want to shut out the world, and again I hid under the blankets, back into my own private world.

Sue, another state ward from Holy Cross, had just given birth to a baby girl. She was in the bed across from me and had seen Steve visiting me and asked me if he was my boyfriend.

I told her that he was. She then asked me if I was scared if anyone found out that he had been to see me. I answered that I wasn't. Hell or high water was not going to stop me from seeing Steve.

Four days had passed, and I still had not seen the baby. A woman approached my bed and introduced herself as being the hospital registrar.

She told me that she had some forms to fill in for the birth registration of the baby. 'What have you decided to call your baby,' she asked.

'Shane Stephan McDonald,' I replied proudly. I had picked Shane because it was Irish for John, and Stephan after Steve.

She started to fill in the forms and when she came to the part where it said father's name she put down, 'father unknown'.

'That's not right. My baby's father's name is Steve Benko. Everyone knows that,' I exclaimed.

'We always put down father unknown for an illegitimate child unless the father has permitted to put his name down at the registration of the baby's birth.'

She then started to ask me questions about Steve's appearance, where I was going to live, and how I was going to look after the baby.

At first, I was curious to know why she wanted to know all this, but I thought they needed to know these things if they were going to make some sort of arrangements for me and my baby.

She left, and I went back to my private little world again.

My baby now had a name. There was a certain satisfaction about having his name written down and acknowledged. *He is mine; his name says so*, I thought as I drifted back into sleep again.

Eight days after giving birth, I still had not seen the baby. The department worker still had not come, and I was losing track of what day of the week it was and how long I had been in the hospital.

Eventually, I woke up out of a dazed sleep to find a woman standing at the side of the bed. She introduced herself as being from the Department of Children's Services. At last, they'd finally come to help me.

'Are you Lily McDonald?' she asked.

'Yes,' I replied.

'I've been told that you have seen your boyfriend while you have been in here; is that correct?'

How did she know? I wondered, and then the realisation hit me— Sue had dobbed me in.

'You can be in big trouble for contacting him. I could send you to Karalla for this.' Karalla was a maximum-security reform school. My blood froze in my veins.

'I haven't done anything wrong; Steve has a right to see the baby.' My mind raced for answers to this woman.

'And what do you think you are going to do about the baby?' her eyes squinted at me while she demanded to know my answer.

'I want him to be put into foster care until I get out of the home. Steve will marry me when I get out of the home,' I told her.

'You are not allowed contact with anyone while you are here in this hospital. We can keep you locked up in the home until you turn eighteen for breaking the rules, which, by the way, is another six months. You can't keep your baby sitting on the fence until then. And if we do put him in foster care, you would have to prove that you can look after him, and that could take at least four years.'

Her malicious voice was ringing in my ears. *Oh my God, what is she saying to me?* I was panicking.

Her voice kept coming at me. 'How do you think your baby will feel when you come along— you, a stranger—and take him from the only people he has known? He would hate you for the rest of his life.'

I couldn't stand my baby hating me for the rest of my life. This woman was right. I can't let my baby stay with strangers, get to know and love them, and then take him off them.

'Your baby will go to people who can look after him and will give him everything he needs. He needs a father and a mother, and you don't know if your boyfriend will marry you in the long run. He may find another girl while you are still in the home.'

I thought that maybe she was right. Six more months until I turned eighteen was a long time. I had already been locked away for seven months, and maybe Steve had been with other girls.

That was one thing I never thought about; maybe he had found another girlfriend. He was so handsome; he could have anyone. My mind was racing, looking for answers. *I want to scream; I want to die. When is this nightmare is going to end?*

It was at this point that this woman must have seen my despair. She brought out the adoption consent form and told me to sign; I had not seen the form before it was passed to me to sign. 'It's in your baby's best interest for you to do this.' I was in shock. I took the pen and thought to myself; *I will sign this as neatly as I can so that if my baby sees this one day, he will know that I tried to do things properly.* I held the pen so tightly in my hand I thought it would snap.

I signed my name where I was told and how I was told: *Lillian Josephine McDonald.* God knows why. The form had already been filled in—that may have had something to do with it.

She went on to say something about having thirty days to change my mind. I did not hear what else she had to say. I wanted this monster to leave me alone. I wanted to die; my baby was going somewhere where I would not see him.

An hour or so later, a nurse came up to see me and asked if I would like to see Shane before I was discharged. It had been eight days since I had given birth to him and my mind could not comprehend what he looked like. To be allowed to see my baby was more than I could hope for. I was given a card by the nurse with my name to hold at the window.

She took me around to the nursery and wheeled a small bassinet up to the window. The sign on his little bed said, *Baby McDonald not to be shown.*

There he lay, a tiny little face wrapped up with a hospital shawl, his fair hair peeping out from under the blanket. I struggled to see his little face as he was turned on his side. I could not get a good look at my precious child.

I stood there, the tears streaming down my face with not even a hanky to wipe them. I was in a dream. *My baby has fair hair; is he my baby? My baby should have black hair like Steve.* My head was hurting. I felt dizzy.

As I stood there looking at the tiny sleeping face, I made him a promise, 'I will see you again, little one. I will see you again.' Five minutes to say goodbye and a lifetime to remember the little sleeping angel in the locked nursery.

That afternoon I was sent back to Holy Cross, my mind empty, my vision blind. It was straight back into the laundry. As I sat on the hard bench folding pillowcases, a distant radio played in the background. I couldn't make out the tune—even music was gone from my life.

I was allowed to sit and fold for a week, and then it was back to standing and folding sheets all day. I felt like a robot walking around in a daze.

The days passed with no visitors, no letters. Had the world deserted me? Where was Jenny? Why didn't she come to see me? *Thirty days, thirty days,* kept going around in my mind. My baby would be gone in thirty days. No phone, no letters, no visitors. My situation and anything to do with it was futile, as I wondered how I could stop this from happening.

The thirtieth day came. I felt as though I was attending the funeral of my dearest loved one; a piece of my heart was gone, and a part of myself had died.

Jenny came to see me after the time had passed to save my son. I was angry with her. Why had she not come and seen me for months before and after my son was born? She told me that she was not allowed. That made sense to me, but all the same, I felt abandoned by her. Trust in my beloved older sister was gone; in the nine months, I was incarcerated, she had seen me five times.

Thirty-five days after I signed the consent form, Sister Isobel came to me to tell me that I would be going home to my mother in a week. It felt like the end of the world. I hated the home, and yet I felt sick at the prospect of leaving.

For the first time in the nine months of my being at home, I was angry. I wanted to set fire to the place. They were getting rid of me, kicking me out, sending me back to the stepfather I despised.

Now that my embarrassing 'bump' was gone, I was promoted to work in the nuns' house, cleaning their rooms with my friend Mary. You could call it a 'premium' job. We had a little cupboard under the stairs where we kept our cleaning materials and a little cupboard where we hid the treats that came with the job, such as hot chocolate mix, and sometimes, if we were lucky, biscuits that were made by the nun who cooked for the order.

I had finished early one day and sat on the lockers thinking about my impending release when a voice clamoured, 'Go and help out in the laundry.' Sister Isobel delivered her order as she walked past.

'Get lost,' I replied.

She turned around and glared at me, her eyes narrowed, 'What did you say?' she roared.

'Get lost,' I repeated.

She came at me with a feather duster she was carrying. I turned and ran down the verandah as she was hitting the back of my legs. She chased me into the laundry, and I jumped over a long bench and sat down.

'Don't get cheeky now just because you are going home. I can stop you from leaving here,' she threatened, her face red from the unexpected exercise.

'I don't care if I stay here forever,' I calmly told her.

It was my first act of defiance in the home for nine months. I had lost everything, so nothing mattered anymore. I had been a good girl for the whole time I was at Holy Cross, probably trying to show that I would also make a good mother and hoping they would help me. If I had caused trouble, maybe someone might have taken notice of me and tried to talk to me. I had been my own worst enemy with my silence.

Why hadn't I been like the other girls who had run away? Why hadn't I climbed over the fences that kept me from my freedom? Why was I so scared that I would hurt myself and my baby? Why, why, why?

The Children's Services worker came to see me the week before I left Holy Cross, taking my bankbook to withdraw my plane fare to Sydney. I was then taken to a factory where they outfitted state wards and given three dresses, a handbag, and a pair of shoes to send me on my way home. A small price to pay for nine months of forced work and the theft of my child.

Days later, I was taken to the airport and seen onto a plane for Sydney.

What lay ahead of me? I was dreading the reception I would receive from my stepfather.

Chapter 4

The plane dipped and jerked as it made its way down the coast closer and closer to Sydney. I had never been on a plane before and was feeling sicker and sicker; this was worse than the car sickness I used to get on long trips.

My mind was wondering what was going to happen when we reached Sydney. Would Mum and the old boy be waiting at the other end? *Don't think about it,* I told myself. *Think of a song.* The only song that kept coming into my mind was Gerry and the Pacemakers' song, 'You'll Never Walk Alone'. It started going through my mind again and again. *When you walk through a storm, hold your head up high and don't be afraid of the dark.* Yes, I had always been afraid of the dark. But then maybe it won't be so bad when I get home, I thought. *Walk on, walk on,* my mind caught onto the chorus of the song.

The plane landed, the bumping and loud roaring of the engines shaking me from my daydreaming. As I made my way down the stairs, I could see the old boy standing near the open door to the terminal. Mum was standing next to him, and my sister Bridget was there as well.

Mum walked over to me. I could feel the tears rushing to my eyes. She quickly hugged me and kissed me on my wet cheek.

'How are you?' she asked.

'All right,' I managed to squeak out of my tightening throat.

The old boy came up and hugged me. 'Glad to see you, Dux,' he grunted as his fat stomach pushed me backward. Bridget came and kissed me, her eyes as full of tears as my own.

The trip from the airport back to the house at Canley Heights where the family lived was silent. I felt sick, and the movement of the car was strange to me.

I was getting paranoid and anxious at the space around me. It had been so long since I had seen my family, and the feeling of openness and freedom frightened me. I had become institutionalised in the home. I thought, *How am I going to deal with this?*

The house was an old fibro place on the main road. On the inside, it looked comfortable.

The rest of the kids were waiting to greet us and clustered around me. It was a year since I had last seen them. They had all grown, and I felt out of place.

The whole scenario seemed strange. Although they were my family, they were strangers to me. I had left my family back at Holy Cross.

The first night of my arrival back home, the old boy was up to his old tricks again. His drinking had not slowed down. I caught him sneaking off to the fridge a couple of times, pouring the Brandivino that he loved to drink when he lived with us at Woodridge. His face was getting redder with each passing hour.

As the drink started to take effect, he started talking to me, his voice becoming slurred and sarcastic. He leaned across the table and said to me, 'Do you know how much trouble you've caused us? Your mother has had a hell of a time worrying about you.' His voice was droning on, accusing me of everything he could think of, blaming me for everything that had ever gone wrong with my family.

I had reached the breaking point, 'I can't take this!' I screamed at him and got up and ran out the door. It was dark outside, and I didn't know where the hell I was. I roamed around for hours in a daze. I ended back outside the house again and sat in the gutter with my head between my knees.

This is where I belong, I thought. *In the gutter.* The nightmare of the past few months swirled around in my head. Distraught and weak, I crept in the back door and quietly made my way to bed. *Welcome home,* was my last thought for the night as I fell into a deathlike sleep.

I had suffered my 'initiation' back into the family, and Mum and the kids kept silent, no one bringing up the events of the past months.

I needed to start looking for a job. I planned to start working and save enough money to go back to Queensland and start looking for Steve and the baby. It didn't occur to me that I would never see them again.

I thought I couldn't go back until I had turned eighteen as I could be arrested again—five months was a long time to wait.

Luckily—if you could call it that—I managed to a job in a chicken factory. It was quite a way from Liverpool station, and I needed to catch a bus there.

I did not know my way around Sydney and was forever getting lost by catching the wrong train. The size of the city made me fearful about going out, and starting a new job made me feel very nervous.

The factory was a large Besser® block building, and a smell of boiled chicken filled the air. The trucks arrived laden with cages full of screeching, clucking birds. I made my way to the office, where I was equipped with a white uniform, a long white vinyl apron, gumboots, and a little peaked hat to keep my shoulder-length hair tucked on top of my head.

After I had put the uniform on, I was shown to a production line over a metal table full of plastic bags containing the giblets of chicken.

The dead and plucked chickens were coming around over our heads, hung up by their feet. There were thousands of them. We were to put the bags into the chicken bums and push them in as far as they would go. I was supposed to do every fourth one.

It was weird. I felt as though I was in an alien world. The warm air and the smell of clean pressed linen from the laundry at Holy Cross was a long way from this place that smelled of boiling flesh.

The other girls on the table looked a bit rough: one had tattoos on her arms, and another had a tattoo of a heart on her forehead. The other two didn't look like they would do anything without the backup of the rougher pair.

I kept my head down and ignored them. I didn't want to talk to anyone. I just wanted to think.

I could hear them talking and laughing, and now and again thought it was me they were laughing at.

The first two days of the job were exhausting and I felt like I was standing up to the ankles of my boots in water. The coldness of the chickens froze my hand even though I had rubber gloves on. On the third day, the girls thought they'd have some fun with me.

The chickens were coming through, and they were missing five and six at a time each time I was rushing to push the giblets into their arses. I was missing a few, and the girls further up the line brought the ones I'd missed back and thrown them on the table for me to do again. The laughter from the girls, especially the rougher ones, was pushing me over the edge.

I stormed up to the shorter one with the tattooed arms: she seemed to be the main instigator. 'If you keep this fucking game up, I will stuff these fucking chicken gizzards up your fucking arse.' She looked at me with surprise and started laughing.

'What your name again?' she asked. 'My name's Regina, and this is my sister Sonia. You don't want to know the others. Come and sit with us at lunch.'

Regina's invitation was too good to refuse, so I then became one of the 'gang'. We all had one thing in common: Regina and her sister had also been in notorious New South Wales girls' homes in Parramatta and Hay.

From the description of those places, Holy Cross sounded like a picnic. For the first time, I was accepted as the person that I had become: a person with a 'record'.

Two weeks after the return to my family, I wrote a letter to Steve. I wasn't sure exactly where to send it, so I posted it to the last place he was working.

In the letter, I told him of my love for him and said that as soon as I had saved enough money to return to Queensland, I would leave to be with him.

I enclosed a photo of myself that had been taken in Sydney. I knew that if my mother found out about the letter, she would have killed me, so I asked him to reply to the post office near Mum's house.

The weeks passed, and each day I went to the post office to see if Steve had sent a reply to my letter. Painfully, I then had to accept that he had either not received the letter, or he did not want to write back to me.

All I could see was his face haunting me day and night. My mind was repeating, *Steve, Steve, Steve. Where's my baby? Where's my baby?*

I had been working at the chicken factory for a couple of months and was invited to go out with Regina and her boyfriend Paul, but I needed a date to make it a foursome.

'Don't worry, Lily,' Regina said. 'I know the perfect person for you.' With that, she pointed her finger at a guy named Alfie, who worked as a cleaner in the factory. 'You're joking,' I gasped, but Alfie was the kind of guy I could take home to Mum and the old boy.

He was very thin, clean-cut, and was genuinely a good guy. He had tried to make conversation with me, but I wasn't interested. He just wasn't my type. 'He likes you, Lil,' Regina commented, 'he told me so. I'll ask him and see if he wants to come with us to the pub on Saturday night.' Regina was confident that Alfie would agree.

I didn't want to go out with him, but it was a chance to get out of the house and away from the old boy.

The incident of my first night back meant I wasn't going to put myself in a position to be attacked by him again, so I went to bed each night at eight o'clock just to get away from him.

It was a release to get back into the social scene again. My memories of Jenny and me going to discos, speedway, and movies made me realise that once, I used to be happy. I thought that if I tried, maybe I could be that way again.

I went out with Alfie that night and many other nights to come. He was a nice guy. Mum and the old boy liked him, and that was a plus; at least it kept them off my back.

I had been going with Alfie for a few months when he asked me if I would like to become engaged to him. We went and picked out a beautiful engagement ring in the shape of a star. He put it on layby and was going to give it to me as soon as he paid it off.

Although Alfie was a nice, caring guy, he could never replace Steve, and each minute of every day kept me wondering where he and our baby were.

It was becoming too much at the factory: everyone knew Alfie, and I were going together, and the jokes and questions about our relationship became too intrusive. I decided to leave and find another job where no one knew my business.

The old boy constantly nagged me when I told him that I was leaving. 'Don't think you're going to sit around here all day on your arse; you get yourself another job. Your mother and I are not going to support any bludgers in this house.'

I started at a fluorescent light factory a week after leaving the chicken factory. On my first day, a girl called Lorraine introduced herself to me and pointed out to two of the guys working on a bench at the front of the factory. 'The tall one is my cousin Geoffrey, and the shorter one is my boyfriend, Paul.' They both gave me a wave, and I nodded my head in turn.

I had been working at the light factory for three days when I became violently sick. I ran to the toilet a few times to be sick. The boss told me to go home. I caught the train to Guildford and started the two-mile walk home. As I walked along, I had the feeling that I was being followed. I turned around, and there was this Geoffrey following me in his car.

'What are you doing here?' I asked him curiously.

'Just seeing how you were going. I told the boss I was sick as well and he let me go home. Do you want a lift?'

'I may as well,' I replied and was glad to get into his car.

'How about going for a drive to Kings Cross?' he asked.

'Great!' I replied. I had never been to the Cross, but I'd heard a lot about it and never thought that I would ever see it.

He reminded me a lot of Mick Jagger from the Rolling Stones. He was skinny and his face was similar, down to the mouth. There was a distinctive Aboriginal look about him; it didn't concern me but made him look more interesting.

Apart from him his looks, there was a cheeky, 'fuck it' attitude about him, an attitude that I could well relate to.

Of course, I thought about Alfie but dismissed it by thinking that I wasn't doing anything wrong anyway.

We drove around for hours, and about five o'clock, I told him to take me home or the old boy would give me heaps.

Leaving the factory and not seeing him every day, my relationship with Alfie was starting to get distant. I wanted him to marry me to take me away from the old boy. Living in that house was driving me mad.

I asked Alfie to move into a flat with me, but he said that he wanted to get engaged and then, in a year or so, we would be married. That wait was far too long for me, and I still had not told him about Steve and the baby.

I had started a friendship with a woman called Margaret at work. She had been married for five years and desperately wanted a baby. She told me that she and her husband had decided to adopt a baby boy and that they were waiting to hear that they had one.

Shortly after, she came in and announced that she was picking up her baby in a few days and would not be back. I didn't know how to feel. I thought of my baby. *Where is he? Someone like Margaret is looking after him now.* I felt like crying for that baby and crying for me.

She was coming in the next morning to pick up her pay. I wrapped up the beautiful crochet matinee jacket and bonnet meant for my baby and gave them to her.

Her eyes lit up with joy at the gift. 'This is beautiful!' she exclaimed. 'Where did you get it from?'

'I bought it for you,' I replied, my lying tongue choking me with grief. I was giving away the last reminder of my baby.

Geoffrey, Lorraine, and Paul lunched with me every day, and after we had eaten, we would all go for a walk.

Lorraine and Paul would walk ahead of us, and we followed. Geoffrey knew I was going with Alfie. 'Why don't you dump this guy? You can go out with me—I'll marry you. What's the problem with that?' I thought he was joking, so I ignored him.

I had been working at the light factory for three months when the boss came up to me and told me he was giving me a weeks' notice, without explanation. I was devastated—I liked it there, and besides, I had become fond of Geoffrey.

I was finding it difficult to get another job. Each day I would go to the employment office only to be told nothing was going at the moment.

Geoffrey would pick me up at the employment office each day during his lunch break and take me somewhere to have lunch. This went on for a couple of weeks.

It wasn't long before the old boy started on me each night. 'Did you find a job today? I bet you're not even looking,' he'd nag. I couldn't handle it any longer.

I've got to leave here. I want to go back to Brisbane and find Steve and my baby. This went on and on inside my head. God knows how I was going to get there and where would I stay. I felt like killing myself; there was no escape from this.

I told Alfie that I needed to leave home, but he was still living with his parents.

'Just hang in there for a while,' he would say. 'We can't get married until we save up some money.'

'What's up with the guy?' Geoffrey said when I told him of Alfie's reaction. 'Look, I've asked Mum and Dad if you can move into our place, and they said it was okay. It just means that you'll have to sleep in the same room as Lorraine and my sister Heather.'

I hugged him, relieved that at least I now had an escape plan.

As soon as Mum and the old boy went to work the next day, I packed my bags, my glory box and moved into Geoffrey's house. I left a letter for Alfie at Mum's house so that he at least knew why I was leaving him. I needed to get away from my parents, and he could not help me with that.

The house was located in Auburn, an older, densely inhabited suburb west of the city. The street was very narrow, with most of the houses having only a narrow front. It was only a two-bedroom weatherboard place, but it was quite long. Geoffrey's brothers Ray and Allan slept in the front bedroom.

The second bedroom was for his sisters Lena and Laurel and cousin Lorraine. Geoffrey slept on a divan in the lounge room and his mother, Clarice, and father, Alan, slept in the dining room, partitioned off by two wardrobes along the hallway.

The place was overcrowded, but it seemed to be a happy place, even though the family was quite poor.

It wasn't long before I ended up sleeping on the divan with Geoffrey. The lack of privacy made it impossible to make love until the early hours of the morning.

I had been there a couple of weeks when I was lucky enough to get a job in a biscuit factory. It was heaven-sent, so I started to save some money after I paid Geoffrey's mother some board.

One night there was a drama with the neighbours across the road, which woke us up. Geoffrey's aunt came over to see if we'd heard anything. She saw us on the divan and must have said something about it to Geoffrey's mother.

Clarice approached us the next night and said, 'I want you two to either get married or Lily can leave here; I don't want the whole street talking about you two.'

'Okay, Mum, we'll get married as soon as soon as I turn eighteen in two months,' Geoffrey replied.

It was ironic that I was marrying a man younger than me when everyone thought that Steve and I were too young. Two months later and true to his word, we were married in the Catholic church up the road.

His family provided us with a little wedding breakfast followed by a train up to Brisbane for a week, staying at the People's Palace, a Salvation Army hostel.

My wedding day, 26 October 1968, had been an exact year to the day that I was let out of Holy Cross.

The honeymoon wasn't a celebration for me—I knew that I was in the same city as Steve and my baby.

On each face I looked at, I was looking for Steve and, in each pram, I looked for my baby. I hadn't told Geoffrey about Steve or the baby. I feared how he would react toward me for keeping it from him. I felt guilty that I had also used him to get away from the miserable life I was having.

I also felt like second-hand goods, and no one wanted second-hand goods.

Not long after we married, Clarice was run over by a car and suffered a fractured pelvis. She was laid up in hospital for six weeks. During this time, Lena had met Terry. He was at least a foot shorter than her and had a chip on his shoulder the size of a gum tree.

It wasn't long before she found out that she was pregnant, and a hasty marriage was soon arranged when Clarice was discharged.

Clarice was diagnosed with heart trouble in the hospital and was told not to exert herself. Even though she was only in her early forties, she looked a lot older—a lifetime of hard work was not kind to her. She was nearly deaf, a situation that had impacted her childhood, never having spoken until the age of twelve.

I took over doing the cooking and housework to help her. It wasn't long before I had to fully take over the running of the house. Although I felt like an unpaid servant, I was glad to be there and be accepted. It was a small price to pay.

Things gradually got better, and Geoffrey's parents had a garage put up in the backyard. We moved into it as soon as it was built. It was only partly finished; we froze in the winter and cooked in the summer, but at least it was away from the house, and we could have a place on our own.

Geoffrey was very possessive and would question me about who I spoke to through the day, where I went and so forth. Anything I did or wanted to do had to involve a discussion about why I wanted to do it or where I was going. It annoyed me, but I thought, *He must love me if he gets as jealous as this.*

We had been married for nearly two years when Lena gave birth to a baby girl. They called her Ann. Terry was very possessive of her and would not let anyone but Clarice nurse her.

I was envious of the joy they had with their baby. It was a constant reminder of what I had lost.

I wanted to get away from reminders of my lost child, so Geoffrey and I rented a lovely modern two-bedroom flat with some money we managed to put aside, and I was also lucky enough to pass the exam to get a job in the public service doing data entry.

Computers were quite new at the time, and the boss told us we would be the most sought-after people in Australia when we were fully trained.

For the first time, I felt like a real person. I had finally escaped the drudgery of working in factories and took great delight in dressing up in nice clothes and shoes to go to work in the city each day.

My husband, on the other hand, was getting more and more jealous of my appearance and starting to question me on every detail of why I was dressing up to go to work.

'What are you putting on that makeup for? Who are you trying to impress?' Each night he kept me up till the early hours of the morning, questioning me until I broke down and cried, forcing me to tell him how much I loved him, and then he would finally let me go to sleep.

Although I had this wonderful job, I was still trying to fall pregnant and once every couple of weeks, I took the day off to make baby clothes. I'd sit all day making little dresses for the baby girl I was going to have. It never occurred to me to make boy's clothes.

The memory of my baby kept going around in my head. I wondered where he was. He would be nearly four now. I still could not fathom how I came to lose him.

I could not logically work out how things turned out the way they did. Things did not seem right—how could they take my baby? But then my mind would tell me it must have been right for them to do it to me.

Even listening to a song on the radio would trigger flashbacks so real that I could even smell the sweet scent of the washing soda of the laundry, and yet reality was going on around me.

My sister Bridget had just returned from New Zealand. She had been living over there for a while and asked us if she and her friend Sue could stay with us for a few weeks until they got a place of their own. We agreed. I thought it was great that, at last, I would have someone to talk to for a change.

Bridget was a real hippie with her long afro hair and her colourful caftans. I envied her sense of fun and freedom. She was outspoken and articulate, and she had something to say about my husband. Geoffrey sensed it and was beginning to resent Bridget and her friend's presence in our flat, and one night after one of our early morning arguing sessions, he told me to tell them to leave at the end of the week. I was upset. I did not want her to leave and be there with him on my own again.

When I told her what Geoffrey had said, she let me know that she and Sue had been listening to Geoffrey going on at me all night and said, 'I don't know why you are putting up with that man's abuse. Sue and I are leaving for Queensland on Friday. If you want to come with us, you are welcome. Frankly, I wouldn't stay with that bastard.'

I thought about Bridget's offer, but my courage was failing me. What if I was pregnant? I had been trying desperately for months to fall pregnant, and what if I left him and found out I was? What would become of me?

My questions were answered in a couple of days when my period arrived and to the realisation of what I had suspected was, in fact, reality: my husband was sterile.

He would never give me a baby.

He could never replace the baby I had lost.

If I stayed with him, I would never have another child.

I was desperate. If I go to Queensland and find Steve, we could search for our baby. It had been nearly four years, and what did that woman say? Something about four years to get the baby back. I made up my mind I was going back to find Steve.

I was terrified to leave. What if Geoffrey came home and found me sneaking off with Bridget and Sue? He would kill me.

As soon as he left for work on Friday morning, I rushed to pack my clothes and some of my glory box. Why the bloody hell I wanted to take the glory box was a puzzle to me; it took up most of the room in the car, but still, we fitted in as much as we could.

I left him a note explaining that I couldn't take things anymore, and we left as quickly as we could.

My heart was pounding until we got out of Sydney and reached the freeway and onto the long highway to Brisbane.

Night fell and, in the darkness, I realised it was too late to turn back. My fear of what lay ahead made my gut wrench. I felt as though I had just committed another failure in my life. 'What are people saying about me now,' I thought?

As the car drove on into the night, I could feel the pull of Brisbane drawing me closer. 'I'm going home,' I thought.

We arrived late the next day and decided to book into a caravan park and were given a nice big van that easily accommodated the three of us. We rested for a couple of days. The major thing now was to find ourselves jobs as soon as possible.

I was lucky enough to get a job in a place that wired telephone switches; I had done a bit of soldering in a job that I had held for a short time, so I had a bit of experience.

I was happy for the first time in a long time, and now it was time to start looking for Steve, but where to start? That was the question.

Driving around Brisbane, I hadn't realised how big the city was.

Panic filled me with despair. *How am I going to find my baby here? This place is endless. Oh my God!*

It dawned on me that I did not know how I was even going to start to search for the baby. And what about Steve? He could be anywhere.

A voice broke into my panicking mind: 'Let's go into the Valley.'

'What did you say, Bridget?' I spoke as if still in a daze.

'I said, "let's go into the Valley." I know a place where we can meet some "heads",' she said as if we all understood what she was saying.

'What are "heads"?' I asked her, oblivious to the 'hippie speak.'

'People that smoke dope and drop acid,' was the informed reply. 'I can see you've been in hiding a long time. Time to get out and have some fun.' She and Sue laughed. Soon, I was out of my daze and ready to get on to the next adventure.

We arrived at a café called The Coconut Grove. It was a small place with an upstairs lounge decorated with palm trees and little huts with benches and tables. The owners had tried to make it look tropical. The music was fairly quiet, and the tables were filled with a mixture of young men and women dressed in hippie clothes.

I looked a bit out of place. I was still wearing the 'mod' clothes I had bought from my time in the public service.

We pulled up a seat and sat and drank coffee, and waited to see if anyone would join us. A young guy with blond hair to his shoulders, wearing a leather cowboy hat, came up to the table and started to talk to us.

He introduced himself as Norman—'But I like to be called Norm,' he said. He had almond-shaped eyes and looked a bit like John Denver, and I loved John Denver. He was cute enough, and although I had an idea that he was younger than me, he acted quite mature and knew quite a bit about life.

As the music played, we talked about the usual things that concerned us: it was 1971, the year of the Vietnam War, drugs, love, and peace. Even though I thought he was extremely cute and he said he was eighteen, he was still far too young for me at twenty-one.

I loved the Coconut Grove, it became the place to meet each night, and each night Norm was there. We got on very well, and he asked me to go with him to his place to meet his friend.

His friend wasn't home, so one kiss led to another, and we found ourselves in bed. *This is not right,* I kept telling myself. *He's too young for you.*

I soon put the age issue out of the equation and thought, *Oh well; I like him, so what the hell.*

I decided to move in with him. We had been living together for a couple of weeks when Bridget and Sue gave us the old car we had driven up to Queensland. It had some mechanical problems, and they told us we could have it if we fixed it.

Norm and I jumped at the chance and soon had the car on the road. It was only a couple of weeks before he was pulled over by the police and charged with driving without a licence. He appeared in court the next day, and the magistrate read out his name and age. I nearly fell off the seat when I found out that he was seventeen!

He was fined a hundred dollars and had to pay within two weeks. Still reeling from the news about his age, I angrily demanded to know why he had lied to me.

'I love you and didn't want to lose you,' he said, his eyes filled with tears. 'You're not going to dump me, are you?' he pleaded. 'No,' I replied, but deep down, I knew the relationship was doomed to fail.

Norm was worried about the fines and decided that he would head back to Sydney. I had thought about going back but did not know how I was going to manage on my own.

Brisbane was bigger than I ever imagined, and having failed to find Steve or have any idea of where to look, and no one to ask for help, I saw this as a good opportunity to return and possibly get a job. We had decided that we would find a place in Kings Cross and look for work as soon as we arrived. Norm knew a boarding house where we could get a cheap room until we found a flat.

Before leaving for Sydney, the gearbox in the car needed replacing, and Norm's friend knew a guy named Brian who could replace it for sixty dollars. Packed for the trip, we drove the car to Brian's place, where they were going to fix it and be off.

I sat in Brian's house and spoke to his wife while we were waiting for the job to be finished. We had been chatting away for a couple of hours when we got onto the subject of discos and bands. It was then I told her about Steve and his band.

She looked at me in amazement and said, 'I know him; he just married my best friend a couple of months ago.' I went into shock. Steve married? Although I thought he may have, the news still upset me.

A splitting detachment of my longed-for hopes came over me. It was as though I was meant to find out news in my last few hours in Queensland.

This was an omen that my connection with Queensland was finished. I thought about it all the way to Sydney. I had to let go of him, but how could I? He was still in my heart. I'd never broken up with him. This went over and over again in my mind.

We arrived back in Sydney on a cold and rainy morning and made our way to the Cross, pulling up in front of a large and untidy boarding house. We rented a room for a couple of nights; Norm was intent on finding a small flat.

I went looking for a job and managed to find one straight away in a laundry. Visions of Holy Cross came to mind the minute I walked through the door—the same sickly smell of laundry powder and steam greeting me back home. Somehow it felt rather comforting, familiar.

Norm found a little basement flat in a three-storey terrace house just across the road from the laundry. I wasn't keen on being so close to my work, but it was cheap, and it had a lot of potential.

He painted and fixed the place up whilst I was working. He also had a part-time job at the markets, which didn't pay much, but it looked like we were starting to get somewhere.

The Cross was a place of endless activity. We wandered the streets each night, taking in the sights. The colourful lights of the strip clubs and the spruikers on the footpaths gave the place a carnival atmosphere. I loved it and for a long time felt just a little bit happy.

The American troops on rest and recreation from Vietnam were also wandering around the streets looking for excitement, giving the place a foreign atmosphere. One could almost imagine they were reliving the Second World War.

Many of them would find their way to the little hippie hangout called Ball Pants. It was a dark, dingy place in the back lane behind the Goldfish Bowl—a pub in the main street.

We loved going there; the place had lots of character, and the marijuana was easy to get, and I had my first taste of it, giving me a feeling of calm. It was our favourite place, and Norm and I hung out there every night smoking and drinking Irish coffee and cola as we listened to a guy sing protest songs.

It was only a couple of weeks back in Sydney before I realised that I was pregnant, filling me with fear. This was the last thing I had expected. The baby that I wanted so desperately had picked the wrong time and place to come. I told Norm the news, and he was over the moon. 'A baby. Wow, I'm stoked!' he declared.

I wasn't 'stoked'—I was terrified. He was too young to give me the security needed for our baby.

I had started to dress in the fashion of the hippies in the Cross: my hair was longer, and long colourful embroidered caftans became my usual wear. I seemed to fit in better and went along with the mood of what was happening around me. It all seemed to be magical to me, living in a place that was so well-known for its colourful, if somewhat seedy atmosphere.

We had started to make a few acquaintances around the Cross, and Norm would invite them to 'crash' in our flat. One night he brought home a girl named Chris. She had been kicked out by her boyfriend and need a place to stay for a couple of nights.

I was pissed off. I was sick of people using the place as a 'crash pad' and told Norm that he would have to stop bringing people home to have 'weed parties'. He was a bit put-out but accepted it and decided that he would smoke weed outside the flat.

Norm was out one night when Chris brought home a guy named Manfred. I walked through the door to see a guy like I had never seen before.

He was dressed in a long black coat with a black shirt and jeans; his brown hair hung down to his waist. He had a feminine face with a short goatee beard and had the most unusual-shaped eyes—like a cat.

I was changing and adapting to the lifestyle in the Cross and had started wearing long black caftans with embroidered flowers around the neck; my hair was halfway down my back.

Manfred stared at me as Chris introduced us, and he said, 'I know you; I've known you from a past life.' I was fascinated and wanted to know more. We spoke for hours on reincarnation and psychic powers. He told me that he was a warlock, a 'white one' of course, and was living in a commune with a group of ten people, including his sister.

He invited me round to his house in Forsyth Street in one of the back streets of the Cross. It was a big two-storey Victorian house with an overgrown yard. The inside was filled with people lying everywhere on mattresses all over the floor.

Although they looked 'out of it', he introduced me to some of the people, and we went out into the backyard to meditate.

I had never been involved with any of this before in my life and found it absorbing and wanted to be involved more. Sitting in the garden and talking to the 'earth spirits' took me back to my childhood, where I read and fantasised about fairies and goblins, and even a leprechaun that Dad had seen every so often.

I felt like the ten-year-old who was given the book of Grimm's Fairy Tales for her birthday.

My relationship with Norm was soon becoming extinct as I spent more time around the commune.

The house was full of interesting discussions, psychic explorations, and the constant smell of food cooking with herbs. Each night after work, I would meet Manfred and we'd go to the library and delve into old books on witchcraft, astrology, and spirituality.

As the weeks passed, It was increasingly obvious that I had to start making decisions on a secure lifestyle for my baby. I had decided that I was going to move into the commune with Manfred and told Norm of my plans.

'What's going to happen to my baby? Are you going to let me see it?' he asked tearfully.

'Of course, I will. I'll let you know how I'm getting on, I promise.' We hugged each other and said our goodbyes.

I felt sad about leaving Norm. We had been together for a few months and did have some really good times, but I just could not see him as the man who could look after me and the baby in the future.

I had been living with Manfred and the group for a couple of weeks when I decided that I would have to book into Crown Street Women's Hospital to arrange for the delivery of my baby. It was close to the Cross and I could walk there.

I was automatically directed to the social worker because I was separated from Geoffrey. Little did I know the notorious reputation of this hospital; I was to find out much later about its dark history.

A thin, long-nosed woman dressed in white took my details and questioned me about my relationship with Norm. I told her that we had separated and that I was living in a commune.

She looked down her nose over her glasses and asked if I had contacted Geoffrey regarding divorce. It was at this point I realised that my relationship with him had to be decided one way or the other.

A couple of days after the hospital visit, I wrote Geoffrey a letter and told him that I was sorry for leaving him the way I did and that we needed to discuss divorce arrangements. I gave my address care of the King's Cross Post Office. I did not want him to know where I was living, fearful that he would turn up unexpectedly.

A letter arrived back from him a couple of days later. He suggested meeting me in a park on the following Saturday to discuss things. If I didn't show up, it was okay, but could I let him know where we could meet next time?

Manfred was against me meeting him. 'I don't trust him; he may hurt you,' he said with a concerned look on his face.

'I'll be all right; he won't do anything to me in public. Don't worry—I have to do this.' He reluctantly let me go without any more debate.

Fear and dread filled me as I approached the park where he sat waiting. As I approached, I could see his face turning into a painful expression trying to hold back the tears. He came up to me and hugged me. 'How are you? You've lost a lot of weight.'

'I'm fine,' I replied, still not knowing what to expect from him.

We went and sat on a bench, and then he burst out crying. 'Oh God, I've missed you. That day when I came home and found you gone, I felt like killing myself. Mum and Dad were so upset. I had to move home with them. I lost my job; I couldn't go to work anymore after you left. I even left the flat; Lena and Terry are living there. I can't set a foot back there.'

The thought of Lena and Terry living in my flat, using my things, made me angry. *How dare they use my things after the way they had treated me?* I felt like yelling at him. *Why did you let those pair pick over my bones?* But I held my tongue. After all, I was the one who walked out on everything.

'Everything in the place reminded me of you. Even the picture frames you painted at Mum's made me cry each time I looked at them.' His voice trembled in pain.

I didn't know what to say. I felt guilty that I had caused all this pain to him and his family. 'I'm sorry,' was all I could manage. He pulled himself together, then said, 'I want you to come home with me. I want you back again.'

I was horrified. 'I didn't come here to go back with you. I came to find out what you wanted to do about a divorce.'

It was time to let him know that I was pregnant so that he wouldn't try to make me go back home with him. 'I've got something to tell you. It's the reason why I can't go back with you. I'm pregnant.' I waited for the explosion, but there was none. He asked me about the father and where I was living, if I had a job and what I was going to do about the baby. I answered his questions, but he listened as though my answers were going over his head.

He just sat there for a while and then said, 'I still want you to come home. How do you think you're going to look after a baby living in a situation like that? What happens when you have to give up the job? Do you think those people are going to look after you? If you come home with me, I'll look after you and the baby and bring it up as my own. I'll never give you a hard time about it. Please, give me a chance to prove it to you. If it doesn't work out, you can leave and go back to these people.'

'I don't know if I can face your family again,' I replied. The prospect of returning to face them was daunting.

'They told me to tell you they want you to come home,' he replied. I could feel myself weakening; his pleading was stirring my conscience, and I felt I had to redeem myself for the way I had sneaked out and left him.

I agreed to go back to see his parents with him. My decision to return would depend on the reception I received from them during my visit.

He seemed to pick up on the drive home. The underlying emotional tearfulness in his voice was gone. As we came closer to his street, I could feel the familiarity of being back in Auburn. I did like the place: it was crowded, and it felt safe.

It was strange pulling up in his car outside the old house again. His young cousins and their friends were sitting in the alleyway across the road.

'Hey Lily,' they yelled, 'welcome back!' I turned and gave them a wave as I walked into the house. Clarice and Allan were sitting in the kitchen when we walked in. They both got up and came and hugged me.

'It's good to see you again. We have been worried sick about where you've been. Geoffrey has been driving us mad; he's been so upset since you left.' Once again, the guilt came flooding back.

I thought, *God, how could I upset these people after all they had done for me, taking me in when I needed help.* I felt so humiliated that I had hurt the whole family. *I have to make things right again.*

We sat around the kitchen table, talking for hours. Night had come, and I asked Geoffrey to take me back to the Cross.

'You don't have to go. Stay here for the night,' he pleaded. 'I promise I won't touch you; just lie here and talk to me.' Reluctantly I agreed.

Manfred would be worrying about me, but he'd know where I was. A thousand thoughts crossed my mind. As we lay on his single bed and talked, I told him about my time in Queensland and Norm.

'Why did you leave me?' he asked.

This is the time for truth, I thought. I finally told him about Steve and the baby.

He became quite emotional and said, 'Why didn't you tell me about this? I would have understood.'

'I didn't want you to think I was a slut. The day I left home, the nuns told me not to tell anyone about what had happened to me. They just told me to forget about it. Only I couldn't. Don't you remember me wanting to have another baby? What about the days I used to take off work to sit and sew baby clothes?'

All my pain was finally being let out. *Oh God, my baby, where is he? Where is Steve? He's married now. He's gone forever.* I started to sob, not telling him what was going around and around in my mind.

He held me tightly, and for the first time in a long time, I thought that he understood. I agreed to return to him on the condition that we move back into our flat. He agreed.

We talked for most of the night. Exhausted, I fell asleep just as the dawn was breaking. Later that day, Geoffrey and I went back to the commune and collected my things. Manfred was upset. He pulled me aside and asked for my address. 'I will come and see you in a week, just to see if you are going all right.' I thanked him for that and told him I'd wait to see him then.

Lena and Terry were told that I was coming back to live at the flat and that I would be using my bedroom. They moved into the spare bedroom with Ann. They greeted me as though I had not been away and with the same indifference that they had always treated me.

This is not going to work with them living here, I thought. Still, I had no choice but to accept the situation as Geoffrey was only working one or two days a week moving furniture, and we could not afford the rent on our own.

I had only been back for a couple of days when Geoffrey made a sarcastic remark to me; it wasn't anything too nasty, so I thought I would ignore it and put it down to him still being hurt over my leaving. After a few nights, he had been having a couple of drinks and kept me awake talking for most of the night. Although he did not abuse me like before, I could feel that he was holding back from saying some of the things that he really wanted to say.

It started to dawn on me that I had made a terrible mistake by going back with him. The feelings I had about him returned, and the reasons why I had left him in the first place resurfaced.

Manfred was coming to see me at the end of the week, and I thought that I would leave with him. Geoffrey was working that day, so I planned to dress in a couple of caftans and make an excuse to go out of the flat when Manfred came.

Terry was home when Manfred arrived. I had barely answered the door when he jumped in before me.

'Who are you?' he asked Manfred.

'He's a friend of mine; he's come to see me,' I told him.

'I'm not letting him in the flat,' he said. I pushed past him and yelled at him to get out of the way. Terry pushed me out of the way and flew at Manfred, punching him in the face and knocking him down the stairs.

'I'm not letting you near my brother's wife. Fuck off out of here before I give you a good hiding!' he yelled at Manfred, who was picking himself up off the steps.

I felt trapped. Terry had the stairway blocked. 'I'm not letting you out' he said. 'Go back in the flat,' he ordered. I obeyed as though he was my jailer. Memories of my imprisonment came flooding back to me. Once again, I was behind bars, only this time I could not see them.

I heard Terry quietly telling Geoffrey about the incident when he came home from work. The conversation ended with Terry saying quietly, 'Don't worry, mate; I'll keep an eye on her.'

Geoffrey quit his job and stayed home with me, going onto unemployment benefits that saw us getting eighteen dollars a week. The rent for the flat was twenty dollars a week.

As we scraped by to keep up our part of the rent and food, it was becoming apparent that we were in deep financial trouble and reliant on Terry and Lena for the necessities.

Little Ann was a delight, and she insisted on me picking her up and waltzing with her to the music of Strauss. One day, Terry came home and saw me twirling her around. 'Put my fucking kid down! I don't want you touching my kid!' he roared at me. I was shocked. Geoffrey was in the bedroom lying down, and I heard him jump off the bed and burst through the door.

'Don't speak to my wife like that, you bastard!' His six-foot frame towered over Terry's short, stocky stature. 'Get your fucking stuff and piss off out of here!' Geoffrey roared at him. Terry and Lena picked up Ann and packed a few clothes in a bag and left. 'We'll be back tomorrow to pick up the rest of our stuff,' he snorted as they piled out the door.

'Good riddance. I hate that little bastard anyway. It was only a matter of time before I punched him one,' Geoffrey said, falling back into the lounge.

'What's going to happen now? We can't afford the rent,' I said, dreading the reply.

'Well, it looks like we have to move back into Mum's place.'

My worst fears became a reality.

Now I would have no chance of ever leaving him again. I would have even more people to watch me. I had the suspicion that Geoffrey was waiting for something like this to happen and use it as an excuse to keep me under the constant surveillance of his mother and family.

Our furniture was packed on the back of a truck, and ten minutes later, we were unpacking it into Geoffrey's parents' house in Auburn. Raymond and Lorraine had moved out of the house, and Geoffrey's brother Al had moved into the garage down the backyard. His parents had the front bedroom and Laurel the remaining room, so it left only the dining room between the lounge and the kitchen to be our bedroom.

We used our wardrobes as a wall and put a long curtain alongside them as a screen to give us some privacy.

Geoffrey had started to play darts at the local hotel and soon found that he had a natural talent for the game. The dart competitions started as a once-a-week excursion and gradually into a five-night-a-week event.

Whilst he was out, I sat and sewed and ironed the little second-hand clothes bought at the St Vincent de Paul shop, my mind thinking about my growing baby. *I wonder if it's a girl or boy. Geoffrey had told me that if it's a boy, don't bother to bring it home from the hospital.* He was sort of joking when he said it but *was he really joking?* I thought.

I never got tired of pulling out the old bassinet holding the things I had gathered for the baby, and I had a sense of wonder as I folded and unfolded the little clothes.

This was my first opportunity to prepare for the arrival of my baby, my thoughts constantly going back to my first baby. *Why hadn't I been allowed to do this for him?* My mind blocked out before I could answer my own thoughts.

Geoffrey was out of work throughout the term of my pregnancy, and this made life difficult.

The eighteen dollar dole payment did not go far after we paid ten dollars board and bought his cigarettes each week. The car had to be sold, and each day was spent washing, cleaning, and carrying home bags of shopping from the street. My mother-in-law was very frail, and that saw me waiting on everyone in the house.

Day after day passed and soon, I was in my final days of pregnancy. *Will I go into the hospital tonight?* I thought as I went to bed each night. Morning came and still, no baby. Depression was starting to set in.

One morning, a week past the due date, I woke to find that my water had broken. 'Don't go anywhere today,' I told Geoffrey, 'I'm going into hospital as soon as the pains start.'

All day, he hung around the house and by four that afternoon, I still had not had any labour pains, so he decided that he would go to the pub and play darts for a while.

We agreed that if anything happened that I would call him, and he would come straight home. It was about six that evening that I went out to take some clothes off the line when I started to have fierce pains.

I stood there thinking, *This is too quick; the pains from my other baby started softly and then got really bad.* I managed to stagger into the house and called Laurel to ring Geoffrey.

I started to panic; the pains were two minutes apart, and we had to get into Crown Street Hospital in the middle of the city. It was Friday night, and the roads would be crowded with traffic going into the city for the theatres and restaurants there.

Laurel had told Geoffrey to hurry. After fifteen minutes, he still hadn't arrived. I lay on the bed in the pains so bad that I could not speak. 'Ring him again and tell him to get home here before she has the baby on the bed,' Clarice ordered. Laurel stood there, her face expressing the panic of a frightened fifteen-year-old.

Ten minutes later, Geoffrey came rushing through the door. 'Do you want me to carry you to the car?' he said, seeing the pain reflected in my face.

'No, just get me to the hospital,' I gasped between the struggle to walk to the utility waiting out the front of the house.

As expected, the traffic was thick and slow. Geoffrey was blowing the car horn, weaving in and out of traffic lanes trying to make his way along the seventeen kilometres that led to the hospital. I sat half-lying and half-sitting in the front seat, holding a towel between my legs.

When at last, we finally reached the hospital, a porter came rushing out with a wheelchair. I got into the chair in a daze and before I knew it, I was on a bed in the labour ward.

The doctor took one look and said to the nurse, 'Get things ready now, or this one will catch us napping.' Before I knew it, a mask was pushed into my face and the sweet sickly smell of gas took me back to the delivery of my son.

I heard the nurse telling me to turn over on my side. Fear and panic overcame me; the memory of being tied down the last time came back to me as though I was reliving my first delivery again.

'Let me lie on my back! Let me lie on my back!' I heard myself screaming, the nightmare of being tied down flooding back to me again.

'All right,' the nurse said as she turned me over.

Five minutes later, my daughter Amanda made her way into the world.

'Let me see her,' I said, still dazed from the gas and needles they had injected into me. A nurse brought her over, and I looked at my baby girl for the first time. Her wrinkled forehead and her almond-shaped eyes looked as though she was frowning at me for bringing her into the world.

I had been sutured up, and the baby had been cleaned and was placed in a bassinet beside my bed before my husband came up to see us.

The nurses had already told him that I had given birth to a girl by the time he had finished filling in hospital information. He was smiling and looked as pleased as Punch when he walked into the post-delivery room.

'Congratulations,' he said as he kissed me on the side of my face. Amanda let out a loud wail and started to scream, the tears rolling down her face. She sounded as though she was in pain.

A nurse came in to see what the commotion was all about. 'Gosh, look at these tears already; this is unusual,' she said as she checked the baby for loose nappy pins.

As Geoffrey looked at the little thing crying in the bassinet, he turned to me and said, 'God, look at her squinty eyes—was the father Chinese or something?'

'No!' I snarled at him. I was angry and humiliated. My baby was only a few minutes old, and I was being reminded of my sins.

'You'll have to go now. Your wife needs to rest,' the nurse said as she came along to do my blood pressure. With that, he kissed me good night and told me that he would see me the next day.

'I have to put the baby in the nursery and feed her. You can see her in the morning,' the nurse said, pushing the bassinet along the corridor.

I was worn out and drifted into a fitful sleep, the pain of labour and the after-pains bringing me back to a realisation of where I was. *I've had a baby.* My thoughts were repeating as I drifted in and out of sleep.

The next day I was awoken by babies crying all around me. I sat up and looked to see where my baby was. She was nowhere to be seen. A nurse came into the ward and walked over to my bed. 'Your baby is still in the nursery; she got a touch of jaundice, and the doctors have told us to keep her in there under the lights until it goes.'

Geoffrey came to visit that afternoon and brought congratulations cards from his family. 'When will you get to see the baby?' he asked.

'I don't know. When they let her out of the nursery.' I had the intention of breastfeeding her, and it worried me that she was not getting any food.

I asked the nurse how the babies were being fed when they were in the nursery. She explained that they gave them some special formula until the mothers could feed them.

It had been two days after the delivery, and Geoffrey came up the following day. I still hadn't seen the baby since the night she was delivered. 'When are they going to give her to you?' he asked

'I don't know—when they think she's better,' I replied.

'Well, I'm going to see the doctor and find out what's going on.' He left and returned a few minutes later. 'I've seen the doctor, and he said that you can have the baby now.'

A sense of relief came over me. At last, I was getting my baby. The nurse brought her in a short while later; by then, my younger sisters had arrived and the whole bed was surrounded with the buzz of cooing and gasps of delight at the little blond angel sleeping amid the commotion.

I was discharged two days later and was told by the social worker to ring her in a week and let her know how I was going. I was thankful to know that there was help there if ever I needed it.

Chapter 5

The first day home from the hospital was filled with excitement for everyone but me. Clarice had not seen the baby until my arrival home. Walking into the house and placing my child into her lap was a gesture of my gratitude for their acceptance of my situation: I had brought home the baby that their son could never give me.

The whole neighbourhood must have come to see the baby. I think it was more of a curiosity for people to see the evidence of my 'sins', but as soon as they saw the tiny bundle wrapped in a pink rug, all the curiosity gave way to wonder at the tiny and perfect baby that slept through the whole inspection.

Things took a turn for the better when Geoffrey finally got a permanent job on the local council. We could, at last, begin to save some money to look for a place of our own. However, that was not going to happen.

I had begun to breastfeed the baby from the first day they had allowed me to have her, but she never seemed to be settled. Each night she would wake up and cry. I would put her to the breast, and although she seemed to be sucking and getting milk, she never seemed satisfied. As soon as I put her down, she would cry again. This went on for six weeks. Night after night, her cries kept the whole house awake.

The sister at the baby health centre scorned me when I told her that I didn't think that my milk was any good for her. 'Just keep going with it. Your baby needs your milk more than she needs a bottle,' she said, making me feel like an inadequate mother who could not even feed her baby.

Finally, I gave up trying to breastfeed and put her on a bottle, the whole time feeling that it was no wonder they took my other baby off me—I was useless with this one.

During this time, I was having thoughts of leaving Geoffrey. He had started to give me a hard time again. More money meant more drinking and more darts; he was now going out seven nights a week.

In desperation, I rang the social worker at Crown Street hospital and told her that I was finding living with him and his family was becoming more and more impossible.

She asked me what I thought my options were if I left and said that I would probably have to put Mandy into foster care until I found a job. Her words brought back the memory of the words of the first social worker ringing in my ears.

Foster care was not an option, knowing I would lose her forever if she went into care. I had to stay with him. *At least I've got a roof over my head.*

Geoffrey was becoming a shadowy figure in my life as I was spending all my time with his family while he went out each night.

My days were spent doing never-ending housework, shopping, and cooking. I had taken over the role of chief cook and bottle washer whilst Clarice looked after Mandy. She sat and nursed and fed her while I went about the daily chores. My nights were filled with television and remoteness.

Days slowly turned into months; the same monotonous routines ground on each day. It was 1974, Mandy was nearly two and she was the special child; her closeness to Clarice was evident. I was too busy running the house and seemed to lose the special intimacy that should have come from spending more time with my growing baby.

If Mandy was hurt or needed anything, she cried out for Clarice or Lena. I felt as though I had given birth to Mandy to give her to Geoffrey's family.

About this time, I was desperate to have another baby. I had rung an adoption agency and asked about adopting a baby, but after the woman asked me a few personal details regarding living arrangements and income, she told me that I would have little chance of adopting a baby because I was living with Geoffrey's mother and father and a child would get confused with having 'two mothers'.

I was angry. They took my baby, and I thought that I now deserved to have one given to me.

I did not bring up the subject of Geoffrey's infertility, nor did he discuss it. It was at this time that information on artificial insemination was becoming widely publicised, and I thought this would be the way that we could have another baby without all the drama of being investigated like adopting a child would have entailed.

I finally took the courage and asked him if he was agreeable to the idea of insemination. To my surprise, he accepted the idea readily, the next step being to inquire into it. I went along to Crown Street Hospital again and spoke to the booking officer, and she directed me to the infertility clinic.

The sister in the clinic took my details and then made an appointment for me to see the doctor the next week. I was so excited at the prospect of another baby. As I walked down the hill to the railway station, my feet did not touch the pavement.

'How did it go?' Geoffrey asked when I got home.

'Great. I have to go back next week for another appointment,' I answered.

'I hope they don't want me to do anything,' he muttered. 'I don't want people poking away at me.'

'You don't have to worry. I'm the one who will have to have all the treatments,' I said to him, reassuring him that he did not have to do anything that might involve some effort on his part.

The next week I was given an internal examination and was asked a lot of questions about why I wanted to have artificial insemination when I already had two pregnancies.

I had to tell the inquiring nurse the whole history of my lost baby, my leaving Geoffrey, and falling pregnant to Norm. Her indifference to my painful recollections made me feel like a beggar asking for bread and receiving a stone.

'We will still have to do tests on you, even though you have had two pregnancies,' she said, peering down her nose at me. She went on to say, 'We also have to do tests on your husband to make sure that he is infertile, and if he is, and why, to make sure that you are both suitable for insemination.'

My hopes were dashed. Geoffrey would never agree to be tested. 'I'll make an appointment for your husband next week,' she said.

'What happened?' he asked when I got home. I told him about the questions and the examinations they had performed on me. He listened interestedly. 'So, when are they going to do it then?' he asked.

Now was my chance to tell him. 'They have to see you first before they will do anything to me. They want to make sure things are okay before they put me on the list.'

'I knew they just wouldn't do it without a big production. You know everything, don't you? A real smart-arse.'

A tightening in my neck as I felt myself getting upset, my eyes filling with tears, getting ready for him to tell me to go to buggery, then he said, 'So, what time's the appointment then?'

My dashed hope was restored. I held my surprise and excitement to myself as I calmly told him one- thirty next Wednesday.

'Right,' was the response.

The following Wednesday, both of us made our way to the infertility clinic. There were other couples there, so I suppose that did something to alleviate his discomfort.

After seeing the doctor and being examined, Geoffrey was told to come back the following month for a sperm count and more tests. I thought that this would be where he would drop the idea, but he showed up the following month and had a sperm count done.

At last, it was finally confirmed: Geoffrey had such a low count he would never father a child. I felt cheated. He received a beating as a teenager that ruptured him, and I often thought that it might have caused his sterility. The reality was that he had to accept the fact that he was sterile and, having accepted it, had to do something about my need for another child.

He went through the next few months of tests, X-rays, and discussions without complaint, and after the doctors exhausted all the required protocol for suitability for insemination, we were told that we were finally on the waiting list.

'Mr and Mrs Fuller, as you know, the service of artificial insemination is one that has attracted a lot of attention, and as such, there are many people on the waiting list. As you already have one child, the waiting time will probably be a bit longer as preference will be given to couples who do not have any children at all. The wait may take some years, so I can't guarantee when you will be called in to be inseminated.' The clinical tone of the doctor's voice made me realise that all our hopes and dreams finally rested on a system over which we had no control, and all our hopes could not make things happen sooner.

I felt so let down that I could not speak as we drove home, the doctor's words going over and over inside my mind: *It could take years. I don't want to wait years.*

I want a baby now. I want my baby back. They took my baby. Why, why, why?' I was angry. I had a right to be. I deserved a baby—my baby.

Geoffrey was more accepting of the doctor's prognosis. 'Oh well, at least we're on the list,' he said. He irritated me. He still had his darts and good times to enjoy each night. I had nothing to look forward to, just housework and sleep and his nagging.

Mandy was growing, and watching my little girl as she approached each birthday gave me a sense that time was passing. My need for another child was diminishing with each passing year.

Every time she turned another year older, my thoughts would turn to Shane. I wondered what he would have been doing at Mandy's age. *I wonder where he is. I wonder where Steve is.* Each day brought the same wondering.

Mandy was seven when we heard that Crown Street was closing down. Geoffrey said, 'Don't you think that you should ask about that waiting list and what is going to happen to it?'

I had completely forgotten about the waiting list. My hope of having another baby had long passed, but I was curious to find out how far we were up the list. He had just awakened my feelings about another baby. I was nearly thirty, and my time was running out.

I rang the hospital the next day and spoke to the sister in the infertility clinic. When I told her that I had been on the waiting list for five years, she seemed to be quite amazed and told me that she would look for my files and ring me back. She rang the next day and said that she had found my file. 'It was put away in a drawer,' and that's why it has been overlooked.

She was quite apologetic and asked me if I would like to come into the hospital the following day to get started on the preparation process to be inseminated. I told her that I would let her know after I had spoken to my husband.

As I hung up the phone, the feelings of excitement did not come rushing back as they did when I thought that I was going to get pregnant five years earlier. Mandy would most probably be eight or nine by the time we had had another child. *No, she'd be too old to enjoy having a brother or sister,* I thought, finally resolving that I was never going to have another child.

Mandy was twelve when Clarice died in the April of 1984. The emphysema that she had been suffering from for years had finally caught up with her. I was deeply saddened as I held her hand as she slipped away from life so quietly that I did not feel her go.

I felt as though I had lost my best friend. Although I had no love for her son, I had a deep sense of gratitude for her. Clarice never reminded me of things I had done wrong, and she always had a genuine love for Mandy.

Time seemed to drag on. We were still living with my father-in-law and taking care of him. He was mostly bed-ridden at that time. He also had emphysema—far worse than Clarice, but he seemed to manage better.

Nineteen eighty-eight was a bugger of a year. I found out my beloved sister Jenny had terminal cancer. I was devastated, and yet she managed to travel for weeks in the back of a panel van from Cairns in North Queensland to say goodbye to our brother Tom and to South Australia to see our sister May, calling into Sydney and staying with me for a few days.

My courageous, beautiful sister who sang with the voice of an angel was now going to be silenced forever. She had been given nine months to live, and it was almost as if she was going to live up to the prognosis that she was given, and nine months later, she gently slipped away to be with our ancestors.

I was devastated. I wanted to go to Brisbane and say goodbye to my beautiful sister, so we drove eleven hundred kilometres to attend her funeral to say goodbye.

We arrived two days before her funeral and went to visit Geoffrey's uncle Laurie and say hello. He had a few drinks, so I did all the driving back to Mum's house, which was about forty-five kilometres.

Mum was frantic by the time we got there. 'Mandy's been trying to ring you all day; it seems she has been in an accident.'

I rang her immediately and asked what was going on. She said that she was okay. It was only a minor accident anyway, and not to worry.

'Get your stuff packed,' Geoffrey demanded.

I pleaded, 'She's okay, she's okay.' Even Mum tried to reassure him that another day wouldn't make any difference; we could leave straight after Jenny's funeral in the morning.

But no, he was determined to leave that night. We drove on through the night and about one in the morning, I could not go on any longer, and we decided to spend the night in a motel on the way.

We arrived back in Sydney later that afternoon. My head was splitting, and the anger of not being able to say goodbye to my sister drove nails through my heart and left me with a resentment for my husband that I could never resolve.

Days seemed to slip by. I barely noticed how time was passing. Each day brought with it the certainty of the same routine, the never-ending cleaning, washing, and cooking. My only escape was to go to play bingo each Friday or Saturday night.

Geoffrey still had his darts competitions every night, and every night he would come home reeking of the beer and cigarettes that he devoured without fail each night. I would either be asleep or pretend to be asleep so that I did not have to speak to him.

Depending on how his night went, he would either leave me alone or wake me to tell of his victories or just to nag me. I hated these nights. He would go on and on about my past indiscretions and how I'd been deserted by the fathers of my children. What little affection I had for him deteriorated with each passing day.

Shane was turning twenty-one in 1988, and I had heard that there was a register where I could put my name down that if he registered his name, they could match us up, and we could be reunited. I was so excited. The prospect of seeing my baby again went through my mind day and night.

Shane's birthday came and went, and with each passing month, I expected to hear the news that he had contacted the children's services department to apply to be put on the register. Each time I thought of my son, the whole nightmare of how I lost him and Steve played over and over again in my mind.

I was searching for answers. *Surely it could not have been right for this to have been done to me. How could they be allowed to take my baby like that?* I answered my frantic questions by rationalising that they must have been allowed to do this to me because they did.

I still had not told Mandy that she had a brother somewhere. She had often asked why she did not have any brothers and sisters, and I would respond that Daddy and I couldn't have any more babies after we had her and that she was so perfect that we could not improve on her perfection. She seemed to take our explanations without querying them too deeply, and the subject would pass until it arose again.

Mandy was a quiet child and spent a lot of the time on her own. She seemed to retreat into a world of her own where she would draw and paint quietly for hours.

Now and then, she would look at me and say, 'Who do I look like, Mum? I don't look like you or Dad.' I would reassure her that she looked like me a little when I was younger and that she got her physical build from her father, who was a big man.

The secret of Mandy's conception was kept from her. Geoffrey refused to acknowledge the fact that he was not her father, so the secret was safely carried by all in the family who knew of my history. Mandy was seventeen now and had her boyfriend Darren living in the garage granny flat with her.

Geoffrey was starting to get even more possessive with me. He realised that I did not have anyone to keep an eye on me, day and night. I had long learned to drive and had my own car. Sometimes, out of the blue, I would look at the trip meter and discover that it had been set back to zero. It was as though he was trying to work out how far I had travelled each day.

I was starting to feel like a prisoner. The constant checking of my every movement and the continual interrogation each night was starting to make me feel as though I wanted to run away, but where would I go? No one wanted me. My despair at my isolation from the world was finally revealing itself to me.

I had given my life to his family and cut myself off from any friends and family to repay my gratitude.

I was going through a reclusive stage. A lot of it was to keep people at arm's length. I was feeling dull, ugly, and stupid, and any other description that applied to a person that had all the self-worth drained out of them.

It was at this point I decided to start to do something with my life, but what? I wasn't exactly sure where to start. All I had ever done was to clean and look after people.

For the first time in a long time, I decided that I would look for a job and was lucky enough to get a two-hour cleaning job at Auburn Girls High School across the road and could also be home early enough to cook dinner.

Even better, now I had no one to look after. I started to go to a local club on a Thursday night, and it was there that I met Russ.

Russ was the secretary of the club and started to join the group that Geoffrey and I sat with each week.

He was an intelligent gentleman who had travelled extensively throughout his life and was enjoying his retirement from his past career in advertising. He was a world traveller who intrigued me with his stories of the places he had visited.

Always well-dressed and with slightly greying hair, his well-kept physical appearance belied his age of sixty-nine. Russ was a lover of classical music and all the finer arts.

Many a night was spent talking about different operas. I felt a bit in the loop as I had been brought up on old musicals, my favourites being Jeanette McDonald and Nelson Eddy.

Russ had brought along a friend of his, Des, to join our happy throng. Des was a brilliant academic who seemed to know everything about everything.

He was the dux of his class in high school and worked for a Commonwealth science research department.

From then on, Thursday nights were the highlight of my week. Geoffrey had started to play snooker with Jan, a woman he had once worked with.

For the first time in a long time, I had two friends who I could talk to. It intrigued me that these two highly intelligent men found me interesting enough to befriend me.

Geoffrey was becoming more involved with Jan. He would play snooker with her each night and come home drunk and start going on about her.

Jan was out of work, so he provided her with drinks and cigarettes to entice her to go out with him.

The expense of his outings was starting to cost us dearly. Essential items were being ignored so that he could continue his nightly visits to the club. Jan was making the most of the situation. I couldn't blame her—if he was stupid enough to spend his money on her, then why wouldn't she make the most of it?

Terry and Lena had moved a couple of years before to Cessnock, a small town two hours' drive west of Sydney, and were down for the week. They had gone to the club with us on our usual Thursday night. Both Geoffrey and Terry had had too much to drink, and when we arrived home, Terry rambled on about my sister-in-law.

'She told me that you told her Geoffrey keeps checking up on you all the time,' slurring in his drunken voice. Geoffrey looked at me, his rage showing immediately in his glaring eyes. Denying it, I felt my face flush with fear trying to find the words to convince Terry that he must have misunderstood what he was saying.

'Yep, that's what she said to me. She reckons that you told her all about the way he follows you around and keeps watching you all the time.' Geoffrey looked at me as though he was only just containing his anger.

He went out to the toilet on the back verandah, and as I watched him through the window, I saw his eyes narrow and lips move to say something like, 'Wait till I get you later.'

I knew I was going to be in for it—another night of degradation and humiliation that made me wish I was dead.

I don't know what made me do it: the couple of drinks I had earlier triggered me into action. I quickly grabbed my handbag and raced out the door and into my car parked across the road. I jumped in and tried to start it.

The key clicked in the ignition—nothing!

'Oh, God.' Fear raced through me as I tried to move the battery cables and get the car started. The radio burst into action, and I quickly jumped into the car and started it.

I locked the door as soon as I got in and took off screeching up the road, Geoffrey standing on the verandah watching my escape.

My heart was beating so fast I could almost hear it. A thousand places rushed through my mind. Queensland was my first thought, but where would I stay up there? It would be the first place Geoffrey would look.

It was getting late, and the prospect of waking people up with my 'drama' filled me with trepidation.

The car seemed to have a mind of its own as it made its way into Kings Cross. The night was cold, and I only had a light jumper on. As I walked around the seedy streets littered with the rubbish of the day's traffic, I wondered what the hell I was doing there.

The sidewalks were nearly bare, and the spruikers of the strip joints huddled in the doorways, trying to keep warm. A biting wind rushed at my face as I walked around the half-deserted streets.

A hamburger place was open, so I stopped and had a hot cup of coffee and a cheeseburger to try to warm me up. The place was just shutting up, so I had to go back to my car. I realised that I was afraid.

The Cross that I had lived in and had been a part of me did not exist anymore. This was a dangerous place for a woman to walk around on her own. I hurried back to the safety of my car and locked the doors.

I wonder what he's thinking now. I hope he's shitting himself, as I thought of Geoffrey. My anger at him was growing as I thought of his threatening face staring at me through the window.

I don't care if I freeze to death. I am not going home to him. The prospect of being kept awake all night and hearing his abuse made me even more determined that now I had run away, I was not going to go back.

I drove around for most of the night, catching a few minutes of sleep until the cold forced me to start the car to get the heater to work. As I lay curled up on the back seat, I started to think of Mandy. I had not said goodbye to her.

She would wake up in the morning to find me gone. I supposed that she didn't need me anyway. As I thought about things, it soon dawned on me that if I wasn't around, not many people would miss me anyway.

The lonely dark night reminded me of my night in the prison cell again.

Curled up like a small child waiting for daybreak and the hope that the morning would make things better was enough to make me hang on through the night and plan on finding a place where I could go and be safe.

The morning was cold as I made my way out to Burwood. I don't know why I ended up there—it wasn't a place that I usually went to. I felt like a mess, my long hair needed brushing, and my clothes looked dirty and untidy. I stopped in at the shops and bought myself a brush and a new jumper to tidy myself up before going to Centrelink to find out where I could get some help.

I was interviewed by a woman who obviously felt sorry for me after hearing my story. 'I'm sorry that we really can't help you here, but I am going to ring a place where you might be able to stay. Wait here until I can see what I can do.'

She returned a few minutes later with a piece of paper that had an address written down on it. It was a woman's refuge. *Thank you, God*, I thought as I took the piece of paper.

Carroll House was also in Burwood and was a reflection of the Holy Cross. The graceful old house represented a welcome haven to all who must have fled to it for safety.

The nun who answered the door to me knew I was coming and, without asking me any details, showed me up the stairs to the second floor.

There was a large sitting area with an old-fashioned lounge and a grandfather clock ticking quietly in the background. The silence and the dark woodwork and furnishings of the old convent made me feel that I had stepped back in time to the dormitory of Holy Cross.

My room was a little bigger than the single bed that took up most of the space, and up the end of the room near the door stood an old-fashioned wardrobe. I fell onto the bed exhausted and immediately fell asleep for most of the day.

I awoke to hear a knocking at the door. A voice called out to me and asked me if I was all right and that a meal was being served in the dining room.

I got out of bed and made my way to the bathroom near my room and washed my face, and tidied myself up. As I made my way down to the dining room, a couple of women introduced themselves to me. They were younger than me and were also on their own.

It seemed that there were small cottages at the back of the convent which were there to accommodate families with children. The main part of the convent was strictly reserved for single women only.

The dining room was a noisy place with women trying to keep their children under control. Most of the women there had been subjected to some form of domestic violence. It seemed strange to me that I should be in the same boat as these women. They were a lot younger than me, and I was slightly embarrassed that a woman of my age—nearly forty—found herself in a refuge. I quickly finished my meal and made my way back to the sanctity of my room.

The peace of the convent was like a blessing to me. For the first time in a long time, I was surrounded by quiet, and at last, I was able to think clearly about all the things in my life, my thoughts only interrupted by the muted Westminster chimes of the old clock.

For the first few days, I kept pretty much to myself. The nuns gave me some second-hand clothes, and I started thinking of looking for another job. Any thoughts of going back to Geoffrey were quickly pushed from my mind.

Although I was really worried about Mandy, I still held back from phoning her. I needed to put the distance of time between everyone I knew.

Ten days passed, and I had still not contacted Geoffrey. I eventually phoned a friend of mine and asked her to contact Mandy and let her know that I was all right and not to worry about me.

The principal of the school where I worked had told me to take two weeks' leave and then let her know what I was doing as I still had the keys to the school and had to make arrangements to drop them off.

I arranged for someone to collect the keys on a Sunday afternoon when I knew Geoffrey would not be working across the road at the council depot.

As I left the school to make my way back to the refuge, fear kicked in; just being in the same suburb as my husband made me very nervous, and I wanted to get back to the safety of the refuge.

The traffic light had just turned red on the railway bridge near my home. *Hurry up and change,* I thought to myself, panicking that someone who knew me would see me. As the oncoming traffic appeared from behind the bridge retaining wall, I could feel my face wince with terror.

There he was: Geoffrey, driving toward me. His face turned into shock as he stared straight at me. He stopped his car with a sharp jerk and yelled, 'Lily, pull over! Pull over!' The cars behind him starting to blow their horns as he was urged to drive on. 'Wait for me!' he yelled as he took off to try to turn around.

The hell I will, I thought, as I sped off down the road at top speed, the next traffic light stopping me in my tracks. I turned around to see if he was following, and as soon as the light turned green, I sped off again.

I had just passed through the next green light when I heard a car horn blowing loudly. I looked around, and it was him. I put my foot down on the accelerator to try to speed as fast as I could go.

He drove up next to me, blowing his horn and waving me over to the side of the road. Fear took hold of me. I thought he would run me off the road if I did not pull over. Terrified, I pulled my car into the gutter.

Jumping out of his car, he came over to the passenger side of my car and got in. He started to sob and tried to grab me. 'Oh God! Oh God!' he wailed. 'I've been looking for you for days. I was getting ready to kill myself. Mandy has been sick with worry. Where have you been?' He rambled on and on whilst I sat in complete terror.

Panicking at what to say to him to get away, I used the excuse, 'I have to go: there are people who are waiting for me, and if I don't turn up, they are going to ring the police.' I was trying to appear calm and imply that the refuge knew of my whereabouts.

'You've got to come home and see your daughter, she's been sick with worry since you left. She's hardly eaten a thing. Please come home and talk to me. I promise I will let you go if you come and speak to us.'

I felt trapped; there was no escape. 'Okay, I'll come, but I'm leaving when I'm ready. I have to get back to the refuge by five, or they will ring the police.' My lie convinced him, and he agreed to let me go after we had talked.

Mandy started to cry as I walked through the door. She hugged me and went and made me a cup of tea. Geoffrey sat next to me on the lounge, his tear-filled eyes, cracking voice, and shaking hands all meant to evoke my sympathy.

'I'm so sorry about what I did to you that night,' he repeated again and again. 'I had no idea that you would run away. Please come home. I need you. Mandy needs you,' he said, his voice breaking into sobs.

There was no sympathy there for him; I had heard this story before.

I blurted out to him how I felt about all the times he sat and watched me work, never once offering to help me as I struggled after a long day's work.

All the birthdays, Christmases, and special days that went by without a card or present. All the nights he kept me awake. I could hardly contain my anger, and him expecting me to come back— you must be joking! I had finally said my piece, and what a relief it had been.

Mandy let out a sob as she listened to the conversation. 'Mum, you've got to come home. I miss you, and Dad has been so upset we don't know what to do.'

Geoffrey piped in, 'I'll go and see a marriage counsellor if you come home. I promise I will never hurt you again. You can leave me and I won't stop you if I hurt you again.'

I looked at Mandy, her face red and her eyes full of tears. She was still my baby, and she needed me. I felt myself being pulled back into a pit as I agreed to return home a few days later.

No one asked me anything about my disappearance at work; they all knew there had been a problem but didn't know what it was. They were glad to see me return, but I felt as though my relationship with them had changed.

The realisation that my friendships with people were only on a superficial level and not the deep, supportive level that I thought they had been made me feel isolated and cut off from them. *What kind of friends did I have when I could not go to them when I desperately needed help?*

I felt like an alien in a strange world. I drew away from everyone.

My fortieth birthday was approaching, and the saying 'life begins at forty' kept going around in my head.

Life won't begin at forty unless I make it begin.

Geoffrey had kept his promise, and we had made an appointment to see a marriage guidance counsellor at the Salvation Army. She sat and listened to me telling her of the loss of Shane, my life with Geoffrey, and the caring of his family.

I went to her twice, and the second time she told me not to come back—she would see my husband on his own each week.

He went to the counsellor a few more times, and then he asked me if he could stop going. 'I know what my problems are now, and I know how to fix them,' he said as he pleaded to be let off his promise.

'Do what you want,' I told him, accepting the fact that he could never honour the promise he had made to me. I was back in the same old situation, and he wanted to be back in his.

It was 1990, just after my fortieth birthday, that I heard on the news that they were going to open up the adoption records and that I could finally find out the whereabouts of Shane.

He would be twenty-three by then, and my thoughts were trying to imagine him and how he would look. The thing that I had waited and prayed for was now going to happen.

Geoffrey was concerned when I told him of the new adoption information laws that were being introduced later that year. 'I can finally find my son now,' I told him.

His response was, 'That's all right, but I hope you don't go looking for his father.'

Geoffrey had put into words the very thing that I had wished for, for the past twenty-three years. *I want to look for Steve and tell him we are finally going to see our son again. We are going to get him back.* At last, I had something to live for.

We had put the house on the market at Geoffrey's insistence. He wanted to buy a dream home so that we could start afresh and have all the things that we wanted instead of using the things left over from his parents.

I wanted to stay in Auburn. I felt secure there. At least we nearly owned the place. We would have to borrow again to buy another house. Geoffrey didn't care. He just wanted to get away to start a new life.

All I wanted was to see my son. As the months passed and the time was getting closer to the new legislation being implemented, it was time to tell Mandy about Shane.

Geoffrey sat with me as I told her about what had happened to me and the news about her brother. 'You mean to say that I've had a brother all this time, and you never told me about him?' she sobbed.

I tried to explain that I thought there was no point in telling her about Shane because I thought I would never see him again.

As we held each other crying, I asked her to forgive me for not telling her about her brother and hoped that we would all have the chance to meet him soon.

She settled down and wiped her face, then smiled and said, 'I can't wait to meet him. For the first time in my life, I've got someone besides my cousins. I wonder what he will think of me.'

'He'll think you're beautiful; after all, you're his sister,' I replied and hugged her again.

The excitement of finally meeting my son again played on my mind day and night. I imagined him as being handsome like his father, with jet black hair and olive skin. He would have a wide-open smile like Steve and probably play some sort of musical instrument, and his eyes would smile just like Steve's did.

A week later, I went to the post office to pay a bill. I don't know what made me do it, but I saw all the phone books for the capital cities and picked out the Brisbane phone book.

My fingers thumbed through the pages to the names starting with the letter B. As my finger ran down the rows of names, it stopped at Benko, Steve's last name. There were only a few of them; I recognised M—it was Steve's brother, Michael—and there it was.

S Benko.

My heart thumped. Steve—it had to be him. I grabbed a piece of paper and wrote down the two phone numbers, and raced home, not knowing what to do with this information.

Over and over, I was thinking, *Shall I ring him? What will I say? As soon I get home tomorrow, I will call him.*

All night, I lay awake and thought of Steve and Shane. The memories of my times with Steve and our little broken song going through my tired mind. *The angels listened in,* my last thought before I dozed off to sleep just before dawn.

All the next morning, as I raced around my work cleaning and polishing the long school corridors, my thoughts were focused on what I would say to Steve when I rang him later that day. I had to think of a good reason for why I was ringing him if his wife answered the phone. I would just tell her that I was an old friend of his and was ringing up to see how he was going.

Oh boy, this is going to be harder than I thought. Oh well—nothing ventured, nothing gained. I resolved to carry out my plan as soon as Geoffrey went back to work after lunch. That way, I knew he would not be arriving unannounced.

As soon as he left, my trembling fingers pushed the buttons on the phone. One ring, two rings, three, rings my ears were becoming accustomed to the sound of the unanswered ringing at the other end of the line.

'Hello,' a man's voice broke into the resignation that the phone was not going to be answered. I gasped at the sound of the voice at the other end of the line. 'Hello,' he repeated.

'Ah, hello,' I muttered, 'could I speak to Steve Benko, please?'

'Speaking,' came the reply.

'Hello, Steve, this is Lily,' I blurted out.

'Lily?' his voice sounded as though he was searching through his thoughts to work out who the hell Lily was.

His voice changed from the happy salutation to the quiet realisation of who it was that was speaking to him.

'Lily! Wow, it's been so long. You threw me for a minute. Wow. How did you find me? Where are you?'

A dozen questions flowed down the line to me, each question starting with his surprised 'wow' and his incredulous reaction that it was me he was speaking to.

His voice, his wonderful voice, it's still the same! Oh God, I can't believe it! I'm speaking to him again. Over and over again, my mind was saying, *It's him, Steve.*

After the initial surprise and shock, we started to talk about our families and how we were going. He had four children and had been separated from his wife for about six years. He was still spray-painting, and yes, he still played in the band.

We chatted for about an hour, and after an exciting exchange of catching up, we finally got around to the painful subject of our son.

'That's why I rang you, Steve, the laws have changed, and I hope to be able to find Shane.'

'Oh, wow!' he exclaimed. 'Incredible. I've always wondered where he's been and what's happened to him. It would be great if we could see him again,' he said, his voice drifting off into a quiet, reflective tone.

'Hey, if you ever come up this way, how about coming to see me? It would be great to see you again.'

'I don't know when I'll be up that way again,' I replied, longing to jump in the car and go straight to him.

Steve and I said our goodbyes, and I had to come down off my cloud and go back to cleaning the filthy schoolyard.

Just for a few hours, I was in heaven as I made my way around, emptying the dirty garbage bins and cleaning the toilets. For the first time in over twenty years, I felt like a real person again.

I lay awake all that night thinking of my conversation with Steve. I imagined how he must look now. *I must see him. I have to go to Queensland,* my mind repeating as I lay there next to Geoffrey.

I planned on how I was going to find the excuse for me to go to Queensland on my own. I could tell him that I wanted to spend time with my mother. I could catch a bus up there. My need to see Steve again was the only thing in my life that was worth doing.

I had decided that I would tell Geoffrey the next night that I needed time away from him to visit my mother and the rest of my family, as I had not had much contact with them over the past few years and seeing that he did not like my family there was no point in him coming with me.

It took all my courage to tell him of my plan the following night. I could see his face searching for reasons not to let me go, but as it had not been long since my return from the refuge, I guess he thought he would have to allow me to finally do something that I wanted to for a change.

I had decided that I would go up to Queensland on the following Saturday by bus and ordered a return ticket. It was a couple of days before my departure when Geoffrey dropped a bomb.

'I have been thinking about you going up there, and I've decided to go and pick you up at the end of the week just to make sure that you get back all right.'

I was furious. His excuse was, 'I'm worried about you. I love you, and I don't want anything to happen to you.'

'Mandy and I have talked about it, and she said that she and I could drive up there on Friday night and we can all leave on Sunday and stay the night at the casino on the Gold Coast. Besides that, Mandy wants to see her grandmother, even if it is only for one day.'

It was all I did to stop from screaming at him. This was his way of making sure that I would be back. There was no point in arguing with him. He had made his mind up, and there was no way he was going to change it.

Calm down; at least you will have a few days to see Steve.

It was more than I expected. If it hadn't been for the promises he made when I returned from the refuge, he would never have let me out of his sight.

Only a few people were getting on the bus at Parramatta, and as I boarded and took a downstairs seat, I felt a liberating sense of freedom even though I knew it was only going to be for a short time. I was finally on my way, and the anticipation of seeing my lost lover was the only thing on my mind.

As the roar of the bus engine continued into the black of the night and the silhouette of the bush whizzed past, John Denver's voice sang 'Sweet Surrender' from the headphones in my ears.

Yes, I was lost and alone on some forgotten highway, but it was leading me home.

The bus arrived in Brisbane at six the next morning. The cool, frosty air hit me as soon as I got out of the heated bus. I had been up all night and was feeling worn out, but the cool air washed over me like a wet towel reviving me, and I started to feel fresh and alive. At last, I was here, and probably only a few miles away from Steve.

The train out to Mum's place at Caboolture seemed to crawl, and I was glad to finally get off it. Mum was waiting for me at the station. Judging by her face, she was glad to see me again.

'I'm glad you're on your own this time. At least that Geoffrey won't be rushing home to see what's going on with Mandy this time.' As soon as we got to her house, I went straight to bed and slept for a few hours.

Mum woke me up later that afternoon with a cup of tea, me telling her, 'I have to ring Steve.' She was not impressed, quizzing me why.

'I need to talk to him and let him know that soon I will be meeting my son and he might want to meet his father.' I replied.

Mum accepted what I had to say, and after settling down, I rang Steve's number again. He sounded surprised to hear from me again, and when I told him that I was in Queensland, he became quite excited. 'Can you meet me tomorrow?' he asked.

'Yes, that's the reason I came up here. I need to speak to you. I have so many questions to ask you.'

We had arranged to meet not far from the place where I used to work. Steve gave me directions on how to get there. It seemed that he had never moved far from the area we had lived in and was surprised when I told him that I did not know where to look for him when I left Geoffrey for the first time.

It took me ages to get to Rocklea, and I had to catch a taxi to the shopping centre where we had arranged to meet. I was at least twenty minutes early and cursed myself for my obsession with punctuality. As I paced up and down in front of the few shops, looking up and down the road, I got scared that he was not going to show.

An old white panel van slowed down as it approached the shops, and I looked to see who was in it. I felt my legs nearly go out from underneath me. All I could see was that familiar wide smile and his dark laughing eyes.

Oh my God! It's him.

I could feel my eyes fill with tears; at the same time, my mouth was trying to smile. He jumped out of the car and raced over to me, and hugged me at the same time, kissing me straight on the lips.

My head was spinning. I felt as though I had been lifted into a vortex and was being carried off to heaven. Finally, after all those years of wondering where he was, he was here in front of me.

'Hop in the car, and we'll go somewhere quiet where we can talk,' as he put his arm around me and opened the car door. A few minutes later, we arrived at Steve's friend's house set up on high piers, reminding me of the little house we shared.

He made me a cup of coffee, and as we sat at the kitchen table, we spoke about the things we had been doing since we last saw each other. I hung on every word he spoke, and now and then, he would lean over and kiss me as he held my hand, his bare feet on mine and his toes caressing mine.

There were a thousand questions I wanted to ask him, and after a while, I mustered the courage to ask, 'Steve, what happened to the marriage papers I signed? I waited and waited and never heard about them.'

He held my hands between his and looked into my face as he told me what had happened. He told me of how he went to Holy Cross with the papers and wanted me to sign the papers while he waited, but Mother Liam the Superior would not allow him to see me.

She told him that he would have to leave the papers with her, and she would get me to sign them, and he could pick them up a day or so later.

He went back the next day, and when he asked for them, Mother Liam would not give them to him. His voice lowered and his eyes fell as he told me how she sat there, twiddling her thumbs, as she told him that he was too young to marry me and that she was not going to give him back the papers.

I felt as though I had been hit by the blade of an axe.

All these years, I had been wondering what had happened and fearing that Steve deserted me. The nightmares came flooding back as I remembered that terrified little girl waiting in that place, wondering when she was going to be rescued and all the time that evil woman knowing that I was doomed to stay there.

Oh my God. How could these people be so cruel?

I started to cry as he went on to tell me how he felt after this woman's cruelty, the dehumanisation of not having the power to do anything, and the futility of the trip to Sydney to get our parents' permission to get married.

My head was exploding with anger, my thoughts racing through my brain: *How dare they? How dare they do this to us? What gave these people the right to destroy our lives and take our baby from us?*

We clung to each other, both crying, his strong hand holding my face as he kissed the tears away from my cheeks. The quiet ticking of the clock keeping time with my silent sobs.

The pain of every time I thought of him and Shane, flooding back to me and stabbing me over and over again. All those lost years, all our lost dreams and happiness, stolen away from us by someone who thought they knew what was better for us than we did.

'Come and lie down with me so I can hold you while we talk,' he said as he held my hands and led me to the bedroom. I followed him as though I was glued to him.

I couldn't stand the thought of ever being separated from him again. As we lay on the bed, his arm under my head, and talked about the thousand things that had never been spoken of for so many years, I held him so tightly I was scared to let go.

I fell asleep from the sheer pain of reliving the trauma of our separation and the emotion of our reunion. I awoke sometime later, the strange surroundings confusing me for a moment.

I could hear Steve gently breathing next to me, and as I stared at his still-handsome face, just slightly touched by time, and his thinning black hair against the whiteness of the pillow, he looked just as young to me as he did twenty-three years before.

Seeing him again, I knew that I could never go back to a marriage that was barren of love and respect.

My love for him was the same as it was so long ago. It was as though I had fallen asleep that night, and the nightmare had been just that. I had awoken to the morning after.

For the past twenty-three years, I had carried the burden of guilt that had been inflicted upon me, not only by my family but also by a husband that used my tragedy to inflict even more abuse.

I knew that after finding out about my experience, I could never live under that oppression again. I decided that on my return to Sydney, I was going to leave the marriage.

Chapter 6

The lights of Brisbane looked like a million coloured stars as Steve drove me back to Mum's place that night. She was surprised to see that he had brought me home, and they exchanged a few comments on how long it had been since they last met.

Mum commented on how little Steve had changed and went off to bed. It was still quite early and when the phone rang, I answered it half-suspecting the voice on the other end was Geoffrey's; sure enough, it was him.

'I thought we agreed that you were not going to ring me every night,' I said. He had rung me the night before, dismissing my wish for him not to ring every day and night. It was as though he was still checking up on me.

'I'm sorry, I know I promised but I'm missing you so much. I feel like getting in the car and driving up there now,' he said, his voice trying to evoke some sort of emotional response from me.

'I told you that I needed time to myself. If you keep ringing me every few hours, it will give Mum the shits. Anyway, we're watching a movie at the moment, so I can't talk long.' He reluctantly said good night and hung up the phone.

I suppose that I should have felt some sort of guilt knowing that I was seeing Steve while my husband thought that I had come up to Brisbane to visit my mother, but I couldn't feel anything: no guilt, no regret, and least of all, no love for my husband.

I had come full circle, and the truth of my love for Steve could not be taken away from me again. It was as though I had been having an affair with Geoffrey for all those years.

Steve came out to see me each night of my stay and we would sit and talk out the front of the house until the late hours just in case Geoffrey rang so that Mum could call me in to answer the phone.

When I was sure that it was safe, we would go for a drive around and stop and have something to eat. He either held my hand or had his arm around me.

I hung onto him, fearing that he would disappear if I let go of him. We laughed and giggled as he told me his corny jokes as we sat and ate the hamburgers he bought at the late-night service station. I could see the woman that served us looking at us as though she knew we had something very special.

I felt as though I was sixteen again and there was no-one in the world but him and me.

'I've got something for you. You'll never guess what it is,' he said on our last night together.

'What is it?' I asked curiously.

He leaned over into the back of the van and pulled out an old airline bag. 'Hmm—here it is,' he said as he fumbled around inside the bag. He pulled out a brown paper bag and took out the contents. It was a heap of old photos. 'I've kept these all these years for some unknown reason—don't know why. I guess that I thought I would see you again one day.' As I looked through the old photos of my family taken at Woodridge, I couldn't believe it—there were photos of me. They must have been taken a few months before I met Steve.

As a grown woman looking at the fifteen-year girl dressed in mismatched hand-me-down clothes, her hair cut like a schoolgirl, an intense feeling of anger hit me. *Oh God—I was no more than a kid; how could they do what they did to me?*

No wonder why I felt like I have for most of my life. They had destroyed my life from my childhood, never giving me the chance to grow into womanhood.

'Remember these?' Steve's voice breaks into my thoughts. He hands me the three little photos we had taken in a photo booth just before I was taken away. I gasped as I looked at them.

'I can't believe that you've had these all these years. How come your wife has never thrown them away?' I asked incredulously.

'She's never seen them; I just kept them hidden away in this old bag,' he replied.

As I looked at the sepia-coloured miniatures, the memory of the day we had them taken came rushing back. We were down to our last sixty cents and Steve insisted that we have them done. Three of the photos were of us looking at each other—the fourth was of us kissing.

There was a ragged edge of the little photos at the end of one side, a reminder of the night he tore one of them off to give to me and remember him.

This is our last day together, I thought as he left to go home in the early hours of the morning. My dream had ended, and I was back to the start of another day in the real world.

The week I had with Steve seemed to pass like a minute. It was agony to watch him depart again; it tore my heart into pieces.

Why does he have to come and pick me up? I wondered.

My resentment built up against my husband, who I envisaged approaching. I should have insisted that I take the bus home. It would have given me time to be alone with my memories of the week and think of where I was going in my life.

Since I had seen Steve again, it became obvious that my marriage had come to an end.

Mum was very quiet about the time I'd been spending with Steve. I think she knew I needed to work things out about the way

I felt for him. I was grateful for this and felt a bit guilty that I had involved her in my deceit.

Almost as if on schedule, Geoffrey and Mandy arrived later that day. They looked tired from the long trip and I undertook my usual duty by waiting on them and cooking them a meal. Later that night, as Geoffrey and I lay in bed, he started to question me about what I'd been doing whilst I'd been at Mum's. I commented that we had gone to a couple of places and spent most of the time talking over things.

'I suppose you didn't miss us,' he said, half-sarcastically. Of course, he expected me to admit that I had. I gave him the appropriate reply, knowing full well that he did not believe me.

We said our goodbyes to Mum early the next morning and made our way down to the Gold Coast. I was trying my best to act as though I was still the same person, but I knew that the events of the past week had changed me into someone I did not even know myself.

I had gone back full circle and found my truth. No more could I ever be told by Geoffrey that I had been deserted, unwanted, and ditched by my son's father. No more could he make me feel second-hand, dirty, and stupid. I had visited the man I had loved for most of my life, and it confirmed my love for him again.

The bright lights and music of Jupiters Casino could never have compared with the lights of Brisbane I saw with Steve. There was more magic in his old panel van than in any other place I had ever been. Mandy was so excited being in the casino, and I put on a façade of excitement for her sake.

My mind was making all sorts of plans to carry out when I got back to Sydney. I had begun to find out what had happened to me and my baby, but not the reasons why.

The long trip home could not go quick enough. I wanted the answers to my questions before I met my son so I could tell him the truth about what had happened to us.

We arrived home late on Sunday night and went to bed exhausted. I felt little sympathy for Geoffrey, who had to get up for work the next day. Even though I had to go to work as well, at least I could come home and have a rest.

As soon as I got home, I sat down and wrote a letter to the Queensland Department of Families. It was the first letter I had ever written about the loss of my baby and although my writing wasn't very good, I had to make it look neat and appear that I wasn't illiterate.

I began.

Dear Jenny Green.

I have been referred to you after inquiries I have made regarding the problem I am having. I hope that you may be able to help me.

The problem began nearly 24 years ago, in 1967. I was living in Brisbane. My mother had just moved to Sydney after a nasty situation. It was a month before my 17th birthday. At the time I was living with my boyfriend that I intended to marry.

One night while he was practising (he was in a band), while I was asleep in bed, the police came. I was woken up, and after questioning me, they found out that I was six weeks pregnant. They took me to the Watchhouse for the night. I appeared in court the next day and was charged with being exposed to moral danger and committed to Holy Cross Girls Home for an indefinite period.

Whilst in the home, my boyfriend, had been to Sydney to obtain my mother's permission to get married. I signed the forms in the home.

After this, I never heard anything else.

During the whole time at the home, I was not allowed contact with the outside by any means of communication. I gave birth to my son on 1.9.67. Whilst in hospital, I contacted his father. This was reported to the social worker who was handling my case.

I feel that I was placed in a hopeless situation to sign the adoption papers after I was told that there was no definite date for me to be released from the home. Approximately five weeks after I left the hospital, long enough for the time limit on changing my mind to lapse, I was returned to the custody of my mother in Sydney.

The reason I have told you all of this is although this happened many years ago, I am still suffering emotionally from this.

I have applied for identifying information for my son and <u>hopefully will</u> one day get in contact with him.

I would like, if possible, to get a copy of my files. I feel that there have been a lot of questions unanswered about what happened to me whilst I was at the home.

I am having difficulty accepting decisions that were made for me without my having any say at that particular time, and my family is not being helpful about the situation.

I know everyone is happy to say let things alone, but this is something that I feel will never be forgotten. If I had some of the answers to some of the questions, I may at least accept it.

My full name at the time was Lily Josephine McDonald.

Born 19.3.50 State ward from Feb 1967.

If you could help me with some information, I would be very grateful.

Thank You
L Fuller

I was finally going to find out what had happened to me. Not one person in my family ever spoke to me about the adoption of my baby or Steve since I returned from Holy Cross. There were so many questions that kept going around in my mind:

Why didn't Mum help?
Why didn't they let me go after I turned seventeen?
What happened to my baby?
Why wasn't I allowed to see my baby?
Why did they take my baby?

Around and around the questions inside my head went, day and night from my first waking moment until my last conscious thought at night.

I lost the courage to tell him I was leaving him after my return from Brisbane. We sold the house in Auburn and bought a beautiful house in Seven Hills that was my dream home. The beautiful brick house represented everything I had ever hoped for—a far cry from the single-fronted weatherboard house in Auburn. It was modern and clean, and the garden was the next best thing to paradise—well, it felt that way for me.

'I want everything new in this house,' Geoffrey proclaimed. 'This is the home we've been waiting for.' Although we had bought Geoffrey's parents' home when his mother died, it was not the same as having our own house that we had chosen together.

In a dream, I went along with the idea of the new house. Maybe this was the thing that would finally make me happy: the prospect of seeing my son again and a new home to start a new life.

I had just moved into the house when I got a phone call from Steve. He was down in Sydney for two days and wanted to see me. It had been two months since I last saw him, and my head was in a spin trying to work out how I could make the excuses to Mandy and Geoffrey and get to see him.

Mandy wasn't working and spent all day at home. I told them I was going out to visit a friend who lived in the mountains. I had arranged to meet him at a hotel along the highway, and we were planning to go to his brother's place near Penrith.

I sat in my car and watched out for him and, sure enough, there he was, riding an old motorbike. Nothing had changed. I remembered the love he had for the old motorbike that he worked on when we were together.

He smiled as he approached my car, his leather jacket slung over his shoulder. I got out and threw my arms around his neck and we hugged each other.

'It's great to see you again,' he said as he kissed me.

'You too,' I replied.

We went into the bar and had a couple of bourbon and colas and later went off to his brother's house. Alone again, and the rest of the world passed by outside the locked door. Reliving our time together, forgetting for a short time all the unhappiness over the years, we spoke more about his family and the work he was doing with his panel-beating business—small talk, happy talk, but we were together again. I could feel again. I could love again, and just for a few hours, he was mine again.

The next day was the same.

Was there a world going about its business around me? I didn't notice.

The two days went as fast as they came and as we said our goodbyes. We knew we would see each other again. It was just a matter of time.

I had thought the Department of Family Services and Aboriginal and Islander Affairs had forgotten my letter when I finally received a reply. The envelope looked too small to contain my records. Panic and fear of the reply gripped me as I ripped open the envelope. The letter read:

Dear Mrs Fuller,

In reply to your letter dated June 1991, I regret to inform you that your records were destroyed in the Queensland floods of 1974. Unfortunately, there is no information available regarding your time as a ward of the state. We are, however, able to send you copies of index cards which give details of your time spent in care.

Yours Sincerely, Jenny Green.

The index cards revealed very little: they had my name and that of my sisters and brother in descending order of age, and the date we were made state wards, and also the dates we were discharged from wardship.

My name was entered twice—first when Dad had left and then when I was admitted to and discharged from Holy Cross. *At least that's something,* I thought. *Now I know the actual dates of my incarceration.*

It had been six months since I applied for identifying information about Shane and I was starting to get impatient.

Stop worrying. They've probably got thousands of applications to go through and mine is just one of them.

I had just arrived home one day when Mandy sang out from the shower, 'There was a phone call from a woman from Queensland.'

'What did she say?' I asked nervously.

'I told her you weren't home; she left her number and told you to ring her and she would ring you back and save you the cost of a phone call. The number is next to the phone.'

This was the moment I had waited for. My heart was thumping so hard I could hear it. I called the number and asked for Caroline Smith. 'Speaking,' came the reply. She thanked me for calling and asked if she could ring me back a few moments later as I was ringing from Sydney in the middle of the day, and this would save me the cost of an expensive phone call.

I hung up the phone and it rang a few seconds later. The woman went into great detail to let me know who she was and her role in the department and then went on to tell me she had some information to pass on to me from my son.

She carefully explained to me the context of objections to contact and objections to information. *What does this have to do with me?* I thought. It was when she said that my son had lodged a contact objection that I felt a jolt. *What is she saying?*

I was grasping to deal with the conversation. *Is she talking to me? She must have me mixed up with someone else. My son would not put a contact veto on me—not my son. He was waiting for me just as much as I had waited for him.* My mind was swirling, and I felt as though I was being pulled into the floor.

The woman went on to give reasons why a young man would not want his life disturbed; then she went on to throw me a crumb: 'Maybe he will change his mind a few years down the track. Young men don't worry about things like this until they have a family of their own.'

After two hours of my begging, pleading, and asking for any hope of something to go on with, she told me that she was preparing me for the message my son had left for me.

'It may sound a little hard to you,' she said, then went on to give me my son's message. 'His message to you is: "I have parents."'

I was in a state of disbelief. I couldn't speak.

Her voice broke the silence between us. 'I had to give you this message first before you received it in the mail. I'm afraid that it looks very hard on paper, and I thought you needed to be prepared for the shock of it seeing it.'

Dazed, I thanked her for her time and hung up the phone, my mind finding it hard to adjust to this different reality—a thousand thoughts rushing through it all at once.

Wait for the letter, I thought, *she may have mistaken me for someone else and the mistake will be found out, and this will all be a very bad joke. I'll just wait for the letter.*

Mandy sat at the kitchen table, watching me as I spoke. I could see the pain and disappointment on her face. 'What did she say?' she asked, her voice trembling to try to hold back from crying.

I could barely drag out the words of the conversation and made the excuse that I had to lie down, the words of the woman going around in my head as I blacked out into trauma.

A few days later, the letter arrived, half-dread and half-hope made me open it as fast as I could to put me out of my misery.

My eyes rushed through the text, words jumping from the page. My son had lodged an objection to contact and information about him, the letter read.

All I could see were the words *fines* and *two-year jail term* if I attempted to break the objection. My mind screeched to a halt. *These people are treating me as though I were a criminal,* I thought as I read on.

The next page delivered another blow. Three lines on their own in the middle of the page:

The message.

Shane Stefan McDonald wishes his birth parents to know the following message.

'I have parents.'

The horror of seeing the words hit me like the blow of an axe. My world went black; my head was split into a hundred pieces. The pain was excruciating, I thought at that moment I was going to die.

Oh God, why can't I die?

From that moment on there was no colour around me. My world had turned to black and grey.

I spent the next three days walking around in a stupefied daze, my eyes unable to see. People were talking to me—what were they saying? I don't know.

The temptation to drive my car into the path of an oncoming truck was almost irresistible. *Just close my eyes and it will be over.*

My thoughts were so focused on the pain that I did not see my daughter's pain—she had been rejected, too.

'Why doesn't he want to know us, Mum?'

I couldn't answer her.

What could I say? I had to face the truth that my son had been living a life somewhere and hadn't been waiting for me. All the years of hoping to see him again, gone.

'Maybe it's better this way. At least you know that he's alive and he must have a happy life if he's not interested in meeting you,' Geoffrey said when I finally found the strength to talk to him about the letter.

His patronising sympathy covered his true feelings: he was secretly glad that my son had rejected me. Now he would not have to worry about my contacting Steve or having another man around who might share my affections, even if it was my son. I knew that he was only going along with my search for my son because it was the only thing that was keeping me in the marriage. It had only been a few months since my return from the refuge and he was as bad as he was before, if not worse.

The continual late-night berating sessions had me to the point of breaking. My son's words going through my mind day and night.

'I have parents.' *What did he mean?*

He must hate me. My despair turned to anger. *How could my own son treat me like this?*

140

He was the child of the man I loved, and he doesn't even know me. I felt betrayed by his rejection of me, and so did Mandy—she never spoke of him again.

My friends were the only things that kept me sane over the next few months. I could pour my feelings out to Russ each Thursday night as we waited for Des to come along and cheer us up. Russ was truly my 'father confessor'—his gentle understanding of my pain acted like a salve to my deepest wounds.

The October long weekend was coming up and it had been over six months since I had last seen Steve. I had to see him again. I needed to have him tell me that things were going to be okay with our son. I needed to feel his optimism. *Oh God, what did I need? I was breaking up. I have to go to Queensland and find Shane. He has to know the truth.*

I rang Mum and asked her if I could stay at her place for a week, and then organised a return flight to Brisbane.

A couple of days before my departure, she rang and said that she and my younger sisters had spoken about my visit and that they thought it wasn't a good idea to go up there and disturb things, and it would be better if I got on with my life instead of looking for my son who was probably adopted by a solicitor or teacher and would feel disappointed that I was just a cleaner.

For the first time, I was ashamed that all I could achieve in life was the lowly position of being a cleaner and that this would be the yardstick by which I would be valued as a person. I felt humiliated that my sisters and mother could devalue me in such a judgemental way.

I never told Geoffrey that my family did not want me to go to Brisbane. He would have taken great delight to let me know that his criticisms of them over the years were justified.

If I had to sleep on the streets, well, so be it. I rang my youngest sister Frances later that week and asked her if she would put me up for a few days. She had just separated from her husband and thought it would be great to have me stay with her.

Just before I was ready to leave, I told Geoffrey that I was staying with Frances and not to bother ringing me up two or three times a day, as we would be going out whilst I was up there. It was my way of telling him not to keep checking up on me.

Although I never really admitted it to myself, this was going to be the trip to Queensland where I would check out the possibilities of finally leaving Geoffrey and moving up there. I just needed courage and the support of my family to achieve this.

As soon as I arrived, I rang Steve to let him know where I was staying. He drove out to Frances' house later that night after he had finished playing pool. He looked worn out as he came in and flopped down onto the lounge.

He had been working all day painting, and after talking for a little while, he fell asleep with his head on my lap. I could have stayed there all night watching him sleep but I was so tired and wearily coaxed him into the bedroom, where we fell asleep on a mattress on the floor.

Each night he drove the sixty kilometres out to Frances' house to see me. We talked about Shane, our families, and the life we could have had if things had not happened the way they did.

I asked him if he thought about going back to his wife and he told me that he would if she would have him back. He spent a lot of time at her house doing jobs and fixing her car, but she would not let him live with her.

I was so jealous of her. If he asked me to stay with him, I would have left everything behind just to be with him. It felt strange I was sleeping with the man I had loved for the best part of my life, and he obviously felt something for me and yet he hung onto the hope of going back to a wife who he had been separated from for six years.

Why can't you see how much I love you? My mind said to him a thousand times, my voice not having the courage to put it into words.

My last night with Steve was almost like being at a funeral. I was saying goodbye to him again, but this time I had a feeling that I would not see him again.

I came up to Brisbane intending to leave Geoffrey, but my thoughts drifted back to the humiliation of my return to him pregnant with Mandy and the hard time he had given me since.

The fear of leaving him and having to return if I failed terrified me more than the prospect of death.

As the plane got closer to Sydney, my courage to leave Geoffrey slowly eroded.

I had told Frances and Mum that I would be leaving him on Friday and would drive my car up there. They listened to my words of Dutch courage, half-believing that I would eventually carry out my plan.

By the time I had arrived at Sydney airport, I had talked myself into giving Geoffrey one last chance and try to resort myself to be a better wife. *Just as well my family didn't believe me when I told them I'd be back,* I thought to myself, half-disgusted at my cowardice.

As I searched the faces looking for Geoffrey at the terminal, suddenly I saw him, his face looking purple with anger.

Fear engulfed me; all sorts of things started going through my mind. Had he found out that I had seen Steve while I was away? Maybe someone told him about what I had been up to in Brisbane. He grunted a greeting at me and stormed off to find my bag.

I ran behind him in the crowded terminal, not wanting him to get angry with me for not keeping up with him. It was a fair walk back to the car. Even though my bag was quite heavy, he marched along at a very quick pace while I struggled to keep up with him.

As soon as we got inside the car, he lit a cigarette and glared at me. 'So, what did your mother say about me? I bet she ran me down the whole time you were up there.'

'She never said anything about you,' I answered.

'Yeah, I bet.'

His sarcastic response warned me that this was going to be a long night.

As expected, he kept me awake most of the night, questioning me about my time in Queensland, wanting to know where I went, who I spoke to, and what was said.

The next day was a holiday Monday, and Mandy had arranged for friends and their three children to come over for a barbeque. He put on his friendly act, and I thought that he had finally gotten over his sarcastic bloodletting from the night before.

He took sarcastic shots at me all that day. I was worn out. I'd had little sleep from the night before and had to start work at five-thirty the next day.

The barbeque wound up around ten that night and I fell into bed. I had just started dozing off when Geoffrey came in and got into bed. 'That's right, fall asleep—do your usual trick,' he scoffed as he lit a cigarette. I ignored him and hoped that he would finish his smoke and go to sleep. 'Didn't you hear what I said?' he remarked as he shoved me in the back.

'Yes, I did. I'm just tired and need some sleep,' I replied, trying not to sound too annoyed.

But it was too late—just my response was enough to get him started. I sat up in the bed and for the next three hours, listened to him running me down, accusing me of anything he could put his mind to.

I was fighting to stay awake; the last few days had caught up to me. He asked me a question and my mind was in such a state that I was barely holding on to consciousness. I must have dozed off for a minute. It was then I felt a sharp jab of his elbow in my side.

Something snapped inside my head. I heard myself yelling at him to keep his 'fucking hands off me'. I turned over just in time to see his angry face and his fist waiting to connect with my face.

'Lay your fucking hand on me and it will be the last thing you fucking do!' I could hear myself screaming at him. His shocked face told me that he was seeing something from me as he had never seen before.

He pulled back in shock as I screamed at him, 'You're worst fucking nightmare has come true! I'm leaving you! Get out of this fucking bed, get out of my sight—as far as this marriage is concerned, you're finished!'

'Get out! Get out!' was all I could say, my voice screaming like a banshee.

He stood at the side of the bed in a daze, probably wondering what he could do to quieten me down. Mandy appeared at the door of my bedroom and stood there frozen, not knowing what was going on. The fear in her face reflected the fright she must have gotten by being woken up by my screaming.

As I started to pull myself together, I pointed to the door and calmly said to him, 'I want you out of this house tonight. If you don't leave, I will get in my car now and go straight to the refuge, as far as I'm concerned, I am leaving for Queensland on Thursday and I am not coming back.'

He started to cry, apologising, pleading with me not to leave. It was as though a rod of steel went through my body—no more would his begging and pleading convince me to stay with him for one minute more.

'You can leave this house tonight. I don't want to see your face again. Don't come near my job or I will pack up and leave straight away.'

I was shocked at what I was hearing. Was it me that was talking to him in such a calculating manner? No more the victim, at last, I could be free. I had finally rid myself of my worst abuser.

'What's going to happen to me?' Mandy asked, looking as though her whole world had fallen apart.

The tears welled in her eyes. A look of panic observing the unfolding drama before her told me she was now going to have to look after herself as I could no longer do it.

'You've got a choice. You can come with me or stay here. You're nineteen now, so you're old enough to make up your mind now. Think about it. You can let me know before I leave.'

I wasn't going to give her any ultimatums to come with me. I would probably have a job surviving on my own without worrying about my daughter. She had enough problems of her own without having to worry about starting a new life with me in a foreign state.

God knows where Geoffrey went that night, and I didn't care. Exhausted, I finally fell asleep and as soon as I lost consciousness, the alarm was screeching for me to get up and go to work.

The events of the previous couple of hours came flooding back to me. It wasn't a dream I had—I actually told him that I was leaving. As I made my way around the job, I was having difficulty believing that I dared to tell him that our marriage was finally over.

The next three days were spent planning on what I was going to take with me to start my new life. I would need as much as I could carry in my car. There would be no money to buy the essentials, so I packed four of everything: cups, plates, cutlery, towels. Mandy's portable television, a sewing machine, a small stereo, some of my precious ornaments, and a few photos—this was what was left of my life as I knew it.

Mandy had decided to stay with Geoffrey. She hated the idea of being around my family and said that she would prefer to stay with the only family she had ever known, and she felt that her father needed her more than I did.

I was glad, in a way. I needed to get away from everything and everyone. Although I lived with people around me every day, and despite being in a marriage, I had always felt alone.

Thursday morning finally came. I was doing the final touches to the work I had done over the previous couple of days when I looked up and saw Geoffrey coming towards me. I was angry and ready to attack him as soon as he came close to me, fearing that he would hurt me.

As he came closer to me, I could see that he had been crying; his eyes were swollen and red.

'What are you doing here? I thought I told you not to come and see me before I went.'

'I just wanted to say goodbye to you,' he said, his face wincing as he looked at me, waiting for my response. 'Please darl, change your mind. I don't want you to leave me. I promise I won't upset you again. I'll do anything you want me to do if you come home with me,' he pleaded with me.

As I looked at him, my resentment rose and I thought my head was going to explode. He was trying to work the same old guilt trip on me again, using my sympathies for his distress for me to slip back under his power again.

'How dare you come here again and use the same old begging and pleading line with me to make me go back with you again? How many times have I listened to you promising me that things were going to change and all you did was abuse me even more? I want you to go now. I never want to see you again, and if there's one thing you ever want to do to repay me, that would be to never treat another woman the way you treated me.'

Finally, I was able to stand there and say these things to his face.

I watched him turn his back and walk away and a sense of relief washed over me. I was free of him at last!

As soon as I had finished my work, I said goodbye to my friends and drove off, taking a last long look at the familiar surroundings of the area that I had lived in for the past twenty-four years. The closer I came to the highway that was taking me to Queensland, the more I felt as though I was leaving my life behind.

The open road lay before me like the runway of an airport, and my car felt like a jet plane that was lifting me off to freedom. There were times when I thought the wheels had left the road. I was free! And a new life lay before me.

As the miles flew past under the wheels of my car, my thoughts raced to dreams of finding a new job, a new home, and the possibility of being with Steve.

I was exhausted by the time I reached Queensland and phoned my mother as soon as I crossed over the border. She was shocked when she learned that I had finally left my husband.

I told her I was going to stay with Frances, as at least she was prepared to put me up. 'Oh, okay. I'll see you when you arrive.' Mum sounded guarded about the news of my separation from Geoffrey, and as I hung up the phone, I suddenly wondered whether or not I had done the right thing—her reception seemed rather cool.

At least Frances was happy to see me when I arrived. Her little villa at Burpengary overlooking a small valley covered with trees was a welcome sight from the crowded narrow streets of Sydney.

'I'm so happy to see you. I was worried that you would change your mind when you got back to Sydney.'

'I nearly did—it was only a fluke that I'm here now.'

Later that night, as we sat and drank a cask of wine, I filled her in on what had happened in Sydney.

A week later, I managed to get a job doing some cleaning, firstly in the morning at the Brisbane International Airport and later in the afternoon at the Roma Street railway centre in town. Each drive amounted to an eighty-kilometre round trip.

I left home at five-thirty in the morning and found my way back home around ten-thirty at night. I managed to keep this up for about two weeks before I decided that I could no longer keep going: the long hours and the cost of petrol hardly justified the cost of working.

With great reluctance, I decided to go on unemployment benefits to help pay some of the bills that I had brought with me from Sydney.

Although Frances did not mind me living with her, I still felt that I had to pay my way. It was by sheer chance that I happened to notice an advertisement in the local paper for a cleaning job at a nearby high school.

This job is mine, I thought as I filled in the application and sent off my resume. It had been nearly a month since I had left Sydney and I was just starting to feel a deep sense of independence.

My thoughts were focused on the job that I had applied for and every moment my mind would wander to thoughts of starting a new life, saving my money, and maybe getting a little place of my own.

Whilst all this was going on around me, there was still that little voice inside of my head repeating my son's words: *I have parents. I have parents.* Suddenly, my mind would wander, and I would start thinking of Shane.

The words of the social worker kept ringing through my brain: *'Your son will hate you for taking him from the only people that he has ever known.'* All I could think about was this angry message that my son had placed on his contact objection. The only comfort that I got each time I thought of his message was, at the least now I was in Queensland, and I was in the same state as him.

Steve came out to see me a few times. I had begun to see less and less of him as his work kept him quite busy and the eighty-kilometre drive from Ipswich out to Frances' place was enough to deter him from coming out too often.

It was a week after I applied for the job that I received a phone call to attend an interview at the school. I was very nervous as I told the school registrar of the reasons for my needing the job.

I came away feeling a little positive and hopeful that the job would be mine and I could finally get some security back into my life again.

A few days later, I got a phone call to let me know that I had been successful, and the job was mine. I was so happy that I could burst.

'Let's go out and celebrate,' Frances said as she danced around upon hearing my good news. I was ecstatic as we hopped into my car and drove up to the local hotel.

'Frances, I want to give you something for looking after me. If it wasn't for you, I wouldn't have been able to leave Geoffrey,' I said, hugging my younger sister.

'If you want to do something for me, you can shout me the cost of another tattoo. I want to get a rose tattooed on my breast,' she replied.

She was always the 'gypsy' in the family who loved to read tarot cards, paint, and wear long flowing skirts to match her long tangled curly hair. She had been in an accident when she was younger, and her personality could change in a split second.

'Oh right! I'll be in that as well; I always wanted a tattoo,' I replied, thinking it would be some form of a statement of liberation and ownership of my body.

Arm in arm, we made our way to the tattoo parlour. Frances had already decided what she had wanted and while she was getting a rose with her ex-husband's name tattooed on her breast, I was looking through the books of designs trying to decide what tattoo I was going to have.

The parlour was a traditional bikie hangout. Apart from the two long-haired bikers doing the tattoos, a young guy was sitting in the waiting area with his feet on the coffee table looking at some biker magazines. He was dressed in a grubby pair of jeans and a tie-dyed singlet with a bandana around his head, his long hair hung down in a plait.

He introduced himself as Mark, and during the time that Frances was getting her tattoo, the parlour was filled with the laughing and joking of the bikers. Mark and I got into discussions on spirituality, and it sort of blew me away that a young guy covered in tattoos could speak of things of this nature.

I had decided that I was going to get a tattoo of an eagle on my shoulder and as the needle dug into my flesh, I felt a deep sense of not only pain, but also a feeling that I was letting some of it out by finally reclaiming my own body.

After we had finished, I invited Mark to come around later that night and have a drink with Frances and me. Although he was ten years younger than me, I liked the happy-go-lucky nature of this little guy who laughingly called himself a walking comic book.

Later that night, we learned that Mark had just split up from his girlfriend, leaving him in a three-bedroom unit alone to pay the rent. He was looking for someone to move in with him to help him out. The thought crossed my mind to move in with him, but I was very reluctant because I had only known him a matter of hours.

It was getting late, and I had had enough to drink; I wasn't a drinker at the best of times. It was about two in the morning when I finally crawled into bed. I must have passed out immediately, but the next thing I knew, I could hear loud banging coming from the lounge room. I went out to see what was wrong and found Frances was lying on top of Mark on the lounge room floor.

'What's going on here?' I didn't know if they were fighting or playing.

'Nothing is going on!' Frances screamed at me. She then started to yell at me, accusing me of things that I didn't even know about. At first, I thought it was the drink speaking, but then I realised that my younger sister held some very deep-seated anger towards me.

I was shocked. *Was this the sister that I had helped so often in the past? She was a stranger that I hardly knew.*

'Come into the bedroom,' Mark said as he gently pushed me past my enraged sister.

I was devastated as I lay there weeping.

'She'll get over it; it's just the drink talking,' he said.

I finally fell asleep and half awoke to hear noises banging away in the kitchen. The events of the night before quickly flashed through my mind, and I wondered why my sister was up so early. I awoke a couple of hours later then went out into the kitchen where I found a note addressed to me.

The note simply said that Frances had decided that we were no longer able to live with each other and asked me to find somewhere else to live.

She had gone to stay with her ex-husband and said that she would be back in a couple of days and hopefully I would be gone by then.

So, this was it then—after all the times I had helped her, she was willing to throw me out onto the street.

'You had better come home and stay at my place until you find something else,' Mark said, seeing my desperation.

I slowly packed my things and put as much as I could fit into my car and drove off to his house.

Mark had a lovely unit, and I was surprised at the way he kept it so neat and tidy. As I looked around the little room that I was going to live in, and the rest of the home, I started to envisage the prospect of being happy there.

The argument with Frances the night before became a distant memory as I started to plan how I was going to arrange my room and the rest of the house. Mark had decided that he was going to go and stay with some friends who were living out in the bush.

The first day of my new job saw me meeting the other female cleaners, who made it quite clear that as a 'Mexican' from over the border taking a Queenslander's job, I was not welcome.

It was quite a strange situation that I was hired into a male cleaner position, becoming the first woman in the state to get the job. What I was not aware of was that due to a union mistake years before, I would be working more hours with less pay than the women at the school.

It took quite a while to get listed on the government payroll system to receive fortnightly wages, so for six months, I received a week's pay up to three weeks later.

Trying desperately to pay my share of rent and food, I ended up pawning everything I had of any value. Mark spent most of his time with his biker friends in the bush, drinking and taking drugs. I never saw much of him—I just went to work and came home.

While I had escaped the abuse of my husband, I was subjected to a regime of harassment every day in my job, the other cleaners doing anything they could to annoy me. Little things like hosing their rubbish over the area I had just cleaned or dumping the dust from their vacuum cleaners straight into the bins I emptied were reminding me that *freedom* was just another word if you were the target of another bully.

Is there any point in labouring on more misery and the day-to-day drudgery of the mundane?

Leaving my marriage, I had jumped out of the frying pan and into the fire and it was time to find my life from the start again.

It was coming up to Christmas 1993, and after two years of living with Mark and his drug addiction and the bullying of the other cleaners, I decided to return to Sydney to live with my daughter. She was in a relationship and had met her partner Bernie not long after I left, and now had a baby boy. Going back to Sydney meant that I would get to know my first grandson and hopefully restart my life.

I had also not seen Steve for some time and resolved that he had his own life to sort out—another reason for me to keep moving on.

Shipping my few possessions onto a back-loading truck, I headed off, watching my mother in the rear-view mirror as I drove off, sadly thinking that she was be going to be a very lonely woman. Her time to help me was long gone and I knew it.

Chapter 7

The traffic was bedlam when I reached Sydney. I seemed to be stuck going nowhere for hours. I could feel the tension rising as I crawled along at a snail's pace. My instinct was to turn the car around and head back to Brisbane, but as the jam flattened out, I managed to finally get to Mandy's house.

She and her partner Bernie shared a big house at Marayong with Mandy's friend Joanne, and I was very lucky to have a room at the back of the house away from the noise of the young ones.

It was approaching Christmas and I was longing to see Russ and Des at the Auburn bowling club again.

They greeted me like a long-lost friend. I felt safe around them; they were my dearest friends, and there were no judgements from them.

I told them of my time in Queensland, the hardships I had encountered, and the way I had been treated, lamenting my broken marriage.

My return to Sydney was to restart my life again and possibly feel what it was like to be happy.

Geoffrey had moved out of Seven Hills and was living with an older woman a long way out of Auburn, so there was no fear of him coming back to his favourite club, so I could enjoy the night with my old friends.

The three of us were invited back to a friend's house later that night for a drink, and Des sat next to me on the couch. I could feel his leg resting on mine and thought it was a bit too close for being just friends. I ignored it, thinking that it was just the size of the couch that put him a bit closer than expected.

New Year's Eve was looming and hanging around with the young ones was becoming a bit tedious—my days of discos every night were long gone—so I invited Des to join us at the local club to bring in the New Year. He had been divorced for many years and had an on-again, off-again relationship with a girlfriend, and at that point, it was in the off-again period.

He also brought along his next-door neighbour, Warren, to match me up with, but Des, after a very close dance session with me, decided that I would be more to his liking. This was a side of Des that I had not seen in my eight years of friendship; the academic friend had turned into a possible companion.

Not long into the new year, I found a job in home care looking after aged and young disabled clients and was in my element, having such an important job away from the hard cleaning work that made me feel tired.

Our relationship grew from friendship into deep and respectful love. He treated me like a princess, buying me flowers every time he saw me, opening the car door each time we went out, and listening to my concerns about life. This was all new to me. I had never experienced being 'cared for' in my life, nor did I have the opportunity to have such a clever man explain everything that intrigued me in great detail.

Eight months later, that concern and devotion saw me move into Des's house in Fairfield, and a year later, on holiday in Hong Kong, he proposed. This was followed a year later, in 1996, by marrying him at the bowling club where we first met.

I was born again: a bride, a princess, desired by a handsome and intelligent man, with a whole new future that was awaiting her.

My dear friend Russ walked me down the aisle to the music of a band playing 'Elizabethan Serenade'.

The golden life I dreamed of became a reality and after a honeymoon cruising to the Pacific Islands, it was back to work for me.

*

Attending to one of the elderly clients that I used to shower every day, I leaned over the back of her wheelchair to pull her up, when a strange sensation, like a bee sting in my shoulder, sent a message that I had injured myself. Little did I know that I had torn a tendon in my shoulder. When I got home, I told Des about what had happened, and he insisted that I hand in my notice as the work was becoming too hard for me.

He loved his job at the CSIRO, where he was employed as an electronics technical officer—his brilliant mind invented and made measurement equipment for the scientists in the laboratory at Lindfield.

The nature of his job meant he didn't work a normal nine-to-five business day, and he would work until the early hours of the morning, leaving me with a lot of time to fill in.

'I'm afraid, old kid'—that was how he used to address me—'that you will have to find something to keep you occupied every day.' Not being able to do any heavy work again, he encouraged me to get some more education so that I could work in an office somewhere.

As I had never been to high school, TAFE would probably be the best solution for me.

I enrolled in a course that looked at community welfare. The units had a lot of interesting subjects that I thought could help me with another job. From the very first class I was hooked!

One of the first units was to look at how organisations were run, and group dynamics.

This meant looking at an organisation, getting to know them, who was who, and who did what. I was at a bit of a loss and wondered what sort of organisation that I should be looking at.

I thought it might be useful to start looking at any organisation that was involved in adoption and that I might learn a bit more about what happened to me.

Looking through the phone book and seeing mostly religious organisations, I came across the name of an organisation called Origins, proudly stating they supported people separated by adoption.

Well, that was me.

With trepidation, I called the number and a softly spoken woman's voice answered, 'Hello, you've reached Origins. Dian Wellfare speaking. Can I help you?'

'Hello. I was wondering if I could find out a little bit more about your organisation. Are you connected with any religious or government organisations?'

I needed to know these things before I started to enquire more about how Origins was run.

The voice on the other end of the line assured me that they were completely independent of religious or any state-run organisations. As the conversation developed, my curiosity became more intense. Instead of telling her that I was a student that was there to study her organisation, I was inquiring as a mother who had lost her child to adoption.

As the conversation continued, she asked me several questions, such as whether I was offered any financial assistance to keep my baby, was offered foster care until I was in a situation to be able to care for my baby, or was told about the lifelong mental health damage that I would suffer if I signed a consent to my child's adoption.

I answered 'No' to all of those questions. 'None of these options had ever been made available to me.'

'Then I have to tell you that the adoption of your child was unlawful,' she informed me.

This was the first time I had heard the word 'unlawful' regarding my situation; my scrambled mind was starting to come out of the fog that had descended on it for so many years.

I said, 'I would like to come and attend one of your support meetings, if that's okay?'

'Yes, of course,' she said, 'we're having one next weekend if you'd like to come along.'

Was I going as a mother who had lost a child to adoption, or as a student disguised as a mother to observe not only how Origins was run, but also witness the emotional revelations of women like myself?

I chose 'student' and had to look at this issue in the sense of being a third party to what was going on around me so that I could take an unbiased and unemotional view of my own experience.

A little grey two-storey cottage surrounded by forget-me-nots was a welcoming sign as I reached the door. A voice called out to me to come through the hallway and into a large lounge room. I was surprised to see at least twenty women sitting around in a circle, all busily chatting with each other.

'Welcome. Can you introduce yourself?' said a friendly-faced woman a little taller than myself. What drew me to her was her large mane of tightly curled light brown hair, reminding me of my sister, Bridget, who wore a similar crop of unrestrained curls.

Being a little bit shy, I suppose, with all eyes upon me, I introduced myself and sat down in the circle. Dian started the meeting by giving each mother ten minutes to reveal how they were feeling, how their reunions were going, and anything else that they would like to talk about.

For the first time, I was able to see and hear other women like myself speak of the pain and distress of losing their child. I was not a student anymore—I was one of 'them', telling my story for the first time to strangers, a burden that was finally starting to lift.

After we had been around the circle, questions were being asked from Dian, and a little more of the former conversation on our legal rights were explained. It clarified the conversation that I had with her on the phone, and started to evoke the student in me.

I put the 'mother' part away; it was now time to observe what was going on around me.

I had to work out who was the leader of this organisation, who was the right-hand person, the mover and shaker, who were the troops, the workers, and the brains behind an organisation whose mission it was to expose what Dian called 'taking the sacred cow of adoption to the abattoir'.

These were questions that needed to be answered for my studies.

Origins had a committee; it usually met before the meetings each month, so there was a structure to Origins. It did meet all the legal requirements, such as being an incorporated association, so it was suitable for me to use as my project.

Looking around Dian's office, it became abundantly clear that this was a group of women who had certainly done their research into adoption. Hundreds of books and black filing folders filled the wall behind her desk. I had no idea that over four hundred mothers had made so many contributions to the library, and Origins had only been going for just over eighteen months.

'Take some of these papers home with you and read them; they might give you a bit more insight into what they knew about adoption,' Dian said as she handed me the material. It was certainly a lot to take in on my first visit.

'How did it go?' asked Des when I finally made it back home. I didn't know what to say—my mind was still trying to process the events of the afternoon.

'I have to do a bit more studying on this; I'm not exactly sure where this is going,' I replied, feeling exhausted.

A paper on civil rights crimes in adoption by Catherine Sherry[1] was one of the papers that Dian had given me. It shook me to the core. Her exposé of the unlawful practices in adoption was graphic and shocking.

When reading that over a hundred and fifty thousand women like myself had lost children—mostly newborns—to adoption from the 1950s, my stomach turned over, and I came out in a cold sweat. In his submission to the New South Wales inquiry into past adoption practices, Dr Rickarby describes it as the 'single mother's holocaust'[2]. I could hardly believe that I was part of this. All those years of thinking that I was a criminal when, in fact, I was the victim.

All these statistics and knowledge of what I had just found out came blurting out of my mouth to Des, who looked at me with grave concern.

'I don't know if you should become involved in all of this—it all looks very radical to me.' Maybe it had something to do with his being employed by the federal government, or fear for me and my state of mind. I don't know.

Having been given all this new information, I was determined to find out as much as I could. The fragmented pieces of my mind and memory were starting to fit into a picture and becoming something that could be understood.

Many more phone calls to Dian followed in the lead up to the next meeting. I was getting quite friendly with her. She impressed me with her knowledge; it was obvious she had done an awful lot of reading and spoken to quite a lot of mothers.

[1] Violation of Women's Human Rights: birthmothers and adoption by Catherine Sherry BA, LLB (Hons) 1992 (Unpublished paper on research conducted on the Adoption Information Act 1990 (NSW).
[2] http://www.originsnsw.com/nswinquiry2/id12.html

Having her own experience, and her medical records, set her on the daunting task of trying to understand how she had lost her child. Her insight was remarkable, and I soaked up every word that fell from her lips.

The next meeting made it more obvious about who did what within the organisation. Dian, of course, was not only the fount of knowledge, but was also what some would describe as the 'mother figure'.

She was the one who comforted and gave insight to all those mothers seeking the truth.

Tracy was the 'mover and shaker': she was the public voice of Origins and the one who could dig out and find the media. Her extroverted personality got the attention of anyone she spoke to.

Wendy, a quiet and thoughtful person, was driven by the suicide of her lost son to find out why he took his life. Her short black hair and dark-rimmed glasses gave her the look of an academic. She was someone to be respected, having had a university education in science, and she had delved into every library possible to find any information on adoption. Her years of research had uncovered a mountain of papers, articles, and books on adoption. It was staggering the amount of information about the legal and mental health effects of adoption that were known and studied throughout the world. I could barely utter the word let alone comprehend what it meant, and yet it had had such a significant effect on my life.

And there it was, in black and white: a subject and process that was going on unchecked and rampant on the lives of people whilst the scholars and academics were studying its impact, the law sitting on the sidelines. Wendy had unearthed undeniable facts that they all knew what they were doing to us and that it was unlawful.

In effect, I had determined the main three heads of the organisation had the roles of leadership, voice, and knowledge.

The rest of the committee was made up of the secretary Denise, and Linda and Rosemary as the public officers. I wanted to become more involved with the committee and asked Dian if it was possible to be more help.

From what I was finding out, it became increasingly urgent that I find my son Shane and tell him what they had done to us. He had to know the truth. It was now 1997, approaching seven years since I received the three words denying me any knowledge of who he was and where he was living. Dian put me in touch with another mother, Jean, in Queensland, who was in a similar predicament of having a contact objection.

Jean's son was taken from her a year after I lost mine. She had been active for quite some time in trying to find out more about what was happening in Queensland.

I contacted her and spoke to her for quite some time. She, too, was desperate to find her son. I found out that she had his first name given to him by his adopters. I was curious, and she questioned why I had not received at least my son's adopted first name.

'You need to write to the department and ask them to give you his first name,' she advised.

The letter was sent that very day explicitly asking for the first name of my son, which was the only piece of information about him that I was entitled to receive.

I still couldn't quite understand how the issue of the contact objection was introduced into the Freedom of Information Act about adoption. At the time I applied for my information, there were going to be no regulations prohibiting me from getting all the information about my son. It came as quite a shock later to find out that he could put a veto on any information on how I might be able to find him.

I spent the next few weeks at the state library, trawling through every copy of the Queensland newspapers, searching for any articles on the releasing of adoption information.

Letters to the editor around the time the legislation was to be changed were swamped by adoptive parents and their adopted children condemning the right of mothers such as myself to know the whereabouts of our lost children.

I had collected quite a number of these letters along with an advertisement for a privacy information meeting held by adoptive parents to contest the upcoming release of information.

It was becoming apparent that there was quite a lobby at the last minute to get the legislation changed to bring in the contact to objection clause into the Act.

I sent off what I had found to Jean. She was highly suspicious that something was 'rotten in the state of Denmark' when it came to adoptive parents having so much say over legislation in Queensland. From what she said, she also thought that her son David (his adopted name) may have been part of this movement of very angry people.

Meanwhile, the TAFE course was going into areas that I thought could be very useful, particularly to my role in Origins.

The Group Dynamics unit was followed by several subjects, including advocacy, child protection, counselling, and lifespan development, covering how a child grows into an adult and the stages of life we go through.

Michael White was a lecturer who held us in awe at the way he described the bond between mother and newborn. His description evoked such emotion in an adopted girl in the class that she ran out the door screaming that she had been in the hospital as a newborn for three months before her adopter came and took her.

I was intrigued and listened to him carefully that the first thing an infant learned was trust through the mother's breast milk that it suckled. My newborn never had the opportunity of suckling at my breast; it made me wonder how much trust he would have in the world.

He also said, as a writer of several books on communism, 'You know you've made it in life when you're on someone's list.' This sentiment was not lost on me as I was becoming more radical by the minute.

I was determined to learn as much as I could, as one day I would be seeking accountability from those who had wronged me.

Every unit of my learning gave me another tool to fight the system. One of the most useful 'tools' was learning about the political platforms of various parties. I related very much to the Labor Party, and joined as a member to access the federal and local politicians in my area.

Becoming more and more literate—with the help of Des editing some of my assignments, and a letter-writing course—I was off and running.

I started a regime of writing to politicians, religious leaders, the United Nations, and anyone else I thought could help me pressure the Department of Families, Youth and Community Care to give me the information to find my son.

I contacted a weekly magazine, *'That's Life'*,[3] to do a story, hoping my son would see it and contact me. It appeared a few weeks later, photos and all. This, at least, would get around the laws preventing me from trying to contact him whilst an objection was in place.

It was 1998, I was becoming more and more involved with Origins, and we were becoming more and more political, starting to demand a parliamentary inquiry into adoption in New South Wales.

This restlessness was brought about by an expose on the 'dead baby scandal'[4] that was being exposed in Western Australia. It involved mostly unmarried mothers who had been told at the time of their child's birth that the baby had died, and the release of the

---

[3] *That's Life* magazine, October 29th 1997.
[4] 'More Reports of Adoption Trickery', *The Australian*, June 12 1996. p5

Information Act throughout the country meant that adoptees and mothers could turn up at each other's doors unannounced.

Many stories were published on the horror of mothers having their 'deceased' child looking for them. The same situation applied to adoptees who were confronted by their natural mother.

The scandal had been exposed some years earlier but had died down, and with a spate of news articles and mothers coming forward, stories of illegal adoption were again becoming prominent in the news.

I even had a front-page story in our local paper titled *'How Dare They.'*[5]

Each week found us demonstrating in front of Parliament House demanding an inquiry, and the media was only too happy to record us for the evening news.

The third demonstration saw us tying some of our younger demonstrators dressed in white shifts to the fence at Parliament House, these young ones representing us as the mothers abused by the system.

The ABC covered the story and then asked Dian to appear on *Lateline*[6] the following night.

An ex-social worker and a parliamentarian appeared along with Dian. It was becoming abundantly clear in the interview that the social worker was unknowingly validating every allegation of corruption that Origins was making, and following the interview, the ABC received countless calls from mothers who shared our views.

Immediately after *Lateline*, we held another demonstration, and it was during this that a politician announced they were going to give us the inquiry that would, hopefully, finally expose the corrupt and illegal practices of adoption.

---

[5] 'How Dare They', *Fairfield City Champion*, 10 December 1997.
[6] 'Birthbond', *Lateline*, ABC, October 1997.

The government gave us six weeks to present our submissions. It was hell trying to record not only the history of the unlawful practices of taking our babies without our consent but the fraud involved in the taking of adoption consents.

Each mother's story was nearly identical to the next regarding the coercion and denial of legal rights we were exposing. The shame of having lost our children and the trauma suffered had silenced us and protected the perpetrators for decades.

I would go down to Dian's place nearly every day to try to help in any way I could. She had an old DOS laptop that she scribed away at. One morning I arrived, she was distraught: the old computer had crashed, and she had lost all of her work.

We managed to get another, and she had to start all over again— over a hundred pages lost in a single moment.

Wendy's submission was mind-blowing. Her research on the mental health damage to mother and child was indisputable, and the words of the professionals on the subject could not be challenged.

Six weeks came and went, and the parliamentary committee had to extend the submission period indefinitely. The extra time gave us more opportunities to send in more information and get the word out to our members.

Our hero, who validated everything we said, was Dr Geoff Rickarby, whose submission to the inquiry was explosive and exposed not only the mental health damage to us and our children, but also the unlawful practices going on behind the closed doors of the hospitals.[7]

It was absolute chaos trying to keep responding to the questions from the committee. A major concern was the drugs given to us to dry up our breast milk. Diethylstilboestrol (DES), or stilboestrol, was banned in the USA but was still being used in Australia.[8]

---

[7] http://www.originsnsw.com/nswinquiry2/id12.html
[8] http://www.originsnsw.com/id76.html

We were concerned about the long-term effects and put out a very detailed survey to our members. Each survey came back with horror stories of cancer and pre-cancerous conditions in our mothers; we had over three hundred stories of trauma and the long-term effects of their hospital experience.

As the last days of the inquiry were being held, we made the unfortunate mistake of sending the original copies to the committee due to time limits and failed to make copies. We later found out that the survey was lost somewhere in the government archives.

While the pandemonium was going on with the New South Wales inquiry, I had also discovered that a Commission of Inquiry into the Abuse of Children in Queensland Institutions (the Forde Inquiry) was announced.[9] This was just the opportunity I had to expose my own story.

I hurriedly put together a submission and a few weeks later was asked by the commission to come and give evidence face-to-face with them.

After asking me about my experience, ex-Governor Leneen Forde looked across the table and asked, 'Didn't you think it was strange that a girl your age was in Holy Cross?'

I was the oldest one there; the other girls—there must've been at least twenty of them—were all years younger than myself, some of them only fourteen and fifteen.

I'd convinced myself over the years that if I had been a month older, they could not have done that, according to the police that arrested me, little knowing the majority of girls were discharged at sixteen.

'I want to get some justice for what happened to me. It was illegal, and I want someone to be held accountable. Can I go to the police?' I asked her.

---

[9] https://www.qld.gov.au/__data/assets/pdf_file/0023/54509/forde-commin-quiry.pdf

'I don't see why not,' she replied.

Driving back to Mum's house in Caboolture, I told Des all that had happened at the meeting and that Mrs Forde agreed that I should go to the police and make a statement.

We went straight to the Caboolture Police Station and I approached the front bench. 'I'd like to make a statement, please.' The receptionist looked up.

'What is this concerning?'

'Kidnapping,' I replied, which caught her attention.

'When did this happen?' she asked, startled by my response.

'Nineteen sixty-seven,' I replied. She could barely contain her amusement; I took the smile off her face by telling her that the state's ex-governor and commissioner of the Forde Inquiry advised me to take that action.

A policeman came out and took me out the back to the office where he made a seven-page statement about my complaint.

'This happened a very long time ago, and I don't know if we can do anything about it now.'

'But this was a crime,' I said, 'and I wanted it investigated.' He agreed that he would send it to his supervisors to see if they could do anything about it.

'The only thing that I could suggest—because you would have to prove 99.9% that a particular person committed that crime or you won't get a conviction—my best advice to you would be that you take personal action against the state of Queensland.'

That set the dogs running. I was now in the chase and eager to return to Sydney and back to where I could do some more research. I wanted to make someone pay for what they did to me. The next plan was to find a lawyer who would take my case on.

Eventually, a letter came back from the department letting me know that my son's first name was now Tim.

Tim. Tim. Tim. Repeating this name a thousand times over, I had to let it sink in that Shane did not exist anymore. At least now I had a name; it was something that I could hang on to and search with. The search for my lost son was now in earnest; I would leave no stone unturned to find him.

The State Library of New South Wales held the electoral rolls of every electorate in the country and week after week, I would go searching through every electoral role that encompassed the Brisbane area.

With a ruler in hand, I would go up and down every column of names looking for the name Tim—or Timothy, just to be sure.

After endless weeks of searching with Mandy and Des when they had the time and approximately two million names, we had a list of forty-six Tims and Timothys.

Armed with that knowledge, the next thing was to go back to Queensland and search the State Archives for the state electoral rolls.

Jean told me with great enthusiasm that the archives now had the admission lists of the primary schools in Queensland, which had not only names and addresses but also the birth dates of children enrolling in primary school, something that the state electoral rolls did not have.

Waiting to go to Queensland and stay with my mother and use that time to go to the archives and finally search, I lay down on the couch and fell asleep exhausted from the weeks of panic.

Dreaming, I felt an enormous wind like a hurricane as I hung on to the side of the lounge for grim death, papers flying all around me. Suddenly, everything stopped and became very quiet. The fear was gone; I had a peaceful and calm feeling that everything was going to be okay, and I was going to find him.

Jean was not as I expected: she was probably about the same height as me, short dark hair, and very wispy in her physique and, like me, passionate in her search for her son.

From all the correspondence and conversations that we had had, I felt that I had known her for a long time, and she felt that she knew me. We had a mission to accomplish together, and she was going to be my companion in that quest.

Des and Mum accompanied me to the archives. I'd given them a little bit of direction on what to search for, but Mum went off on a tangent of her own and decided to see if there was any information about our arrival in Australia. She was overjoyed when she found the passenger list that held our names on our arrival in Australia and the letter introducing us to a priest in Townsville.

The state electoral rolls were another thing: three days going through them cut the list of Tims down to about fifteen.

Jean was devastated—she was going through the microfiche looking at the school admission books. Her belief that the archives contained all of the books in Queensland was a mistake: there were only six schools in Queensland that had given their books to the archives.

Coming to the end of the third day, I was feeling quite defeated and had a sinking feeling that this search was going to become fruitless.

'I think I've found something!' Jean exclaimed, holding a piece of paper in her hand. 'I found a Timothy; he was born on the same day as your son, the first of September, at the women's hospital.'

'But the woman at the department told me specifically that his name was Tim, not Timothy.'

She replied, 'They often change their names or the dates of birth to try to stop us from finding them.'

'Okay, I'll chase this one up then.' Although I didn't think it was going to be a positive result, I thought it may as well be at least something to look into.

A few minutes later, she came out again, holding up another piece of paper. 'I found another one,' she said joyfully. 'His name is Tim, and he lives across the road from the other Tim, and his birthday is the tenth of September. Don't forget I told you that they often change the birth dates as well.'

That was the end of it, we had reached the end of our search; it was now a matter of looking up the names that we had collected, but firstly we would seek out the two Tims.

We drove back to Jean's house. She was more brazen than I was, and she was going to see if she could track down the first Timothy that we found. He had a very unusual name, and it was easy as there were very few with that surname in the phone book.

She rang a couple of numbers and ended up finding the sister of Timothy. He worked in a coal mine in North Queensland, and she had not heard from him for a while, but she said she would call him and let him know that we were searching for someone who may have been adopted.

Timothy's mother had died when he was four and he and his father travelled around Queensland for many years, so whether he may or may not have been adopted was not known to any of the family.

Calling back later, she let us know Timothy's phone number.

We did not have the contact details of the other Tim and I was going to follow that up the next day.

Driving home in the dark, and still excited by the day's events, thinking nervously of what I would say to the young man I was about to call.

'There he is!' Mum yelled from the back seat. A utility in front of us heading towards Caboolture proudly displayed the signage on his tailgate: *Tim's Painting*. We all laughed, thinking it was not going to be that easy to find him.

We arrived back at Mum's place. I called Timothy and asked him if he knew anything about his birth.

We chatted for quite a while. He sounded like such a lovely young man. I was hoping that he was my son, but he was very doubtful. 'I don't think I am your son, but the funny thing is the boy across the road. He was my little mate. His name was also Tim. I'm sure he was adopted, and we were both born on the same day at the women's hospital!'

I said, 'But it said on his school admission list that he was born on the tenth of September.'

'No, I'm sure he was born on the same day as me. Let me ask my sister; she still lives in the same street as his adoptive parents.'

Shortly after, he rang back and confirmed that yes, the other Tim had been born on the same day as him. I was blown away, I now had my son's full name, and it was not difficult to find him.

Now the search was on, it came down to now searching through the electoral rolls to find out where he lived.

Needing time to process all this information and to settle down, I asked Mum to come to the local federal politician in her area to let him know what was happening in New South Wales about the adoption inquiry and also to see if I could garner some support to get something like that happening in Queensland. The Forde Inquiry was still gaining a lot of attention in the media, but I was hopeful, with a little support politically, that we may get an adoption inquiry going as well.

Gary Campbell was a pleasant sort of chap—young for a politician and quite knowledgeable. I suppose he must have been bored that day and had a bit of time up his sleeve. We spoke for about an hour and a half, and my political lobbying was broken up now and again by a reminiscence of his days when he was a local councillor in the seat of Mount Gravatt. He recalled a young adoptee: 'Yes, I think his name was David; he was one very angry young man and opposed the idea of the records being opened.'

My ears pricked up. We knew there was an adoption privacy group that was running around lobbying to keep the records closed— maybe this young man could be Jean's son!

The time to face the music had come at the electoral office. I scoured the list of names and finally came across Tim. I could hardly believe that he lived just a few streets away from my mother.

With a pounding in my chest of excitement and fear, I drove down the dirt road with Des and pulled up in front of a beautiful rambling ranch-style house.

I knew from the size of the house and the surrounding land that my son must be doing well. Fearfully approaching the front door, I knocked, and a very attractive dark-haired girl came to the door. Nervously, I greeted her. A questioning look on her face indicated she was wondering why a stranger would come to her door.

'I don't know if you can help me. I'm looking for my son. He was adopted a long time ago.'

Her eyes widened in disbelief. She took a deep breath, asking, 'How did you find us?'

'It was very difficult,' was my response.

She asked me to wait on the verandah while she called her husband. He was on his way home from work, and I heard her saying, 'No, this is not a joke!'

Panicked, she asked, 'Did you go and see Tim's parents? I hope you respected their privacy. He's on his way home now—he'll be here in five minutes.'

I was scared to death. I didn't want to meet him at that moment. I didn't just want to crash into his life—he needed time to have this visit sink in.

'I've made these journals for him,' I said, passing them over to her. The journals we made in the event my son was found contained photos, media articles, copies of letters I had sent, and my story. I told her, 'If he is my son, he can keep them. If not, can you please call me on this number and I will pick them up?'

I had to get out of there fast and nearly ran down the circular driveway into the car.

'Quick, get going. I don't want him to see me,' I said, lunging down as I saw a white utility coming around the corner. Des sped off as the utility turned into the driveway. Looking back, I saw that familiar painted tailgate we had seen the night before.

Hours passed. The night never seemed to end, and over and over again my mind was picturing my son turning over the pages of my journals, each page indelible in my mind.

Morning finally came. Mum and Des were sitting, chatting happily around the kitchen table. My stomach was rolling over and over again, waiting expectantly for the phone to ring.

All of us had a casual staring session with each other—waiting, waiting.

The loud ring of the phone on the wall still caught us by surprise, even though we were expecting it. I urged Mum to answer it for me—I was too cowardly, and I needed my mother to break the ice.

'Hello,' she said cheerily.

'Yes, it is. I'll pass you over to her.'

She handed me the phone, pointing, and indicating it was him.

'Hello, is that Lily?' His voice was soft and did not sound threatening.

'Yes,' I replied. I briefly told him that I was looking for my son, who had been adopted, and after a short conversation, he stopped thoughtfully.

'I think I'm your son. I think you can stop looking.'

Those words rang in my ears and relief washed over me. My search was finally over. We arranged to meet an hour later in the gardens of Caboolture Lakes.

I sat there for what felt like an eternity, and then a familiar face approached. I recognised Tim's wife and realised the man holding her hand next to her was my son.

As they came closer and I could make out his features, he didn't look like Steve—he didn't look like the baby that I'd imagined for so long. He was not much taller than me and quite thin. His hair was a colour I couldn't describe—it was a combination of light brown and blond with a touch of red.

He had the Jewish nose instantly recognisable as my mother's, and as he turned his face and looked at me, it was a combination of every one of my siblings.

Being confronted by a young man in his thirties was a shock to me. I had lost a baby and grieved for him for most of my life. It was hard to reconcile that this young man standing before me was that newborn.

I quickly hugged him and he froze as stiff as a board. I pulled back, embarrassed. I wasn't a showy person of my affections at the best of times, never really hugging my only daughter.

His reaction made me feel that I had done something wrong. He was holding a couple of picture frames of his children in his hand. It looked like he picked them up on his way out the door.

He was quietly reserved, and after our greeting, we sat on the park bench for a couple of hours discussing how I found him, lost him, and I asked him about his life.

He was the oldest of four children the parents had adopted: two younger brothers and an adopted sister followed.

He had had a good upbringing and thought a lot of his adopters. I, on the other hand, was feeling quite resentful that these strangers could get four children while I could only have one.

When it came to the discussion of the journals I had given him, he remarked that his mother and father had seen the *That's*

Life article that I had sent him. I was amazed, and asked him if he had been told of it.

No, was the response. Worst still was he had not been told of his adoption until he was twenty-three, so all my longing and the efforts to find him were completely unknown to him.

He said that as he was picking up his brother at the parents' house at 6 am, his adopters wanted to see him later, telling him he was adopted and to sign the 'contact to objection', thus sealing his records and my fate forever.

So, this is how the game is going to be played, I thought to myself. They had known my story and never told my son that I was searching for him, so it took me another eighteen months to find him!

I thought that it could not get any worse and as the afternoon wore on, I discovered that his adoptive grandparents lived three doors down facing the back fence of Holy Cross.

Panic kicked in. Maybe the adoptive grandmother had been observing me whilst she volunteered at the home's kitchen. Maybe she was watching and waiting for me to have the baby that may have been intended for their daughter. I was getting paranoid; they were just too close to Holy Cross and me.

This revelation filled me with anger that I had been used to provide a stranger with a family.

The visit came to an end. I was completely worn out by the exhilaration of finally meeting my firstborn and the emotional toll, which well and truly overpowered me.

We arranged to meet the next day, and they were going to bring their children, my grandchildren, to meet Des and my mother.

It was nice to see them again the next day. Some of the trauma of the previous day had subsided and the prospect of seeing the children was something I looked forward to, despite being told by his wife not to mention that I was Tim's mother.

I was only too happy not to disclose such news, and as she and I chatted, I looked over and saw my mother showing Tim the family photos explaining who was who.

It was obvious that she was enjoying the moment and that he had her characteristics. Ironically, this was the grandson and nephew that my family did not want me to meet.

I had been in touch with Steve for a while during my search and called him to let him know the news. He was delighted and asked if he could come and meet Tim. I had to let him know that Tim was not ready for a meeting with him at that time. He took it very well and said that he would wait until Tim was ready, which at least made me feel better that he was prepared to wait until I got to know Tim and his family a little better.

The headline 'My Darling Boy' adorned the front page of my local newspaper. It was a great Mother's Day story on our reunion.[10]

I had found him a couple of weeks before Mother's Day and wondered if there would be any chance of getting a card from him. It was sheer hope, but I always lived in hope anyway.

Yes! There was a card in the letterbox the Friday before the big day. Hurriedly I opened the letter, and a flowered card appeared. As I pulled it out of the envelope, a few pieces of paper fell to the floor.

They were photos. I picked them up and there were a few little black-and-white photos of a blond smiling baby. The writing said *twelve weeks old*, and his bib said *Tim*.

I went into a state of shock with each photo. There was one of him at about two riding a little trike. The next one was of him about four, a little blond boy smiling and holding a football flag—his first day at school. This was my child.

I had missed all those years of him growing up. In each photo, he was smiling at a stranger and not at me.

---

[10] 'My darling Boy', *Fairfield City Champion*, 6 May 1998.

Death would have been more acceptable to me at that point. I rang Dian to tell her what I had just encountered. She saved me, talked me down from hanging myself off the clothesline.

Anger quickly replaced grief.

If you could imagine a wolf running down a street with blood running from its mouth that would be me. I was raging and I was going to make someone pay for what had been done to me.

It wasn't easy to find a lawyer who was prepared to take my case. I'd approached the Public Interest Advocacy Centre (PIAC), who said they were unable to help me; Legal Aid Queensland refused because of financial restrictions; women's legal services; the Law Society, and many lawyers each said my matter was beyond their reach.

Trawling through the Brisbane phone book, I spotted a law firm that I hoped would help me sue the state of Queensland for the theft of my son.

I contacted Jones and Associates, a young team who were eager to take my case on for a fee, not pro bono.

The chase for justice was on.

Needing to get as much evidence I could, I contacted the Sisters of Mercy and asked for any information on my time at Holy Cross.

A few weeks later, I received an admittance form under the Children's Services Act, giving the name of Lillian Josephine McDonald and also noting that my father was in Boggo Road Gaol, and my mother was living in a caravan park in Sydney.

It was ironic that both my father and I were locked up at the same time. Looking back, I believe that my father would never have left me behind bars—even though he may have given us a hard time, he would not have let anyone else harm us.

Another very interesting piece of information was included. It was the visitor's list for the duration of the time spent in Holy Cross. It appeared that for the first couple of months on the list, I was visited by two older women from the factory where I'd worked. They visited me nearly every fortnight for the first three months of my incarceration. We were not told if a visitor was coming—we just had to sit around and wait every Sunday and hope that our names were called out. I suppose that I was lucky: some of the girls never saw anyone.

In the fourth month, my sister Jenny came to see me. She then visited me for the next two months regularly, so she had no idea what was going on with my release or what was happening with my parents. No one had told her what was being done regarding my release.

Her last visit before the birth of my son was on the thirtieth of July. Her next visit was on the fifteenth of October.

I remember getting angry with her at that visit—her reason for not coming was that she was told she was not allowed to see me.

Putting the pieces together, I was starting to see a picture here. The nuns had deliberately kept me without a visitor or support leading up to and after the thirty days revocation period where I could get my child back. It was all starting to make sense to me now.

Determined to get more information, I wrote to the department again and asked them to provide any documents about my son's adoption, as I supposedly had all the information about my state wardship.

Not long after my request, I received some photocopied forms, one titled, *Report of Investigation* and another *Birth/Death of an Illegitimate Child*.

The *Report of Investigation* was sent by the registrar from the hospital to the Department of Children's Services on the fourth of September. It contained my name, address, my description, where I was living, and my hobbies.

It also had a section for the putative father that described Steve, his occupation, and that he would not support me and the child.

At the end of the form, in the comments for notes is asked 'baby for adoption?'

I also noted that I'd signed my name wrong, calling myself Lillian instead of Lily. I don't know why I did that—I had never called myself Lillian.

The *Birth/Death of an Illegitimate Child* form was also sent by the Registry of Birth, Deaths, and Marriages to the Director of the Children's Services Department. It contained my son's date of birth and his name Shane Stephan McDonald, again recording my name as Lillian, not Lily.

On doing a little bit of research, I discovered that under the *Infant Life Protection Act of 1905* (Qld)[11] that every illegitimate birth in Queensland was to be reported to the district register within three days after the birth, and on notification, the circumstances of the illegitimate birth were investigated by a departmental officer or the police.

In effect from 1905, every woman in Queensland who gave birth to an illegitimate child was reported to the state authorities.

Sickening outrage was not the appropriate feeling I used to describe how I felt about getting this information—it felt far worse. Young women like myself were reported on and hounded down by the 'wolves' of the state for our newborns.

The worst part of all of this was that, according to the Act, the fathers of those children were forced to make provision for the upkeep of the child and its mother or face jail. No-one had sought out Steve, they just wanted our baby.

---

[11] *Infant Life Protection Act of 1905* (Qld).

Chapter 8

In December 1999, it had been nearly two years since I started the TAFE course and my discovery of Origins. The fragments of memories that could never take shape were starting to reveal a very large picture of my experience that I could finally understand.

My classmates at the college took my journey with me, using each unit that I studied as a tool for me to undertake the next move that I was going to make.

My story, and how I used the skills I had obtained in the course, saw me being paid by the college to do presentations on how it helped me with an impossible mission. The new students were intrigued by the search and my reunion.

Despite having a positive outcome, I knew I had to see someone and speak to them about the conflict still going on inside my mind and trying to get around every day to act normally and still dealing with the nightmare.

The demons inside my head needed identifying so I could fully understand what I was dealing with and get some help. Looking through the local paper, I discovered a community counselling service. They only allowed a few sessions and referred me to a child psychiatrist.

Mary seemed to be a kind and considerate person; given she understood the trauma children suffered, I guess this made me feel a little safer with her. She asked me about my life, and I told her about my childhood and what had happened to me in Holy Cross.

A few weeks later, I received her report and diagnosis: her opinion was that I'd suffered recurrent depressions and post-traumatic stress disorder, which was the result of major trauma in my life.

She acknowledged that I had suffered significant emotional damage as a result of those horrific circumstances, thus leading to subsequent difficulty in my relationships and communicating my emotions.

Her treatment advice was that I would need at least two to three years of weekly therapy with someone with whom I could form a trusting relationship. She concluded her report with the statement that my difficultly in interpersonal relationships and closeness with others is probably going to be lifelong.

Her view was that, as far as taking a court case on, she acknowledged that I did not have access to the information regarding my time in care to take legal action sooner and that my depression would have prevented me from carrying it out, anyway.

The year 1999 was hectic: it was coming up to the deadline for the NSW adoption inquiry, and we rushed to get in Origins' last-minute submissions.

The Forde Inquiry had also handed down its final report; it was a scathing condemnation of the abuse that state wards like me endured in Queensland institutions.[12]

Reading through and finding parts of my submission and comments recorded for history gave me a sense of validation at having them put on the record.

With the end of the year approaching, and trying to find the next step that would take me into the year 2000, I decided that I would try to enrol in university and study law.

---

[12] https://www.qld.gov.au/__data/assets/pdf_file/0023/54509/forde-commin-quiry.pdf

I had little faith that I would be accepted, but if I was thinking of legal action against the state, I needed to have some idea of how the law worked to improve my chances of getting some justice.

The highlight of my life came in mid-December when I was accepted into Macquarie University. It was overwhelming that a girl who had never completed high school was going to university.

*

In June 2000, Des and I decided we would take Mum over to England for her seventieth birthday. We would also spend a week or so over in Ireland.

We hired a car and spent quite a bit of time sightseeing around the Lincoln area, and after a fortnight drove across to Wales and onto the Irish ferry.

The Irish Sea was like a sheet of glass. I was expecting a rough trip, but we managed to make it over there in a few hours listening to the Irish band and watching everybody have a few drinks. Well, more than a few drinks; by the time we landed in Dublin, the boat was well and truly rocking.

The minute my foot touched the ground, I knew I was on familiar soil. My parents had lived in Ireland for a while when I was a baby, and it almost felt like a homecoming. There is a certain feeling you get when you stand in the land of your ancestors. It is difficult to explain, and it was like a centring of myself, a yin and yang, resetting my emotions and my identity.

We spent a week over there touring around while staying in the small whitewashed Irish cottage in the middle of the field. The cows wandered around up to the window, having an occasional look in. In the distance was the steeple of the church where the Brontë sister's grandparents got married.

I understood why it was called the Emerald Isle—the lush green grass that circled the remote farmhouse gave me a sense of peace, stability, and connection to my past.

It was time to go back to England and stay with my father's brother, uncle Mike. I hadn't seen him since I was nine years old. He hadn't changed one bit. He was still as funny and loving as I remembered him.

'I have to take you down to London, so you can see where your father is buried and say hello to him.'

Yes, I wanted to see where he finally ended up. The last time I saw him was not under particularly good circumstances. He died at the age of fifty-one, a year older than I was at that time. Uncle Mike told me he had to go to Ireland to find him and finally discovered him in a barn half-frozen to death and had well and truly lost his mind. He was eventually placed into a psychiatric institution, where he died.

Standing by his grave, no bigger than the width of his coffin, I had finally met my father again. His gravestone—weather-beaten and barren, not a flower to honour him—was engraved with his epitaph, *A loving brother*; no mention of the words *Father of nine children*.

A feeling of bitter-sweetness washed over me as I stood there at his grave.

The anger of the child in me was gone. As a fifty-year-old, I had been through my own wars, and I could finally understand the frailty of a man who had fought every battle possible in his life.

Now in his grave, he was probably lying there wondering what the hell it was all about.

Was I, too, going to end up the same way?

*

My return to Australia was a return to the real world and all the problems that came with it, and despite knowing I had a problem, I was also becoming more and more involved in speaking up about adoption in Origins.

There had been a split in the first few months of the parliamentary inquiry that saw some of the committee going their own way. Tracy saw her role and knowledge as being inferior to Dian's—she did not have the historical knowledge to prove the intent behind the illegal adoption market and how it evolved. This saw her trying to start up another group to rival Origins.

On 8 December 2000, Dian and I sat in the dining room at Dian's house with two other mothers and a crew from the ABC. We had waited most of the day for the NSW adoption inquiry report to be handed down in parliament, and the tension was building. The wait seemed to go on forever.

Finally, a copy was hurriedly couriered over to Dian's house, where we had just minutes to respond before the 7 pm news. A one-page overview came with the report—a covering statement that revealed that 'some practices were unlawful'.

The weekend papers screamed *Babies Stolen for Adoption*[13] and after the initial exposé, the whole damning exposé. That was it: a damning report, *Releasing the Past*,[14] on illegal adoption in New South Wales was released in the last minutes of parliament on Friday evening, not to be discussed again until at least four months later. The two-and-a-half-year inquiry with over three hundred submissions was basically swept under the historical doormat.

Although I had thought about legal action, it had taken me a while to get over the initial reaction to the reunion with my son and it was time to decide whether or not I was going to sue the state of Queensland and the nuns.

[13] "Babies Stolen For Adoption", Daily Telegraph 9th December 2000.
[14] "Releasing the Past" Adoption Practices 1950-1998. Final Report. Standing Committee on Social Issues, 8th December 2000.

I told Tim of my intention to take them to court, and I think he was a little bit bemused and possibly seeking some accountability for himself. He never really said much about my decision, and I think he went along with it to see how things would play out.

After trawling through the Brisbane phone book, I spotted a law firm that I hoped would help me take legal action. David Webb, my lawyer, looked as though he had just received his law degree: slim, blond-haired, with a medium build and very enthusiastic personality. He seemed to be keen to take on the church and state.

I'd given him a fair bit of information and was told that he could not take the case on pro bono and I would have to pay for his services. I had just received a small workers' compensation payment for my disabled right shoulder, and I thought that would kick-start my court case and see where we would go from then on.

University had me completely immersed in every unit that I'd taken, and funnily, I was able to relate it to my own experience, especially when it came to Criminal Law. Whilst gathering the evidence for my court case, I was being triggered time and time again at the realisation of the crimes that had been committed against me. False imprisonment, assault, fraud, breach of duty of care, kidnapping—it went on and on, through every unit that I studied. My mind was starting to go into a tailspin.

The worst revelation came when I discovered that the age of consent for sexual relations in Queensland was sixteen. I was eleven months over that. It now made sense to me why Steve had not been charged with carnal knowledge.

So, my 'crime' was non-existent, and I had been held illegally against my will.

Following on from Dr Mary's report, and in light of my deteriorating mental state, it became abundantly clear that I needed some help, and I asked my doctor if she could refer me to see a psychiatrist.

Dr Peters was a very distinguished-looking man; his dark balding hair and his prominent moustache not only gave him a look of authority, but his large stature gave rise to an element of fear. Hopefully, this man was going to help me.

I had been given one-hour visits to see him and my first visit passed very quickly. Skimming over my story, he responded positively, saying that he was well aware of the experiences of girls like me as he had been an obstetrician in a Sydney hospital that also took babies from their unmarried mothers at birth.

I had been to see him several times when he suggested that I should try hypnotherapy to get beyond the trauma that was blocking my memory. My mind had been playing tricks on me for decades— every time I would try to make sense of things, the 'demons' would put stumbling blocks in my way, imprisoning me again behind the bars of the Holy Cross.

Lying back in a large comfortable chair and closing my eyes, I heard Dr Peters' voice drifting off into a low methodical tone, repeating, 'You are going down a long set of stairs, lower and lower and lower, slowly descending into the depths of darkness; one step, two steps, you are drifting back into the past. What do you see?'

This journey into the darkness of my mind was to go on for years to come.

A year later, and after my lawyer conferred with a barrister, a statement of claim was lodged in the Supreme Court of Queensland.

I was the plaintiff—Lily Arthur—and the first defendant was 'the state of Queensland'. The second defendant was the 'Corporation of the Trustees of the Order of the Sisters of Mercy in Queensland.'

The statement alleged a breach of fiduciary care as my guardian. I had Dr Mary's report that confirmed the damage that had been done to me. I was ready to go.

It was now getting serious, and I was going to have to prove to my son first and foremost that not only was he loved, but that he had been stolen from me.

Needing to find as much evidence as I could to establish that the nuns played an active part in the loss of my child, I decided to look into the home to provide more historical background for my court case, thinking that every little bit of research could help, especially when it came to the nuns having a primary interest in adoption.

It was no secret what was going on in that place as far as the unmarried mothers were concerned: they were visible, they could come and go as they please, but the state wards were a different story—they were hidden.

The history of Holy Cross was a bit vague until I came across the Brisbane Centenary Official Historical Souvenir.

It was built by the donations of a number of eminent people and officially opened in 1889, described as 'Magdalen Asylum-Holy Cross Retreat, Wooloowin'.

The above-mentioned institution is under the care of the Sisters of Mercy. Its objects are:

1. *to provide a home for the destitute and needy irrespective of creed or country.*
2. *to aid and reform the erring.*
3. *to shelter the weak-minded.*
4. *to train the wayward and uncontrollable to habits of self-restraint by necessary instruction and kind but firm discipline.*

It went on to say, 'In connection with the home is the Holy Cross steam laundry, well-equipped with up-to-date machinery and all labour-saving appliances.' [15]

---

[15] Brisbane Centenary Official Historical Souvenir of 1921. Page 265. State Library Queensland.

As far as I could tell, there were no 'labour-saving appliances'. I certainly didn't see any that untangled the mess that was disgorged from the washing machines, and folded sheets, pillowcases and tablecloths for eight hours a day!

A Magdalene laundry. The state put me into a place where I was forced to work for the Catholic church. That threw me!

I had seen the movies *Sinners* and *The Magdalene Sisters*, based on the Magdalene laundries in Ireland. Those movies also showed there were older women in the homes in Ireland that were never released, which intrigued me. Holy Cross also had older women there, and among them, three women with Down Syndrome. Little was said about why they were in there.

Strangely I felt unique that I—like the Irish girls—could call myself a Magdalene. Stranger still that I had an Irish background.

There was a picture of the building itself—it was just as miserable as those in the films I watched. It was mysterious: a three-storey, austere, foreboding structure that housed secrets from those who passed by its gates. The lower part housed the front office, the recreation hall, kitchen and dining room, and a large kitchen area at the rear of the building where we used to have cooking lessons on a Saturday morning. I could even pick the window in the middle storey that held a dormitory sectioned off into cubicles of two beds.

A toilet and shower block was at the end of the corridor, and at the end of each corridor was a steel gate that was locked at night. The picture didn't show that the windows had bars on them.

So, according to the Directory of Social Services Queensland 1968, Holy Cross Retreat's purpose was 'the rehabilitation of pregnant and underprivileged girls, and adoption is encouraged, either direct from the hospital or after the mother has returned to the retreat.' [16]

---

[16] Directory of Social Services Queensland 1968. p168.

A bit more research revealed a newspaper article, with the headline, 'Adoption Worry on Illegitimacy: Boy babies 'bank up'. This article hit me right between the eyes. A few months previous to the taking of my son, it seems they could not get enough baby boys adopted out. The preference for adopters was for baby girls. The waiting list for them varied between six to twelve months on the application, the department admitting that the 'banking up' of baby boys was 'an embarrassment'.[17]

I was floored that they took so many baby boys that they had a problem finding them a home, and mine could have been included!

Another article appeared a few months later in the *Sunday Mail*, 'One Birth in Ten Illegitimate (Adoption Lists are Shrinking)'. In the article, Mother Liam, the head Nun at Holy Cross, described us girls as 'sweet and wonderful' and said that it was apparent that most of us had been kind and loved by our parents.[18]

Dr Bertrand King, a psychiatrist, noted in the same article that almost any girl, given the wrong set of circumstances, could become an unmarried mother, and went on to say, 'The larger proportion of unwed mothers ends up having a nervous breakdown.'

So, there it was in black and white: they knew in 1967 that girls like me were likely to suffer mental health problems.

The New South Wales inquiry report had given us a lot of information on the legal rights of mothers and gave me quite a bit of direction on what sort of evidence I would need for my forthcoming legal action.

Dian was directing me on what to look for whilst she was building another case to take New South Wales back to court.

'We need them to actually admit their crimes,' she said firmly.

So, I needed confirmation that my son was taken from me at birth without my consent. How was I going to do that?

---

[17] 'Adoption Worry on Illegitimacy: Boy babies "bank up"', Sunday Mail, 16th April 1967.
[18] "One Birth in Ten Illegitimate. (Adoption Lists are Shrinking), Sunday Mail, 16th July 1967.

I had written to the Minister for Health previously and asked them for my medical records and was told that they had been destroyed after a period of twenty-five years.

In my letter, I specifically asked for the reasons why my son was taken from me immediately after the birth. The minister's response was that 'it was felt the pain of separation may be less for the adopting mother if she did not see her child. With the benefit of greater information and insight, this has not been the practice in recent years.' So, yes, the minister admitted that this was the usual practice.

She could not, however, give an exact answer regarding the administration of diethylstilboestrol, a drug given to dry up my milk, noting that the practice was ceased because of the small risk of some women developing clots, particularly older women.

The letter from the Minister of Health was a goldmine. She confirmed everything that I had been saying regarding my time at the Royal Women's Hospital. At least I didn't have to prove that part of my claim.

The ink had barely dried on the statement of claim when I received a phone call from David Webb asking me to go to Queensland and express my concerns to the nuns.

I was curious that they wanted to sit down and listen to my story. A few weeks later, I met with the head sister at their headquarters somewhere in Brisbane. We sat around in a circle: my mother, David, the nuns' lawyer, and the nun. The nuns' lawyer asked me if I could tell them about my time at Holy Cross.

The long, sad, sorry saga fell from my lips until I glanced over at the nun, whose face expressed not only her disdain, but also her resentment at having to sit and listen to me.

Words could not express my feelings—suddenly, I felt as low as the cockroach I saw crawling across the floor at the back of the room. I was frozen and unable to speak. David stepped in, stopping the conversation and asking for us to be excused for a while until I could compose myself.

What the hell am I doing here? I had no idea. I wanted to see them in court, not in their stronghold where they held all the power. Their intention soon became apparent when David came out to speak to us.

'The Sisters want to offer you ten thousand dollars to withdraw your claim.'

'They have got to be kidding. I want to see them in court—that's my response.'

He went back to see them and came out a few minutes later with the new proposal of twenty thousand dollars. I wanted to get out of that situation quick smart. I wasn't there for a settlement; I was there because they had offered to listen to me and my concerns, and, for an apology.

We made our way back to my barrister's office, where Mr Neil gave us a rundown on the response from the nuns' lawyers.

'Lily, the nuns have offered you twenty thousand to withdraw your claim. In my opinion, you should take that money and put it in your war chest. It is going to be very difficult for your legal team to be up against two defendants with their legal teams. So, my advice to you is just to deal with the state and get rid of the nuns. Their lawyer said they would fight your claim and say that the state had authorised them to treat you in the manner that they did.'

Reluctantly, I agreed with their advice and a few weeks later signed a confidentiality agreement for the settlement of twenty thousand dollars, co-signed by my husband, daughter, son, and Steve, that they would not seek any action concerning my treatment. If the media asked any questions, my response would be, 'I am fighting for justice against the state of Queensland and am continuing my litigation against the state. I have discontinued my action against the Sisters of Mercy.'

Nineteen thousand was deposited into my bank account—I don't know what happened to the remaining thousand—and the promised apology from the nuns floated off into thin air. Nothing was said by the nuns about the unpaid forced labour that I was subjected to inside the Holy Cross laundry. To any observer, they got off very lightly.

The focus was now to be directed at the state.

After the settlement with the nuns, the discourse between my lawyers and me became very sparse—time was getting on to get a court date, and numerous phone calls and letters went unanswered. The settlement from the nuns went to paying the lawyers who got it, so not much was achieved in that exercise.

The state had indicated that it was prepared to fight the action, so it was imperative to get things going again. Once again, out of desperation, I started looking for another lawyer who was prepared to take me on. Fate would have it that I stumbled upon Grant Deering.

We had a little bit of a chat and he asked me to send him my court documents so that he could look at them. A few days later, he called me to let me know that the deadline to bring the action was perilously close. We had to act fast if we were going to take the state to court.

Dian was still devastated at the response of the New South Wales inquiry—even though they had admitted their practices had been unlawful and harmful, they would still not be held accountable.

A further insult to its victims occurred six months after the handing down of the report, when the government funded a past perpetrator of unlawful adoption that had morphed into an adoption support organisation, with ex–consent-takers as its counsellors.

Despite the injustice of it all, we just couldn't give up! The past few years had seen Origins ignite a fire in the bellies of women demanding justice, and we just couldn't leave them without a sense of hope.

'We either have to grow or go,' I told Dian, and that meant having exposed the unlawful practices, Origins now had to fully expose the harm that they did to us and our children.

A national mental health conference was one way of doing it, and two years after the handing down of the report, we held our first national conference on the mental health of people affected by family separation.[19]

We advertised as far and wide as we possibly could, including the Aboriginal media.

It was astounding and mind-blowing over the two days of the conference that Aboriginal people came from as far away as Western Australia, far across the country in remote areas, and from places in the Northern Territory, North Queensland, and beyond to come to our conference in Sydney.

Just the stress of organising such a huge event saw me collapsing on the first day. My energy was restored as an Aboriginal lady completely unknown to me let me rest my head on her shoulder.

Sixty-three speakers gave presentations over those two days, including psychiatrists, doctors, nurses, Aboriginal mental health workers, and of course, our mothers.

Origins was the first unfunded organisation to even attempt such a challenge. Even without the help of state or adoption agencies, we proved that we were capable of our own self-determination. We were well and truly established by then. Elizabeth Edwards in Victoria was following Dian's lead in exposing adoption crimes in that state.

Although she was a little bit older and came across as more conservative than the rest of us, Elizabeth was a firebrand, and she had no intention of holding back from demanding the Victorian mothers have a voice and were determined to turn over every stone in Victoria to get at the truth.

---

[19] 1st National Mental Health Conference on the Effects of Family Separation, Liverpool Hospital, NSW 2002.

In Queensland, Linda Bryant was leading Origins and lobbying for changes to the legislation concerning contact objections. Linda was a veteran of adoption activism, having been a member of an adoption support group for several years. She had seen the coming and goings of various adoption regulations and legislation in Queensland and also knew the political manoeuvrings of adoptive parents.

The internet proved to be invaluable to our cause, and Des started to put up web pages that would send our message and what we were doing in Australia across the world.

Branches of Origins in the United States and Canada—with smaller branches in the UK and New Zealand—delivered loud and clear our message that these illegal practices were being carried out worldwide.

The same coercive blackmailing by social workers, and the unlawful practice of taking our babies without our consent resonated with mothers everywhere.

The Forde Inquiry had brought out a lot of interest into the abuse suffered by state wards and triggered the formation of an organisation of ex-wards that spread nationwide. I became one of the first to become a member and invited their committee to co-host our first mental health conference. The very first meeting of the ex-wards was held in Ashfield in a local church. The place was swarming with aging people and the atmosphere of pain and suffering was suffocating. I felt myself going into a tailspin when one of the organisers asked me to counsel a ward who had also lost two children to adoption at Holy Cross.

*

It was October 2003 when I was summoned to Queensland to have my mental health assessed by the state's expert witness, who saw me for just over one hour.

His first report was quite lengthy, acknowledging that I had shown him the papers associated with my son's adoption and pointing out the incorrect names and information.

I was described in the report as being very bitter regarding being taken to Holy Cross, and he acknowledged the fact that I was having difficulty dealing with the information that had become available to me.

The focus was on all the negative aspects of my life. I made no secret of my childhood and subsequent marriage—they were not the reasons I was there to see him.

He described me as being angry and, at times, too distressed, so it was difficult to have a rapport with me, and his report goes on to say I had a number of 'overvalued ideas and what could be considered persecutory themes' in the way that I thought, specifically related to the actions of the authorities at the time that they had put me into Holy Cross and taken my child.

His opinion was that I had revealed evidence of depression, anger, and bitterness related to the theft of my son.

In his consideration, I had a mood disorder, depression, and atypical anxiety disorder with obsessional features.

He acknowledged that, from the information available to him, the removal of my son was a significant contributing factor to my condition, and that the other adverse life effects would have contributed to my psychological distress.

He concluded that it would be likely that I would have a degree of ongoing psychological distress relating to my son and acknowledged that several years of regular psychiatric treatment had not resolved this distress.

He also considered that I was capable of bringing the relevant legal proceedings to court before 1995.

Was he aware that every piece of evidence to bring a court case was hidden from me until I found my son and asked him to take off his information objection in 1998?

It would be hard to take a court case when you never had one piece of paper to prove that you even had a child, let alone lost one.

Obviously, that report was not good enough for the state, so they got him to do a second one.

In his second report, he agreed that there appeared to be little doubt from the medical record in the transcripts provided by Dr Peters that I had been particularly depressed and distressed, and at times, suicidal.

Still, backing up his first report that I had 'persecutory or overvalued ideas', the fact that I was now starting to see too many coincidences and was thinking that there was some sort of a 'baby racket' going on confirmed his comments.

He went on in his second report to say that he was unable to identify a causal association between the forced separation of my son and the separation of my parents when I was eleven and that I had become obsessed with extracting what he believed to be 'appropriate retribution' for the actions of those who removed my son.

Was he saying that seeking justice through a court of law for the damage caused to me was retribution, given it came at great financial and emotional cost?

There had been a separate inquiry into child migration two years previously, and Australian care leavers started to attract a lot of political support as well. The stories of abused and neglected children forced the call for a senate inquiry into children brought up in state care.

The senate inquiry into the 'forgotten Australians'[20] was announced, following on from the 'Bringing them Home' report that exposed the horrific abuse of Aboriginal children.

[20] https://www.aph.gov.au/Parliamentary_Business/Committees/Senate/ Community_Affairs/Completed_inquiries/2008-10/recs_lost_innocents_ forgotten_aust_rpts/report/index

To recognise each group, they were described as the 'Stolen Generation' for the Aboriginal children and 'forgotten Australians' for the ex-state wards. We didn't have a description for ourselves at that point and just called ourselves 'mothers who had lost children to adoption.'

A West Australian senator who had been a child migrant himself and was involved in the child migrant inquiry had supported us before the state ward inquiry was announced.

We had previously met with him to discuss getting his support for a senate inquiry into past adoption. However, state wards and child migrants were more of a focus to him and we lost the support we needed to get our hearing.

I was fortunate: as my story fitted into both issues, I was able to put in a submission not only on my behalf but for Origins as well. The Origins submission addressed the fact that many mothers were minors and incarcerated voluntarily or involuntarily in religious and state-run institutions. This was another avenue of getting the issue investigated again and into the focus of the government.

The senate inquiry into the forgotten Australians released its report in August 2000.[21] Although it gave a comprehensive account of the treatment of ex-state wards, the thirty-nine recommendations mostly pointed to the states and various institutions in collaboration with the Commonwealth to be responsible for the harm caused to ex-wards.

Things were moving along for us that year: not only had Linda opened an Origins office in Queensland at the Mental Health Association and started preparing for our second national mental health conference at the Parks Centre for Mental Health at Wacol, she was also consulting with the Queensland state government on an adoption act review.

---

[21] https://www.aph.gov.au/Parliamentary_Business/Committees/Senate/ Community_Affairs/Completed_inquiries/2008-10/recs_lost_innocents_ forgotten_aust_rpts/report/index

Elizabeth, in Victoria, was also stirring up a storm, taking the Victorian government to court and winning a battle for freedom of information, so it was all happening around us.[22]

Dian was still reeling from the outcome of the New South Wales inquiry and also from her lost court case. It was very difficult to watch her spiralling into hopelessness.

She was still trying to get her mind around the judgment of her final appeal. The judges' reason for dismissing her case just didn't make sense.

A young journalist became very interested in our cause, and when she learned that I was taking up a landmark court case against the state of Queensland, asked me if it was possible to make a documentary around it if she could get funding. She later worked with Kate Smith, a journalist from the ABC, to get the funding and the script written.

I'd had quite a bit of media exposure, so another person interviewing me didn't faze me. Half the time, most of what I said never appeared publicly anyway. So, it came as a great surprise that Film Australia decided to fund the documentary and aptly named it *Gone to a Good Home*.

My reunion with Tim, although it started with great promise, went through times where we had little or no contact with each other. Months on end would pass when I wouldn't hear from him.

A sense of entitlement for anything in the way of a relationship was too much to expect considering the way I had 'crashed' into his life. I was on the back burner of his life. Just to be a small part of it would be considered by many a situation to be grateful for. Tim and his wife still hadn't told the children about my relationship with them.

I had tried to compensate my son and his family for all the lost Christmases, birthdays, and any other event that I had missed out

---

[22] https://www.theage.com.au/national/women-forced-to-give-away-babies-fight-states-silence-20040804-gdydz8.html

on. Endless amounts of information and gifts were sent to him and his family. I thought that giving him everything possible would prove my love for him.

Love, and the willingness to show it through those gifts, turned to resentment when I had to address each letter and parcel to his adopted name—a constant knife in my guts and reminder of his theft and connection to strangers.

As 2004 was grinding to an end, the court case was going to bring finality to a very hectic year, the date for the hearing being set for the first of November.

Apart from the endless round of study, Origins business, and my personal life, the Democrat Party nominated me as a candidate for the seat of Prospect. I had previously met an Aboriginal senator who had a keen interest in the Stolen Generations and he needed all the support he could get to keep his seat in the senate. The party needed representatives, so every vote was going to count, despite me not being a serious candidate in a safe Labor seat.

My foray into politics was quite interesting. Finally, I had put some of my political studies into action. It gave me an insight into, 'it's not what you know, but who you know', and my curiosity had brought me face to face with politicians who I thought could further our cause. Needless to say, my first political stand only brought a few hundred votes and did not contribute to the election of the senator.

I was still contacting the department for more information as the court case was getting closer. I just wanted to make sure there would be no surprises during the hearing. Much to my surprise, the last approach yielded a departmental form that was not included in previous freedom of information inquiries.

It's amazing that a few sheets of paper can reveal so much, and the *Expected Child for Adoption Form* was no exception. Four sheets of paper that looked on the face of it to say little, but the intent behind them said a lot.

The *Report of Investigation* from the hospital to the department to notify them of the birth contained my wrong name, the wrong name of my mother, a description of Steve and me to match up with the potential adopters, and asked the department if my baby was up for adoption. Worse still, it said the father would not support us, despite having not even asked him.

The *Birth/Death of an Illegitimate Child Form* sent by the Registrar of Birth, Death and Marriages to the department was to notify of my son's birth and to also register him for adoption.

If he had not 'legally' existed, then he would have had to go through the court to be made a state ward before he could be adopted.

The *Adoption Consent Form* had my name and address wrong, I had signed my name incorrectly, and it never made any mention of a revocation period of thirty days. So, the thirty-day period that was implied was a ruse to give me hope that I could get my baby back.

Finally, the *Expected Child for Adoption* form, filled in on the day I signed the adoption consent, still referring to the wrong name, had a description of me: hair colour, height, skin complexion, nationality, and hobbies, and Steve's description as well.

What came as a shock to me was that my baby was 'offered' to his adopters on the eighth of September, the day I signed the consent, eight days after he was born.

So, within hours of my seeing him for the first time, he was already being off-loaded to strangers, being described as a 'nice small baby with fair hair.' The five-dollar fee for his adoption was duly paid on the thirteenth of September, and the adopters took custody of him on the sixteenth of September. My baby lay for sixteen days in the hospital nursery before he was finally taken to a home and 'mothered.'

Having done quite a bit of research on the attachment of newborns, I was sickened to the core to think that my newborn had lain in his bassinette for days on end, crying, screaming, and traumatised, waiting for his 'mother' to bond with him, while I—in a drugged and confused state, lay in hospital, and then, shipped off to fold pillowcases in the laundry—was oblivious to the torture my baby was going through.

Did this start to his life have anything to do with his reserved reaction when I met him for the first time? The New South Wales inquiry had taught me a lot about what they knew about the effects of separation for the newborn. They had been researching the mental health effects of adoption for decades worldwide and the research had uncovered that adopted children were over-represented in mental health institutions by one hundred percent.

How could I forgive them for what they did to us?

As the court date approached, things became quite frantic. I spent most of my time answering endless questions sent to me by my lawyers. A statement of claim for loss and damage was needed for any potential compensation payout. I had to go back over my whole working life, lost educational opportunities, if there were any physical and mental health damage that I'd suffered, and any other consequences that I had suffered from my experience.

A twenty-five-page document was submitted to the court, along with nearly five hundred other documents, with an estimation of the loss and damage caused by what had happened to me. According to my lawyers, it amounted to over two million dollars.

Considering that a woman at that time had been unlawfully incarcerated in a migrant detention centre for about the same duration of my incarceration and received a similar payout, it was not such a great expectation that I should be treated the same for the harm caused to me.

Des was behind me all the way, not only emotionally but also financially. Although I still had a bit of money left over from my worker's compensation, he was prepared to help me pay for my legal fees. At that point, we had no idea just how much this was going to cost us.

The concept of the court giving me some justice was paramount, and as a student of law, I expected that the law would punish those who broke it.

Chapter 9

Des and I had flown up to Brisbane two days before the court case, which was due to start on the first of November. Grant Deering had engaged a barrister, Keith Williams, who wanted to see me on the Sunday before going to court the following day.

It struck me at the time that all barristers seem to look huge, dark, and foreboding, and Keith Williams was no exception. He was over six foot tall and had a stern brooding look that looked as if he was summing me up to see if I could last the distance of what we were about to undertake.

He looked directly at me, straight into my eyes, and said, 'Give me one good reason why I should take this matter into court tomorrow.'

Fear grabbed my throat in a chokehold as I fought for the words to respond to his direct interrogation.

Not the student nor the activist, I reverted to the young woman— the child, the victim. 'They committed a lot of crimes against me and stole my baby,' I responded.

He stared at me for a little while and his face seemed to soften at my response. 'I'm not going to give you any false hope: I don't see much of a chance of you winning this case.'

My stomach sunk and a feeling of nausea washed over me, but it was too late. I had waited many years to get to this point and any retreat now would show my son everything I had told him was not the truth.

Judgment day had arrived. I met Grant at his office, and we took the long walk around to the Supreme Court. I was quite fatigued by the time I got there—he was tall and could walk fast, and I was overweight and slow. Turning the last corner toward the court I saw a large gathering of media.

The Lady Justice statue loomed large at the front of the court. It was reassuring that justice was represented by a woman. Was she going to give me the justice that I had waited for?

'Something big must be happening,' I thought to myself, and as we approached the front door, the media surrounded me, asking me questions about why I was taking the state to court.

Arthur v Queensland[23] was to become a precedent case after all, and I hadn't realised the importance of it.

Kate Smith, the journalist producing the documentary, followed closely behind with a cameraman to record all the attention. Mandy and her family had flown up from Sydney to attend the court as well. My mother was there to give evidence if she was going to be called. Steve also was prepared to have his say but, surprisingly, my son Tim had also flown down from Mackay. Everyone in my life who meant anything was there for me, but Des, my strongest support, was the one who held my hand.

Jean and two other mothers who had been coerced by the same consent-taker were also there to give evidence. The door to the furnace was opened. There was no going back now—it was Arthur v Queensland.

The ex-ward, the child of the state, was going to hold them—her so-called parents—to account.

I didn't take much notice of the courtroom. The judge was perched on the bench with two other people near him. Grant Deering, Keith Williams, and another young lawyer sat on the left-hand side front table and the state's barrister on the right-hand side with his colleagues.

The onlookers and my family sat in the back of the courtroom. I was horrified to find out that one of the principal players of an

---

[23] Arthur v State of Qld Dec 22, - [2004] QSC 456

adoption privacy group was there to watch the proceedings. It made my blood curdle that this person was going to be privy to my life, a pariah that fed on the blood of mothers like myself.

Keith Williams gave his opening address, saying that my claim for equitable compensation for breach of duty of care was a novel one. He went on to explain that my relationship with the state as its ward was a fiduciary one: in effect that I was under the age of eighteen and under the care and control of the Department of Children's Services, and that the department had breached its duty of care to me.

He asked if my claim would be defeated by the defence of laches, meaning it had taken too long to bring it to court, and if not, what compensation would I be entitled to.

Mr Williams then gave an overview of my claim and presented some of my state ward's documents as exhibits, which included the *Report of Investigation*, the *Authority to take a Child into Care*, and the *Birth/Death of an Illegitimate Child* forms. He also pointed out the anomalies in my name and address. He spent more than an hour giving great detail into the information on the forms and the history of my experience. I was then called into the witness box and affirmed to tell the truth on the Bible.

Keith asked my name and address and whether or not I was working; I responded to his questions, forcing myself into feeling quite calm and composed.

He asked if I had ever gone by the name Lily McDonald in February, and if I had ever called myself Lillian McDonald.

'Of course not,' I answered.

Having established that I'd never called myself Lillian, Keith went on to ask me about the history of my childhood, education, and then about my time with Steve.

He went into great detail talking about my relationship with Steve and then and about the night that I was taken to the watchhouse. He questioned me about where I was taken to. At the time I had no idea of where it was. Only later did I discover that I had been taken down to what I know now was the South Brisbane Watchhouse. For many years, I thought they had taken me to Boggo Road Gaol.

He then asked me if I stayed at the watchhouse, or if I was allowed to go home.

The picture of what happened that night had been burnt into my memory for decades. I could see it in my mind like the scene of a horror movie as I relayed it to the court.

'When I went to the desk, there were two policemen and the sergeant behind the desk said, "What did you bring her here for? You could get hung for bringing her here", and they said, "Well, it was too late to take her anywhere else," and then the desk policeman told me to take off my jewellery and the belt holding up my skirt. I had to take that off and then he said I was going to get the 'deluxe' cell because it had sheets on, and they took me up to the cell and locked me in there.'

I was asked if I stayed there overnight.

'Yes,' I responded. A quick flash of memory froze me in that moment. The screams of women in the other cells, the yelling and swearing of drunken men, and the opening and shutting of the hatch on the cell door every few minutes. Yes, I stayed there all night.

The 'deluxe' cell with the hard cold mattress and a grey blanket that felt like sandpaper, the steel toilet that I vomited into endlessly and the cold water tap that I washed away the tears that could not be held back.

Memories of a night that I could never erase from my mind.

Back to reality.

I was then asked what happened the next morning.

'The same policeman came and took me to the court'. I recounted the events.

'I was in a courtroom and the two magistrates asked the policeman if he had contacted my parents.' He said that I could not tell him where they were as they had just moved to Sydney. All I knew was that they were in a caravan park. I was told that I was going to be sent to Holy Cross at Woolowin.

He then questioned me about whether Steve intended to support me, to which I replied 'yes', and if my parents knew that I was with him; I replied that they did. He then asked me about the four days between my first appearance and the second one at the children's court. I told him about being locked up for those days until my next appearance.

I was asked if I recalled, other than the presiding members of the children's court, if there was any police officer or someone from the department.

My answer was 'no'. And did I know what complaint or charge was brought against me?

'I was told that I was exposed to moral danger.' He asked if I knew how long I was going to be held at Holy Cross.

No, I was not told how long I was going to be kept there.

I was then asked, 'Did you make any attempt to contact anyone?'

'I couldn't because there was no telephone, no friends, no letters—nothing.'

I described how we were allowed to write letters every Sunday when I eventually found out where my mother lived, and also that the nuns read those letters before they were allowed to be sent.

He asked, 'As your pregnancy advanced, were you still required to work in the laundry?'

I described that 'I was forced to work in the laundry every day from Monday to Friday, and apart from that, I had to clean half the recreation hall and my part of the dormitory where I was sleeping. I then went down and worked in the laundry. I worked there for the duration of my pregnancy, standing up all day folding sheets.'

I went on to tell of signing the marriage papers and waiting to hear from Steve.

'Did anyone from the department visit you at any stage?'

'No.'

'Did anyone from the hospital ask you what you intend to do with the child?'

'No.'

'Did you tell anyone at the hospital at that stage before you gave birth that you intended to put the baby up for adoption?'

'No.'

'Immediately after the birth, were you able to or were you shown the baby?'

'No.'

Several questions followed: did they tell me what the baby was? Was I given the baby to nurse, and why? My response was they took him straight out of the labour ward to the nursery.

Did I see the baby again and what had happened after I'd given birth? I told them about me being stitched up and that I had asked to see the baby.

More and more questions followed on. I described every detail of what went on that day I gave birth, and in my time in hospital.

I was exhausted from the hours of answering the questions from my barrister. Each response led to another question covering every aspect of my experience and later about the reunion with my son.

It was now the state's turn to interrogate me.

The state's barrister also exceeded my expectations on what a barrister should look like: my visions of large, dark, and foreboding figures were doubled at the sight of him. He had a way of trying to look intimidating when he put his hand on his hips, expanding his gown to look even more overpowering. He was waiting to tear me to pieces, I could feel it, and in those circumstances, the words of my father—'Never bow down to any man'—raced through my mind.

I was here for justice: not a child unable to defend themselves, but a woman who was well and truly aware of what had been done to her.

'You were engaged in campaigning this time a month ago, weren't you, Mrs Arthur?' he asked.

'I started to. I didn't do anything at the beginning of this year, and I had started discrimination law mid-term in the second half and couldn't cope with it because I had too much going on, and I was under instruction by my psychiatrist to stop all study. I was asked to stand for the seat of Prospect a couple of months before the election—that had nothing to do with my studies.'

I was thinking to myself, *What does this have to do with the theft of my son?*

After going into great detail about my 'political foray' and having established the fact that I'd been a 'political animal', he then went on to question me about my childhood.

His questions about our arrival in Australia, my family, and my father covered just about every incident of my childhood, pointing out the poverty and the abuse doled out by my father.

Not once was he interested in the fact that my father had fought for the duration of the Second World War, and later continued to spend another four years in Palestine fighting for a country that was not even his own.

Of course, the issue of us being made state wards came into the equation, and the stabbing of my stepfather, all his questions painting a picture of squalor and violence.

The first day was over, thank God! The inquisition by the state was to drag out every miserable chapter of my existence caused by others.

The second day opened with the state concentrating on my stepfather and his behaviour towards me and his subsequent stabbing by my father.

Again, he went over my marriage to Geoffrey and his possessive behaviour and the circumstances of my pregnancy with my daughter.

He then changed his interrogation and asked questions about Holy Cross.

Did I remember the nuns?

Did my mother come to see me?

Why didn't she come to see me?

Did I remember Steve coming to see me?

He questioned me about the *Report of Investigation* and handed me a copy.

'What can you tell me about this document?'

I commented that they put my mother's name down as Felicia, but her name is Lily.

Brushing that aside, he asked me to look at the form and confirm the information that described my hair colour, eye colour, complexion, height, weight, educational standard, special interests, and hereditary traits.

He went on, saying that most of those, or at least some of those, were matters of information that only I could have given to whomever was filling out this form.

I agreed. 'Yes, someone would have had to ask me those questions, and I would have told them the information.'

What he did not ask me was if I remembered the person asking me those questions.

He did not ask me if I remembered much of what was happening for the eight days I spent hiding under the blankets, drugged and writhing in pain from the cutting and tearing caused by the way they delivered my son to expedite his delivery.

The questions hammered at me, asking me how I said that Steve was not going to support me, knowing full well that I had not seen him for over six months and was still under the belief that we were going to be married and that I would be released after the baby was born.

They knew he was the father of our child, and yet no one bothered to ask him or let him know of our son's birth.

He asked if I tried to contact Steve when I was released from Holy Cross?

'Yes, of course I did,' I replied.

He went on to interrogate me about the person who filled in the form. I didn't know anything about her.

There was no mention of the fact that the *Report of Investigation* was a compulsory form under the *Infant Life Protection Act* that was sent from the hospital to the department to notify of the birth of an illegitimate child. Even though I was interrogated on minor information on the form, what was not questioned was why it was sent from the hospital to the department four days after my son's birth. The form recorded my name wrongly, the wrong address of where I lived, the wrong name of my mother and misinformation about whether or not Steve would support me. Worst of all, it asked the department if my baby was to be adopted without asking me or even letting me see him.

All the wrong information was written on the form and yet there was no mention that the form could have been filled in at another time without confirming whether the information contained on it was true.

Throughout the whole of my interrogation by the state, there was not one admission of the fact that from the instant of my arrest that they, the state, were responsible for everything that happened to me.

Keith Williams re-examined me again and asked me quite a lot of questions to add a bit more balance to my childhood. Yes, we had a hard childhood, and yes, my father was a very damaged man, and yes, we were all brought up together, and yes, my mother looked after us after my father left. He brought up my lifestyle as a teenager and the happy times I would go dancing and to the speedway with my sister—all the normal things that a teenager would do.

He asked if my life with Steve was happy. I said yes—we had our own place, and it was furnished, we used to play music and go to parties, and were in love.

My time in the witness box was spent. It was now Steve's turn.

Steve was far more upbeat than I was. Instead of being fearful after seeing me being 'grilled', he couldn't wait to get into the witness box to tell his side of the story.

After a few background questions about how we met and where we lived and when I moved in with him, Keith Williams started asking questions about the night I was taken away.

'So, you continued to live with Lily until fifteenth February 1967, is that correct?'

'Yes.'

'Were you aware as of that date that she was pregnant?'

'Yes.'

'How did you feel about that?'

'Great.'

And what were his intentions as far as his and my life were concerned?

'Well, we were pretty much inseparable. We were probably head over heels with each other. There is no question we were going to get married.'

He went on to ask Steve what had happened that night.

'Did you make any inquiries as to where she was going?'

'Yes, the police told me to ring up Moorooka police station the next day, which I did. They said that she was at the Holy Cross and "it is out of our hands."'

He went on to tell how he contacted my sister Jenny and how a few days later, he came with her to see me for the first time since that night.

'How long were you allowed to see her?'

'About five minutes.'

'Was your visit supervised or unsupervised?'

'Mother Superior was right in front of us.'

Steve went into great detail about how he went to Sydney to

get our parents' permission to marry and how he found my mother without a proper address to go to.

His memory for detail blew me away as I sat and listened to what was going on at the time. We had discussed what had happened to us, but now I was hearing it as a far more detailed description than ever before.

'Did you get Lily's mother to sign those documents?'

'Yes, and my father.'

'Where was your father living?'

'At Blacktown in Sydney.'

Keith Williams asked him if he had owned a vehicle, to which Steve responded no, that he relied on public transport.

He then went on to describe his reception when he went back to Holy Cross with the papers. He was not allowed to see me and instead gave the papers to the mother superior. When asked if he was given the papers back after I had signed them, his answer was no.

'Now, did you find out that Lily had had a child?'

'Yes, her sister Jenny got in touch with me and said that Lily had the baby.'

'What did you do?'

'I got in touch with a mate, and he came and picked me up in his car to take me to the hospital and come and meet our son and see Lily.'

'How did she appear to you?'

'Different. She just wasn't the same woman. She wasn't the same bubbly woman I knew in the seven months. She didn't even have an idea of what was happening.'

'Were you able to talk with Lily?'

'Yes, sort of. We decided we'd go and see the baby. We were all standing around just looking at all the other babies. We didn't know; she couldn't point the baby out.'

'Just describe what happened when you did that?'

'We just stood there, sort of in the background, because there were a few people right at the glass front there. Waited our turn and we looked, and we didn't know which one we had to look at.'

'As of the time you went to the hospital after Lily had had the baby, what were your intention regarding yours and her future?'

'At that time, I still thought we were going to get married. I was waiting for her to get out. Had I had known, I would have taken her out of the hospital.'

I was shaking to the core listening to Steve. He would have taken me out of the hospital.

So many times, I had thought of running away: climbing over the fence, running through the church, each time stopping myself from trying to grab my freedom, protecting my baby. I complied with everything that I was forced to do, unknowing that my fate and that of my baby was already sealed and promised to strangers. And here was the father of my child declaring in a court of law that he would have taken us away and protected us, and there wasn't a bloody thing that they could do about it!

When asked about what had happened after we lost our baby, he told how we had lost contact with each other. He had moved several times and didn't know where I had ended up, and I had moved as well.

He did receive the letter that I'd sent him months later, and surprisingly still, I had it. When asked did he reply, he responded that he had written a letter back to me but never received a reply.

Did he think our relationship was over?

'I thought she would probably come back to find me, but it never happened.'

'Did you subsequently marry yourself?'

'Yes, four years later.'

It was now the state's turn to cross-examine him. Steve showed no fear at that prospect, having witnessed how I was interrogated, I was expecting him to be wary at the questions that were going to be asked of him.

His opening questions weren't very different to those from Mr Williams. It was about lunchtime and the court was adjourned.

After lunch, the barrister interrogated Steve on where we were going to live after I'd had the baby. He responded that he was waiting for me to be released and then we would get a house together. He was waiting for someone to get in contact with him. When asked why he hadn't made any plans, his response was, 'You can't make plans if you don't know what's going on.'

When asked why he hadn't contacted the hospital or Holy Cross to find out when I would be released, he responded that he had not been allowed any contact with me during my whole incarceration.

It was obvious that they were trying to make Steve look like a deadbeat, abandoning father, but what he was doing was exposing the futility of a nineteen-year-old man fighting a system that had stolen his 'wife' and child.

And yes, I was his 'wife' despite not having the piece of paper to validate it—the *Commonwealth Marriage Act* allowed me to marry at sixteen.

Dr Peters was called as the next witness. His questioning by Mr Williams was very brief, basically asking him if the report sent to my lawyers in respect of the diagnosis was 'honestly held'. His response was, yes, that it was.

The state's barrister quizzed Dr Peters, asking more questions about the doctor's knowledge of my father and my childhood. He was trying to get away from my incarceration and the loss of the baby, even going into the night my stepfather was stabbed.

Dr Peters agreed that he had been told all the gory details of my life—there were no secrets there for the state to expose, covering every aspect from my first marriage until my first appointment with him.

There was a pattern emerging from the state's questioning: going over and over my life previous to my experience at Holy Cross and after, focusing very little on the crimes committed against me by the state. After having repeatedly questioned Dr Peters about every inch of my life, the barrister started to ask him about his diagnosis of my condition.

He asked him if his diagnosis of post-traumatic stress disorder was as per DSM 4 [codes that are the classification found in the Diagnostic and Statistical Manual of Mental Disorders].

He confirmed that yes, it was.

'The first of the DSM 4 diagnostic criteria for post-traumatic stress disorder is as follows: the person has been exposed to a traumatic event?'

'Yes.'

The barrister asked if both of the following had been present: one, the person experienced, witnessed or was confronted with an event or events that involved actual or threatened death or serious injury or a threat to the physical integrity of the self or others; and two, the persons' response involved intense fear, helplessness, or horror.

Dr Peters responded, 'Yes.'

Well, that had certainly happened to me!

He pointed out that several things could have been responsible for my condition. Dr Peters disagreed with him, responding with his belief that the forcible separation of a mother from her newborn infant *did* fit the definition of post-traumatic stress disorder.

Dr Peters was reaffirming Dr Rickarby's diagnosis of what happened to mothers who lost children to forcible adoption practices.[24]

The next witness was from the post-adoption services with the department. She was asked what records were kept on me and responded by saying there were eight documents.

---

[24] http://www.originsnsw.com/id86.html

'Do they correspond to the three or four documents that you have spoken about in your evidence?'

'The first two documents relate to the adoption record that I was referring to, and the third document relates to the *Infant Life Protection Record*.'

'About an *Expected Child for Adoption* form?'

'Yes.'

The document was tendered as evidence.

A little questioning about its contents also revealed the damning information of getting my name wrong and not mentioning Steve's name where it asked for the father's name—strange, given all the information from the *Report of Investigation* was on it.

What did not get mentioned was that my baby was offered to his adoptive parents that day, 8 September. It would have been that afternoon of the taking of my consent. They paid their fee on 13 September. I was told it was the equivalent of $5, and they collected him from the hospital on 16 September.

Despite telling me that there were thirty days to change my mind and get him back, his adoption order was made on 25 September 1967. The lying bastards adopted him out seventeen days after I signed the consent.

While I was still suffering the wounds of his difficult delivery and folding sheets in the laundry, counting the days until I was going to lose him and praying to God that someone would come and release me, he was already gone.

Back to reality!

The worker went on to say that only relevant documents were put onto microfiche and anything that did not have a legal nature was disposed of. She had never seen in her eighteen years of working with the department anything other than a few sheets of paper were kept as a record on adoption.

When asked about file notes by the departmental workers who spoke to the mothers, she responded that she had never seen on the microfiche any instances where a departmental officer who attested a consent in the 1960s having any case notes, if they ever existed at all.

The next witness was from the Department of Health, who explained that the medical records were only kept for a period of twenty-five years and destroyed after that. The only record that they had of my time in the hospital was an entry in the birth register and a card showing the birth having occurred in the Royal Women's Hospital.

Mr Williams went on to ask, 'Was there any involvement of the Department of Children's Services, any documents relating to communications between the hospital and the department that were kept on the file?'

'There may have been—I can't guarantee,' she responded.

She had seen some of the old files: a letter from whichever department was responsible advising that a particular person was authorised to pick up the baby, and it would only be a one-page letter which would be brought by that particular person.

This revealed another lie from the government, which told mothers like me that adopters would never know who we were— my son's adopters knew who I was from the day I lost him. A letter sent to the adopters to pick up *the child of ***** from the hospital gave them my name and that of my baby.

She went on to add that there was rarely any actual correspondence. However, there may have been social worker's notes.

She acknowledged that there was a social worker from 1962 onwards in the Royal Women's Hospital and they would have a separate entry on the mother because she would have been referred to the social work department.

When asked about the doctor who delivered my son and the person who witnessed the forms, they were unable to find any reference to them in the hospital records.

The next witness was the registrar of the magistrates and children's courts. Although she'd never seen the *Authority to Receive a Child in Care* form committing me to Holy Cross, she did agree that it probably did come from the children's court.

As the lunchtime adjournment approached, Mr Williams asked if the three other mothers with whom the consent-taker dealt with could be granted permission to give evidence.

On returning to the court, he gave an overview of the threatening and coercive treatment they received from my consent taker to sign adoption consents.

The state objected to the other mothers who were going to give evidence, effectively putting some of the victims out of the picture and citing the fact that, as the consent-taker had passed away, they couldn't get her side of the story.

Only one of the mothers had seen and nursed her baby, but she had given birth in the Salvation Army hospital. The remaining two had given birth in the women's hospital and, like me, had not seen their babies until after they signed the adoption consent.

The judge overruled the objection saying that the proposed evidence was intended to logically prove that my account is reliable, offering some material support for that version. However, to introduce their evidence and have it investigated by the state, the court case would have to be deferred for at least another five to six months. I didn't want to drag it out that long.

My evidence would have to stand on its own two feet.

Keith Williams, after taking my instructions, proposed that the evidence he was prepared to introduce describing the witness's story would have to be withdrawn. The state was concerned that there may have been reporters in the back of the courtroom when the evidence concerning the mother's stories was opened, but was content that the judge would proceed as if the evidence had not been opened.

The judge noticed that he did not see any journalists there and if the state wanted a restraining order, the state would have to give notice.

As he was adjourning for the day, the judge asked Mr Williams if any other cases may be useful in mine.

Mr Williams referred to two Aboriginal cases that went before the courts, and both were Stolen Generation cases that had failed.

Sitting in one of the meeting rooms at the back of the court with Grant and Des, we discussed the day's proceedings and what it all meant; I was still in a daze after everything that was being said.

Keith Williams was having discussions with the state's barrister in the back room. He came over to the table and sat down. 'I have a proposition from the state,' he said. 'They want to come to a settlement.'

'What sort of settlement?' I asked.

'That each of us walks away from this now without any costs.'

'They have got to be kidding. I want a judgment so it can be recorded in the law books—win or lose.' That was my response. I was prepared to see this through to the bitter end.

On day three of the court case, I knew it was going to get very interesting after the offer made to me by the state the day before.

Dr Mary gave her evidence by phone. I was surprised that they contacted her—it had been so long since I had been to see her.

My barrister questioned her.

'Are you a psychiatrist by profession?'

'I am.'

She then listed her qualifications. She had obviously been well-trained in child psychiatry and was asked if she had prepared a report dated 22 December 2000 on me.

'Yes', she replied.

He asked if the information I provided was accurate and her diagnosis was honestly held, she replied in the affirmative.

'No further questions.'

The opposite side asked her just about every question that he asked Dr Peters, once again going over all of my childhood, teen years, and my married life. Had she told you this, had she told you that? he quizzed.

Her answers were yes, yes, and yes.

Taking her to the diagnosis and opinion part of her report, he asked if I suffered from recurrent depressions and post-traumatic stress disorder in her diagnosis of post-traumatic stress disorder and if it fit the criteria in DSM4.

'Yes.'

He then went on to ask her whether all the incidents throughout my life could cause me to suffer from post-traumatic stress disorder. She agreed that they were extreme stressors.

She was excused.

The letter I received, ironically, on my son's birthday—1 September 1998—from the Minister of Health's department that admitted to the way they delivered my son—with me tied down and shackled—and confirming they separated him from me at birth was tendered as evidence. The letter also confirmed that I was given drugs against my will.

The state then proceeded to tender the death certificates of the consent-takers, nuns, and nurses; all the witnesses to those crimes were gone.

He then announced some witnesses that he was prepared to call, which would include the Queensland police, a person from the department, and some ex-departmental workers.

The judge responded that the letter from the health department indicated that there was no standard operating procedure such as the attendance of a witness when the consent was taken, or whether the hospital staff would be expected to be consulted to confirm that a mother was in the physical and psychological condition to discuss the question of adoption.

The letter from the health department would suggest the probability that there was no standing instruction that would have required such things to occur.

Keith announced that the court would hear evidence from two workers who were employed in the adoption section of the department at the same time, performing a similar job to the person who took my consent, and who would describe what the procedures were.

My ears pricked up at this announcement. I'd seen these names on other mother's records and couldn't wait to hear what they had to say, and neither could Linda and some of the other mothers in the courtroom who had a history with them.

The first witness would tell that because of the number of babies at that time being given up for adoption, she had visited the hospital three days a week in order to take consent for the adoptions.

I was to hear that there was a period of time after the birth during which the mothers were not allowed to sign a consent for adoption and not till a legally qualified medical practitioner had issued a certificate stating that the mother was in a fit condition to give her consent.

I was now going to find out from the 'horse's mouth' (so to speak) that the Department of Children's Services only became involved upon a referral from the *Report of Investigation*, and it would only have been if whoever filled out the form had marked that the baby was for adoption, or there was a query that the baby was for adoption that the childcare officers became involved and went to see the mother.

Along with the other mothers in the courtroom, we were to hear from another witness who was employed as a childcare officer in the department from about August 1965 at the Brisbane Women's Hospital.

For the first time, these people would be called upon to explain their practices that were hidden from our view and decided in the halls of government buildings.

We were told that they would confirm that it was up to the nursing sisters whether or not the birth mothers visited their babies.

And they would confirm the procedure by which the registrar would complete the *Report of Investigation* and ascertain whether or not the mother wanted to adopt the baby. It was also her role to register the birth.

I was finally starting to see who was who, and who did what to me. Only the main culprit was dead, but her cohorts were here to explain.

A childcare officer of the department was also going to be called. Now, that was going to be interesting!

I'd seen a letter written to him by the CEO of a regional hospital when we were collecting evidence for the senate inquiry saying that the unmarried mothers at that hospital were getting angry about being kept there for anything up to two weeks awaiting their release. Their release was dependent on the results of the venereal disease testing that was done on them before their babies were accepted for adoption.

Mr Prince from the Department of Families was called. He was aware of me but didn't take it any further, other than knowing that I'd given evidence before the Forde Inquiry. He was also aware that I was heavily involved in locating my information for the inquiry and that I had been unsuccessful.

The floods of 1974 were said to have destroyed over fifty thousand adoption files and information on infant life protection records. Some of them had been retrieved, but not mine. All he did was confirm that there were no records of mine. I was lucky I had the few documents that I had.

The next witness was from the police department, who confirmed they were unable to locate any documents about my arrest in 1967. So, my arrest was not recorded—there was no mention of a registrar kept at the watchhouse.

Mr Williams cross-examined her, asking her if Moorooka police station had any records. No was her response—they had even searched police notebooks, but to no avail, and most police officers from that time had passed on.

Obviously, the state had gone to a lot of trouble to dig up some of these witnesses. They even found a midwife whose name appeared on some of my documents and asked her if she remembered my name and that of my baby. Of course not! Why would she? I was one of the thousands.

She did, however, remember being spoken to by the police four years earlier during the investigation of my complaint, instigated by the Forde Inquiry.

She was asked if she was able to assist them.

'No, not at all,' was her reply.

Mr Williams confirmed her qualifications and went on to ask a few questions. She was a trainee midwife at the time. She was employed at the women's hospital and worked in various areas at that time. She had worked in the delivery wards and also in the nursery, but not always in the labour ward.

She was asked in her employment at the hospital if she would have been involved in the birth of hundreds, if not thousands, of children.

'Oh, yes, yes.'

So, it wouldn't have been possible for her to remember any individual one of them?

No, of course not.

She confirmed that yes, there were always children for adoption in the nurseries, and there was a separate nursery for children to be put up for adoption. The babies had alias names so the nursing staff didn't know who the children belonged to. She confirmed again that the babies were given an alias name. We listened in disbelief. A mother sitting near me gasped in horror: we were now having an insight into what was happening while we were lying in our hospital beds, wondering what was happening to our newborns.

The nurses only knew the baby by alias names on the cot, not knowing whether the mother had given the child that name or not because that was in the hands of a separate department to the nursing staff.

She agreed that the children who were going to be adopted would be placed in a separate nursery.

This person was confirming everything that I had alleged, and her evidence was exposing some of the practices that were going on inside that hospital, but the next revelation was quite explosive.

Asked if the mother asked to see her child, would she be given the child?

'Well, she wouldn't ask the nursing staff, that's for sure,' she responded.

Who would she ask?

The 'adoption children' were kept in a different ward, and the mothers were seen by a different section of the hospital. Thinking back, it was no wonder I couldn't see a baby that could possibly be mine: he was hidden in a different part of the hospital.

The social workers would go and see them and speak with them; she emphasised that it was separate from the nurses' work. She confirmed that the nurses had no part in deciding whether or not the baby should be taken to the mother.

The department consent-taker was called up next. She was a short, dark-haired woman with sharp features. Funny thing—I had a Scottish friend whose name was the same as hers, and they looked very similar. She, too, had a very definite way of thinking of things and was very judgmental of those she thought were not up to her standards.

Sitting nervously in the witness box, she gave her name and address, and confirmed that she had been previously employed by the Department of Children's Services and had worked for the department from about 1965. As an ex-nurse, she used to work in the labour wards in other hospitals. She had also undertaken training in obstetrics at the Crown Street Women's Hospital in Sydney. That shocked me!

Crown Street was one of the most notorious hospitals engaged in unlawful adoption practices and the prime focus of the New South Wales parliamentary inquiry into unlawful adoption practices. This woman was taught by professionals how to get adoption consent— that appeared to be the case based on the evidence given at the NSW parliamentary inquiry!

It became blatantly obvious that these government departments employed women mostly unmarried, without children, and women with a midwifery experience in the background. The majority of them would not have had any empathy for young mothers who found themselves in a very vulnerable situation.

I came to this realisation after witnessing the evidence of many mothers who had been dealt with by similar workers from the same department.

She was supposedly employed as a childcare worker in the department. God knows exactly what that meant.

When asked where the babies were kept after birth, she replied that if they were to be for adoption, there was no specific nursery that they went to—they were dotted around each ward that had a nursery attached to it.

And where were the mothers kept?

Most likely with the mothers that didn't have babies. They were to be placed with the stillbirth mothers, other adoption mothers, or maybe the mothers of small premmies that were ill—anywhere they didn't have nursing mothers around to upset them.

The state asked about the babies where the mother hadn't given any indication before birth that the babies would be adopted out.

They would go to the normal ward. The mother and her baby would be there, the baby was her responsibility, and they were both in the care of the hospital.

The babies for adoption, whose responsibility or say-so was it to visiting or having contact with her baby?

She replied, 'Well, that would be at the discretion of the sister in charge of the ward in whose nursery the baby was placed. She would say whether she or how often she could visit the baby because it would be upsetting to visitors and what have you if she was hanging around distressed all the time.'

My mind was screaming, *Liar, liar, liar! We just heard from the nurse who testified that it was your role to decide if we could see our babies or not!*

She admitted that until the consent was signed, the baby was still the mother's. In that case, why was I not allowed to see my baby?

I looked around the room, watching the responses of the other mothers, whose shocked faces were horrified that this woman could sit there so casually and tell the story from her side, while young mothers like myself had no idea of what was happening to us.

The state asked, 'Did you have your own method of proceeding with getting an adoption consent?'

'Yes, more or less. I would talk to her and explain the process of adoption. I would show her the form. I'd explain each item on the form, explained to her what it all meant, the rights of revocation, the thirty days after she had signed it in which she could change her mind, and I explained, I felt, in full detail as to what it really meant.

'I would spend between thirty to forty-five minutes; it would depend on her state, her mental state. Some of them would be very upset, and you would have to spend longer with them.'

One of her 'victims' was in court; I could hear her whisper under her breath, about me, 'Liar, liar; it's all lies.'

She went into great detail to explain how she thought it was only fair that mothers would be made aware of the difficulties they had if they decided to keep their child, reiterating that there were no financial benefits in those days for a mother.

She had known my consent-taker for about thirty years and had no hesitation in saying that she was a very kind, caring, and considerate lady, and she wouldn't know how to be domineering.

If that was the case, why was it that my memory of her over forty years was of the threat and coercion she used to swindle my child off me?

She went on to describe her as a quiet, caring lady who was a missionary with the local flying doctor. She also had a very, very, strong deep, religious conviction and was very much involved with the Presbyterian Church, and altogether was a very good, honest, reliable person.

Yes, I thought to myself, *just like all the other religious zealots who broke the law hand over fist, as revealed in the New South Wales parliamentary inquiry.*

It was now Keith Williams turn to examine her. He asked her if she was aware of stilboestrol. She answered that it was used for mothers who were not breastfeeding their babies—that included the babies for adoption. He quizzed her on whose decision it was to administer the drug. She replied it was the doctor.

He asked, 'So, the doctor would have made a note of the decision to adopt the baby?'

She agreed and stated that the doctor would also talk to the patient and ask if she decided on that.

This was news to me. I never saw a doctor the whole time I was in there, except for the birth.

We knew there weren't many consent-takers in the department, and this was confirmed when the worker admitted that there were only four of them that did this kind of work.

He asked if she went on her own to take consents.

Yes. And she further agreed that nobody else was present when she took them.

When asked why, her response was that there was no need for anyone else to be there.

Keith asked several questions about the *Report of Investigation* and where it was kept. She agreed that it was kept at the hospital. He showed her mine.

He asked, 'When you went to the hospital, did you sit down and speak with whoever had completed the report of investigation to get some background information?'

'Well, sometimes, perhaps—perhaps not, some other times. I really can't specifically recall who I spoke to on each occasion I went.' She was fumbling to answer the obvious question.

He then asked her if she was ever given a form with a question mark regarding whether or not the baby was for adoption and if they ever came in.

'Occasionally. I see this one has one,' she replied.

'Would that have signified to you that the mother hadn't made up her mind?'

She agreed, 'Absolutely, yes.'

He grilled her on whether it was inappropriate to approach mothers and attempt to persuade them to adopt out their baby. He asked if the mothers had placed any trust in her. After all, they were trusting her with their newborn. She was the person who was taking their child from them and giving them to strangers.

Her response was she didn't see why they would trust her: she was a stranger, after all, and they were a 'bit stressed' with the situation.

'A bit stressed' was an understatement!

I could hardly contain my anger listening to this woman: cold, calculating, and indifferent to the suffering of young mothers about to lose their babies, like me. Women like her sat in judgement over us and sentenced us to a life of grief and loss. My contempt for her as a human being tested my conviction that good could always overcome evil.

More questions, in terms of her approach, he asked, 'Did it make any difference to your approach whether the mother was under twenty-one?'

'No,' was her response.

'So, if a mother was aged fifteen, you took the same approach as one aged twenty-six?'

'Oh no, not a big age difference like that. I'd expect a fifteen-year-old to be somewhat more immature than a twenty-six-year-old would be.'

Yes, an easier target that could be kept in an institution like me, I thought, *locked up and the key thrown away.* Of course she would take into account the maturity of the mother.

She was asked whether a fifteen-year-old could understand the process of adoption. Her response was that she would explain once or twice, or how many times seemed necessary, and asked if they understood it. She could only accept the fact that if they said yes, they did understand.

So in terms of mothers who were in the care and control of the Director of Children's Services, was that a relevant factor that she took into account when taking the consent?

Her response: 'Well, you'd have to give it some thought. If she was in care and control, then once again, it's in the director's too-hard basket.'

He asked what she meant by 'the director's too-hard basket'.

'Well, the director of the department, he determines what will happen to them, not the childcare officer, and that would be a difficult decision to make. That's what I mean by the too-hard basket.'

I could hardly think; her words rang through my mind. My life—and my son's life—was tossed into the fucking 'too-hard basket' by fucking strangers—how can anyone respond to that? I could have bit my tongue off, I was so angry!

Anyone could see after repeated interrogation she was breaking down under the stress, being asked to explain how she and her cohorts operated.

She had finally let the cat out of the bag on the tactics they used to treat young mothers, and we were there to hear it.

The final question of whether a young unmarried mother had rights, being under the age of majority—at that time twenty-one— put a nail in the coffin.

Had the department taken any steps to have a parent, family member, or some other independent person at the signing of the consent?

Her response was, 'No.'

She came down off the witness stand and sat next to the adoption privacy woman.

The gallery witnessed the truth that could have only been exposed under oath about what happened to us. It was there for all of us to hear.

I was hoping that Tim could understand what had just gone down and that our lives had been decided by people like these.

A muttering loud enough to hear from the other side of the courtroom, 'those women were nothing but bags of trash anyway, and they deserved to lose their baby.' We all heard those words—it was evident even up to that day exactly what they thought of us and still do.

Divine intervention would have the adoptive mother falling on her face as she went to lunch.

Another department consent-taker was next.

She was one of the four. They could have been compared to the 'Four Horsemen of the Apocalypse'—that thought had crossed my mind, by the misery that had been left in their wake destroying lives like mine from the few minutes they came into it.

Another of her victims was in the room and was desperate to hear what she had to say.

She explained in great detail how she took an adoption consent. It was almost as though she was reading it from a manual. Unlike New South Wales, which had a welfare manual, none could be found in Queensland, so obviously, she was prepared for the questioning.

She said that she emphasised the part on the form so that the mother understood the nature of signing the consent. She would cross out the part that gives the information of the father as also not required and get the mother to initial as it wasn't a legitimate child who was being adopted.

Supposedly, she gave the mothers a card with her phone number so if they changed their mind, they could call her later. This was all new to me, it wasn't my experience, but maybe she had a different tactic.

As for the thirty-day revocation period that was to be explained to the mother before they took her consent, well, that was one of the biggest lies to get a mother to sign the consent form, as most adoptions were approved and signed off by the director within a few days after the form was signed, and not a month later.

My son was given to his adopters eight days after I signed the consent—liars, all of them!

The state asked her, 'Did you forbid mothers to see their child?'

'No, no, no, never.'

She confirmed the babies that were up for adoption were always on a different floor in the hospital from where the mother was.

She said she would take the mother down to the nursery where the baby was, and would speak to whoever was in charge. The baby's cot was then wheeled over to the glass door of the nursery, allowing the mother to look at the child through the door.

Did she remember if any mothers ever asked her if they could hold the child?

No, she didn't remember anyone ever asking her to do that.

He then asked her about her training and whether she knew my consent-taker. She confirmed they had been friends for several years while they worked together, and she was still there in 1984. Although never seeing her taking an adoption consent, she portrayed her as a woman of integrity, and a religious one at that.

It was now Keith Williams turn to cross-examine her.

He asked her, 'What notes have you got in front of you?'

'Just notes I've been jotting down trying to think of what I might be asked today, and a copy of the adoption consent form.'

She agreed that there were only four consent-takers within the department and, as she was a childcare officer and a justice of the peace, considered that her qualifications were sufficient to make her capable of taking an adoption consent.

I thought to myself as she spoke, *Really? I'm a justice of the peace too; that did not give me the authority to take the consent of a minor.*

She fumbled around in the questioning, unsure exactly of what she was working as during her time in the department. She also didn't know in her training at the department if there were any procedures that she should have followed in taking consents.

Keith asked the question again, 'When you went to take consent, did you do that by yourself?'

'Yes.'

'There was never anyone else present?'

'No, no.'

She confirmed that even if the mother was a minor, it didn't make any difference to the procedure that she followed. She recalled that she had never taken consent from a mother who was the subject of an order for care and control under the director. She also went to see the baby first. Mr Williams asked why.

'It was just to tell the mother if the baby was well or not and if the paediatrician said the baby was medically fit for adoption.'

She would then make a few notes about the mother and physical characteristics, her occupation, and education and confirmed that she would only approach the mothers whose forms were marked baby for adoption.

She was then excused.

Another exhausting day listening to these people. I was feeling quite sick at the thought of it. It was liberating, however, to have them dragged into court decades later to hear them justifying their actions that ruined so many lives and kept it hidden from public view.

I had nothing but contempt for these people who made their living on the misery of people like me.

The mental health expert was the first of the state's witnesses on the fourth day, giving the judge a copy of his curriculum vitae, affirming the professor's qualifications and experience. They went through the psychiatric reports that he had prepared, a similar exercise to that of Dr Peters, only from the state's perspective. I won't go into great detail—it mainly focused on whether or not I had the symptoms of post-traumatic stress disorder.

It was Keith's turn to examine him. He confirmed from the professor that I had told him all the significant events in my life, so nothing was withheld. The doctor agreed that medication would probably alleviate my symptoms after two years.

Keith questioned him on his diagnosis and his disagreement with Dr Peters' diagnosis of post-traumatic stress disorder: 'You are both talking about anxiety disorders, aren't you?'

'Yes.'

And this is where a prominent psychiatrist dismissed the bond between mother and child when he was asked, 'Is it that you don't consider the removal of one's baby a significantly traumatic event as to satisfy the criteria of PTSD?'

He replied, 'I don't.'

So as a vulnerable seventeen-year-old, my false imprisonment, incarceration, sixteen-hour labour, and the torture suffered, with the outcome being the theft of my child from the labour ward, would not cause me a trauma?

Not in his opinion.

A collective gasp from those listening to the words that fell from his lips caught him covering his mouth with his hands as if to try to take back exactly what he just said. Watching those in the room, especially the mothers, they appeared shocked that he could say that the forceful taking of the baby at birth from its mother was not a trauma.

The next witness was employed as a childcare officer by the department in 1967 and knew all the consent-takers. He was also the Director of Children's Services in the 1980s.

Questions to Mr Prince were focused on his knowledge of the consent-takers. He confirmed that most of them were qualified nurses and rejected the suggestion that mine was in a position to threaten me with Karrala House. That was about the extent of his evidence for the state.

Keith Williams asked him if he had ever attended her when she took an adoption consent from a mother. His response was, again, no, and agreed that consent-takers usually took adoption consents on their own, sometimes accompanied by a trainee.

'Was there a surplus of babies for adoption in 1967 and in the late 1960s?' Keith asked.

His response was, 'I wouldn't like to use the term "surplus", sir, in respect to babies.'

He could not comment on whether there were more babies than adoption applications, so Keith read from the annual Director's reports to the Queensland Parliament, showing him the year 1966.

'You will see there is a report of how many applications were received?'

'Yes.'

'What's the number?'

'1,401.'

'And the adoption orders issued.'

'1,398.'

Pointing out a deficiency of three, asking him, 'The difference is three, between those two numbers?'

Keith Williams then referred to other years where the adoption applications exceeded the number of adoption orders issued.

This confirmed there was a demand for our newborns and the department made sure that almost every order was filled. Even those babies who were rejected at birth later found homes with the disabled or pensioners on low incomes. Every adopter and child was put into a category numbered from one to twenty. Tim came in at category ten, listed as "tradespeople", the first being judges and lawyers, etc.

Finally, that was it: the last witness!

Both sides gave quite lengthy closing arguments, and at the end of the fourth day, the matter was referred to the judge for his consideration, saying, 'I will consider the matter in an attempt to deliver a judgment before Christmas.'

The next six weeks leading up to Christmas were spent trying to distract me from the outcome. Des and I busied ourselves buying presents for the grandchildren and Mandy.

A few days before Christmas, Grant called us to let us know that the judgment would be handed down on the twenty-second of December.

Kate arranged to go up to Brisbane and booked a hotel room for us so they could finish the documentary—that was to be the outcome of the court case.

I couldn't sleep and spent most of the night tossing and turning. It was about five o'clock in the morning when I got up and sat on the balcony watching the grey dawn rise to a burst of brilliant sunshine.

Arriving at the courthouse again, there was a barrage of media there, all awaiting the outcome of this precedent case.

Again, the observer's area was filled with mothers, adoptees, and the media. The judge, endowed with his wig and gown, sat down in his chair, his bearded face looking down over his glasses at the papers in front of him, and finally spoke.

I was determined to look at him directly in the face. I wanted him to see my face and remember it. His judgment was going to affect every child that was under the guardianship of the state, every mother who had given birth in a hospital and had her child taken without her consent, and every Aboriginal child that had been abused in care—this was not just all about me.

On 22 December 2004 came the final blow of the axe.

'In the matter of Arthur versus the state of Queensland, the matter is dismissed. You will read my reasons in my judgment.'

The state's barrister rose to his feet and said, 'Your Honour, we will not be pursuing costs.'

With that, we left the courtroom and were guided to a room out the back. As my lawyers sat around the table, Des and I watched Grant read the resulting judgment, his face greying at every word he was reading and just highlighting some of the reasons why my case had failed. Grant couldn't go on, saying it was too difficult to read it and for me to hear it, saying the judgment ruled out any future action if taken to the High Court.

We left the court to face the media waiting outside, asking me questions about the judgment, my response saying there was no justice for people like me and that the state could abuse its wards and get away with it.

The whole day, and getting through it, was a nightmare.

Tim was there as well to see the outcome. I was wretched and felt that I hadn't been able to prove to him that he was stolen from me. I had failed him, and the law had failed me.

Yes, the state had succeeded in portraying me as a tortured wreck, abused by many before I came into the so-called care of the state, the judgment failing to expose the many criminals and the crimes that were involved in my abuse under its care.

The judgment also failed to recognise that I should not have even been incarcerated in the first place. Given that I was above the age of consent and under the *Commonwealth Marriage Act,* I could get married and have consensual sex at sixteen.

Well, after all, I wanted a judgment and I got it! One thing was obvious: that I was going to pay for the sins of my fathers. I'd been told early on in the piece that I'd be punished for bringing too many 'heads of damage' into the court and how right that prediction was.

Des read the judgment when we got home and said it was the most depressing piece of work he had ever read, hiding it from me so I would never have to see it again.

On our return from Brisbane the day before Christmas, Des was attempting to buy me a present. I didn't want anything to remind me of what had transpired that year, but he chose a gold bracelet, and with all of its memories, I could not bring myself to wear it.

How I managed to get over the next few days, I don't know. It all seemed to be a blur to me. I finally understood how Dian felt after she'd lost three of her appeals—she had taken more of a battering than me.

Des was very concerned about my state of mind and asked Linda to come down and spend some time with me and try to distract me from what I was going through. My brain couldn't associate itself with my body. I felt that all my skin was ripped away from me, and I was a walking skeleton. Was there any point in going on?

Every day I thought of doing away with myself, and many options were explored, but my conscience dragged up every excuse for not going through with it. How could I punish those who love me by taking an easy option?

If I thought things were bad then, it got even worse when my daughter announced a month later that she was moving to New Zealand with her children and her partner. On 26 January—Australia Day—they all boarded a plane and left.

My only memories of that day, and the next three months, were of continual crying. I don't know what hurt more—the denial of justice or the leaving of my family.

Chapter 10

I didn't want to face the world again, but *Woman's Day* wanted to do a story with me, so I agreed. To tell my story about the loss of my court case to a national women's magazine was an opportunity to have a thoughtful response in hindsight to the judgment. I was quite glad that I did, as the magazine gave an accurate account of why I had taken the court case.[25]

Des had an extension built on the back of the house—a sunroom with lots of windows so I could look out into the backyard and see the trees and watch the birds feed off them. It was to be my private world where I could escape to. That idea didn't last very long; outside influences were dragging me back into the real world again.

Dian and I spent quite a bit of time together doing a post-mortem over our respective court cases, and as we had both failed on the issue of negligence, she thought that she would try another tack and focus on the criminal side of what had happened to her.

She decided, after looking at quite a lot of cases, that she would again bring an action against the state of New South Wales for fraud and fraudulent concealment. She poured over every conceivable judgment in fraud cases to establish her argument. Day after day, she would ring me several times and we would discuss every new aspect she felt related to fraud. As there was no statute of limitation on a criminal act, she felt that this would be the best way to bring her case back into court again.

[25] 'My baby was taken away'. Woman's Day. 7 February 2005

I was more or less trying to put things behind me and trying to distract myself in anyway I could, and Dian's relentless focus on the criminal element of her son's adoption brought out a lot of unresolved issues with me and how the state got away with the crimes they committed.

We had rented a council office out at Bonnyrigg Plaza a couple of years previously to use for Origins and I would go out of there on the days that the Aboriginal playgroup met there. It was lovely to see the little Aboriginal children coming into play there, and I got quite familiar with the group's coordinator. She was a lovely, gentle, soft-spoken person, and it was quite easy for me to speak to her about the pain of my grandchildren being in another country.

I hadn't had much contact with Aboriginal people before, but did strike up a very good friendship with my friend Rita, who I met in the first unit at university. We spent quite a bit of time studying with each other and, as she was an Aboriginal health officer at the Children's Hospital, she allowed me to go along to some of the events that she held at the hospital.

Rita was very generous with her time and helped me with some of the cultural issues of Aboriginal people. She was mad keen on Elvis, and I was privileged to see her emotional response years later when we walked through the gates at Graceland.

She would sit by the 'king's' gravesite every day for the three days we stayed there—a lifetime dream for her that came true. She also advised me on how to speak with respect for Aboriginal culture and to understand the structure of Indigenous communities.

Origins was still doing a lot of work with ex-state wards, and I was contacted by a woman who had been in a state-run girls' home at Parramatta. She also was a mother who had lost two children to adoption. Parramatta Girls Home[26] was opening its doors for a reunion of its ex-residents and there had been a lot of articles in the media about the place.

---

[26] http://www.parragirls.org.au/parramatta-girls-home.php

The forgotten Australians inquiry had exposed a lot of very negative attention about what had gone on there, and the tales of brutality and abuse subjected on the girls there horrified the general public. It also had a place of torture in the basement the girls used to call the 'dungeon'.

Denise had asked me to go along with her as the thought of going on her own terrified her. I took a video camera along with me because she asked me if I'd take a record of the place so that she could keep and show her family.

The home in parts looked quite attractive. Its white cottage style buildings built over a hundred years before gave it a non-threatening appearance. The covered walkway that led to the main part of the institution with its dormitories looked quite different from Holy Cross, where I'd been kept, less archaic and more like a boarding school. Obviously, if its walls could speak, it could only tell of the misery and trauma it was hiding.

We went down to the basement of the main building, past the showers and into the dark alcove that was known as the dungeon— this was the place where the girls told of being sexually abused by some of the male workers there.

Denise described how she was abused there and started to suffer an anxiety attack, so we needed to get out of there quick smart. Strolling along the walkway, there was a group of Aboriginal women sitting in a circle talking to one another. I asked if they minded me taking some video footage of them and they agreed so long as they got a copy of it.

I took down all their names and addresses and promised them a video of the whole footage that I'd taken and gave them my name and phone number for them to contact me. Keeping my promise, I did, of course, send them all a videotape of the open day, never expecting to hear from them again.

Two thousand and five was pretty busy—that year, there were several senate inquiries that we gave evidence at, one being a mental health inquiry, our submission based on the mental health effects of what we had suffered by losing our children.[27]

At every opportunity, we called for our own senate enquiry. Nearly all of our pleas fell on deaf ears. There was also a parliamentary inquiry into intercountry adoption to speak about the effects of adoption.[28]

It had been nearly a year since the Parramatta Girls Home reunion and well past my recollection of what exactly happened on that day. The phone rang and after confirming my name, a husky voice responded, 'Hello, Lillian, this is Aunty Val.'

I was confused. Who the hell was Aunty Val?

'You remember me—you took a video of me and my sister, Rita, at Parramatta Girls Home, and you sent me the video?'

Although I couldn't visualise her, I remembered the Aboriginal ladies and was quite surprised to be contacted by one of them.

Lillian. Funny she should call me that—I put it down to the fact that she must have forgotten my name. Anyway, she went on to say, 'I've got some work for you. I want you to come and see me.'

After taking down her address details, I arranged to go and visit her. I was quite surprised to see a short, dark-haired Aboriginal lady with a very authoritarian voice and the personality of a true activist. Not backward in coming forward, Auntie Val was not scared to speak her mind.

She introduced herself as Val Linow, but her original name was Wenberg.

Aunty Val was one of the Stolen Generation. Along with her four sisters and two brothers, she and her sisters had been raised at

[27] https://www.aph.gov.au/Parliamentary_Business/Committees/Senate/woc/wocjanjun05/c13

[28] https://www.aph.gov.au/parliamentary_business/committees/house_of_representatives_committees?url=fhs/./adoption/prelims.htm

Cootamundra Girls' Home. I later learned that she was the first Aboriginal woman to receive compensation for abuse whilst in the care of the state. Aunty Val wanted to set up a support group around the Liverpool area and she needed someone to help her with it. We already had the Origins office at Bonnyrigg, so that was a useful start to help the group get going.

Bonnyrigg was in the centre of a fairly large Aboriginal population. Many of them came from around the Redfern area and moved into housing developments that were built about twenty years prior. It was quite a picturesque area with a lot of open spaces and duplex villas. The shopping centre was the heart of the community.

Aunt called the group the South-West Sydney Stolen Generation Support Group, and we set up a website and started to introduce ourselves through the Aboriginal community, attending and speaking at various events that were happening in the local area.

As there was a lot of focus on the Stolen Generations at the time, Aunty Val was asked to go to a lot of places to speak up about her experiences and the need for a national apology. I went with her most of the time for support and we became great friends.

I was meeting a lot of Aboriginal people and getting to know their stories. Most were sad, tragic, and, at times, could be humorous.

They were such resilient people that I thought to myself, *I was probably more fortunate than they were—at least I didn't have the racial discrimination that they suffered, along with the lifetime of abuse that went along with it.*

I felt less sorry for myself after seeing the trauma of years of separation from families that the Stolen Generation had inflicted on them, and found myself being able to relate to them more than most non-Aboriginal people.

Gone to a Good Home[29] was finally finished late in the year and was due to go to air the following year. That was a relief—it had been two years in the making and I was looking forward to seeing the end result.

Aunt Val and I had been kicking around with each other for a couple of years, and we had the opportunity to advise on production on a play called *The Fence* that was being shown for Arts Week and proved to be a very popular event showcasing Aboriginal artists.

Origins was fortunate to receive funding from the federal government that year to hold a Sorry Day event at Mount Annan, Botanical Gardens. I was asked to speak at the launching of the Stolen Generations memorial that was being planned for the garden and although I spoke as a non-Aboriginal person, I felt that I should not be speaking on behalf of their experiences.

We had the same good fortune the following year with funding. That year saw a hundred children and adults attend the event.

The beautiful sandstone monument of an Aboriginal mother, father and children was carved and stood proud and tall; a little pond at the base of the statue meant that water could be poured over the statue signifying the tears of the Stolen Generations.

The garden was a fitting place to remember the sorrows of Aboriginal people.

It was 2006, and that period was seeing a lot of Aboriginal people speaking up and demanding the wages stolen from them by past individuals, so a parliamentary inquiry was formed to investigate the states and organisations that exploited them for their labour.

A submission was sent to the 'Stolen Wages' inquiry, giving evidence on the young girls at Holy Cross that were forced to work

---

[29] https://www.screenaustralia.gov.au/the-screen-guide/t/gone-to-a-good-home-2005/21216/

for no wages—young wards that were not a visible part of the inquiry at that stage.[30]

So many times, I would look at the group photo taken at Holy Cross with three of my Aboriginal friends and Sister Theo and wonder where they were and if they had survived. The photo was taken a couple of days before I left. The nuns gave me my suitcase containing the belongings I had brought to the home. My little Brownie camera was still there in my case, with a few exposures left on the film, and I was fortunate to be able to take photos of girls whose fates were never known.

I sent the photos to the *National Indigenous Times* to see if I could find them again, but no luck.

In response to the forgotten Australians inquiry, the federal government had called together a conference of over 200 organisations and state representatives from all over the country for a two-day conference.

It was at that conference that the recommendation was made to ally with ex-care leavers to speak on behalf of forgotten Australians. There was to be one representative from each state. Origins recruited Pamella Vernon as our delegate on the alliance to represent us and New South Wales. There was a lot of opposition to us being a part of the alliance, as we were seen as an organisation that only dealt with adoption.

It didn't occur to the objectors that many young mothers were also ex-state wards and their children who were lost to adoption, every one of them became state wards until their adoption order went through. Many babies deemed unfit for adoption languished in orphanages in homes, forgotten and unwanted from birth.

---

[30] https://www.aph.gov.au/parliamentary_business/committees/senate/legal_ and_constitutional_affairs/completed_inquiries/2004-07/stolen_wages/ submissions/sublist

An estimated 150,000 babies were placed under the guardian-ship of the state, plus mothers like myself.

So, people affected by adoption contributed heavily to the quoted half million children that were included in the scope of the inquiry. Those impacted by adoption had a right to have a say as well, and we took it.

Shedding the Light on Adoption. Yes, we were certainly shedding light on adoption, and this was the name given to the conference in 2006 in New York, sponsored by Origins USA.

The conference was a great success, and it was also a wonderful opportunity to finally meet our American and Canadian coordi-nators Karen and Valerie, and the wonderful psychotherapist and author Joe Soll—an adoptee who has been supporting adoptees and mothers for decades.

Listening to the stories of American mothers and adoptees, I couldn't help feeling angry that our illegal coercion tactics were also used on young women across the ocean in not only America and Canada but also Scotland and England.

Immediately on our return from America, Origins Victoria held our third national mental health conference in the Melbourne Town Hall. Elizabeth had fought hard to get the funding to present it, and once again, it proved to be an outstanding success.

Surely our hard work and our research somewhere along the line would be recognised and get us some funding to keep our organisa-tion going and growing, but time after time, our funding applications would be rejected.

We had to keep going on the memberships that were slowly drying up, forcing the committee to keep dipping into its own pocket if we were going to keep going.

Gone to a Good Home was shown in November 2006 on SBS National Television. I sat and watched it awestruck—this was about me, my story.[31]

The portrayal of me as a teenager and the images in the background looked exactly like the memories that flashed through my mind: the jail cell, the dormitory, and the verandah at the back of Holy Cross.

Flash, flash, flash. My mind was going in and out of the past and present—one second an observer, and one second a victim, still trapped in my nightmare.

The award-winning documentary certainly portrayed my reality and also the stories of other mothers. It was an outstanding success and travelled to places across the world, including India. The documentary was my compensation for a court case lost, and for justice.

Finally, Dian's court case against the state for fraud and fraudulent concealment had been given a date in the supreme court. She had spent the last couple of years, night and day, putting together an impressive folio of the state's unlawful practices.

It was just her and me who were going to present her case—two women passionate for justice who still lived to fight on. We wound our way around the supreme court, passing many of the empty courtrooms down into the bowels of one of the smaller courts at the back of the buildings.

The room was pretty sparse apart from the judge, the state's solicitors and the court recorder, it was just Dian and me.

For any other person without legal training, this would have been a daunting task: to take on a state government and accuse it of stealing her only child. For Dian Wellfare, this was not a challenge— it was war, and she declared it.

---

[31] https://www.screenaustralia.gov.au/the-screen-guide/t/gone-to-a-good-home-2005/21216/

She read out her complaint and presented her evidence, focusing on the fact that they knew the practice of taking a child from its mother without her consent was an unlawful act, admitted by adoption workers from the mid-1960s.

She took her place in the witness box and was questioned by the state's solicitors. For every question they asked her, she answered back, exposing the collusion of the state's hospital workers, social workers, doctors, and midwives—all employees of the New South Wales government.

It was obvious from what she was saying that she had thrown a grenade at the state that day. Whilst the legal people were trying to maintain a look of neutrality, the court clerk and the recorder looked up in horror.

I sat there watching her, probably feeling more nervous than she, but we were there on a mission, and this was going to be our last chance to make somebody or something accountable.

The matter lasted the full day with Dian giving her final address and bringing her case to its close. We were told to expect a judgment in a few weeks.

Leaving the court and going out into the busy streets of the city, we both felt that we were ready to collapse. Now we would have to go through the painful process of waiting.

A few weeks later, she received the judgment by courier. She was alone as she read the verdict to me. As with my court case, the same words jumped out from the page: *Matter dismissed.* They may as well have shot an arrow through her heart and finished her off there and then. I had no words to give her, but I knew exactly how she felt.

Her slow decline saw this courageous warrior retreat into the corner of her lounge room, guarded by her two faithful Tibetan terriers. Her world had become a very small place that she was unable to move out of. No amount of encouragement could bring back the fiery lioness that fought so hard for justice.

Dian was retreating from the world, and my involvement with the Stolen Generation was becoming more and more time-consuming, so much so that I was invited to attend an exclusive two-day conference at Picton. Aboriginal people had come from all over the country to discuss forming a national alliance to represent the Stolen Generations.

I was a bit out of my depth. I didn't know what I could contribute. It was a case of just sitting back and learning from what people were saying and what they wanted to achieve at the national level.

A few weeks later, a delegation met in Cairns to form the National Stolen Generations Alliance (NSGA).

The Alliance was to be founded on the principles of reconciliation where Aboriginal and non-Aboriginal people would work together.

There would be a committee that would be headed by two co-chairs, one Aboriginal and one non-Aboriginal. The Treasurer, secretary, and several other positions would make up the rest of the committee.

Each state had an Aboriginal and non-Aboriginal state delegate who reported back to the committee. Unbeknown to me, I was nominated as the non-Aboriginal delegate for New South Wales. Aunty Val excitedly told me of my new and unexpected position that I knew very little about and also what was expected from me.

Fortunately, we had the office and all the equipment, plus quite a large volume of media covering the 'Bringing them Home' report. At least that was a start for my new role.

It was quite a hectic time and, after much lobbying and public support, on 13 February 2008, the Rudd government gave a national apology to the Stolen Generations and the Aboriginal peoples of Australia.[32]

Aunty Val asked me to go to Canberra with her to support her through the emotional event.

---

[32] https://www.creativespirits.info/aboriginalculture/politics/stolen-generations/ sorry-apology-to-stolen-generations

It was an incredible experience to be surrounded by so many Aboriginal people. They came from every part of the country, their faces showing the expectation and the unknown outcomes from such a long-awaited admission that would acknowledge their pain, suffering, and loss.

I was in the Great Hall at Parliament House and listened to the collective weeping of the nation's children as they listened to the words that fell from the prime minister's lips.

Outside, hundreds sat on the gravel and grass just to be there and be part of such a historical event. They had a cup of tea or coffee or a bottle of water, and maybe a biscuit. No fanfare, no banquet— nothing to celebrate such a significant event.

The thing of most importance was a piece of paper they held in their hands, with the words of apology and hope for equality.

*

I was burnt-out. What does a girl do to get away from all the trauma of dealing with very difficult situations? My answer was to take up what my father taught us to do, and that was to sing, so I took up karaoke.

It was a great way of inspiring some confidence in myself to stand up and expose myself to being ridiculed—wonderful for public speaking! Three nights a week—the big one on a Saturday night—at Cabra-Vale Diggers Club gave me the much-needed escape to help me keep balanced in my head. I couldn't have been too bad, and after each song got a bit of applause. If I thought the world of politics was dirty, karaoke—and the antics used to get into the grand final every three months—saw people playing even more dirty games than the worst politicians.

Tony was the ringmaster, and every Saturday night was like a circus, where people vied and charmed their way into the grand final for the major prize of a thousand dollars.

No doubt about it, karaoke was a killer sport, and in its benign way, taught me a hell of a lot of things that people would do to grab the spoils and, of course, do it with a smile on their face!

It was the night before New Year's Eve when the phone rang about ten at night. I wondered who could be calling at that hour of the night. It was Dian.

'This is a nice surprise; it's a bit early to be wished Happy New Year's Eve,' I greeted her, wondering why she was calling so late, although it wasn't unusual.

'You'll never guess where I am!'

'Where are you?' I inquired.

'I'm in the hospital.'

'What the hell are you doing there?'

'I've got some good news and some bad news.'

'Tell me the bad news first.'

She obviously was in shock as she told me, 'I was robbed. I was fast asleep on the couch, and this beautiful smell woke me. It was the most beautiful perfume that I've ever smelt. Funny thing is, the dogs never barked.'

She told me how an intense sense of fear had grabbed her, and she raced over to the kitchen table where her purse had been sitting. Her mother had given her a large sum of money, and it was gone. She said that her chest began to tighten, and she felt like she was going to have a heart attack, so she rang for the ambulance and they took her off to the hospital.

After trying to console her for a while, I asked her what her good news was.

'I've been diagnosed with cancer,' she said as if it was secondary to what she had told me before. I didn't know how to take that news. Why did she think it was good news?

'What sort of cancer?'

'They think it's pancreatic cancer, but I won't know until they do some more tests. I have to wait a few more days until I find out for sure.' She sounded pretty hopeful that it was something that could be overcome and dealt with. I knew she wasn't well, but I certainly wasn't expecting that sort of news.

A few days later, she told me it had been confirmed: she had pancreatic cancer and had about three months to live. The committee knew we had to have direction on where Origins needed to go and fulfil any wishes that Dian wanted fulfilled. Gathering around her bed, Elizabeth, Linda, Wendy, and I listened to our leader's instructions on how we would continue to keep Origins going. We promised her that we would continue and that we would publish her book.

What about her son—was she going to tell him that she was dying?

We were quite prepared to let him know of Dian's condition, but she was adamant that he was not to be told. 'I don't want him to come to see me out of pity.'

Unbeknown to her, the committee talked about it and decided that if he found out later about her condition and was not given the chance to say goodbye, he would have to live with that for the rest of his life, probably causing him a lot of regret.

As I was the one who was in sporadic contact with him, I would be the one to let him know what was happening. He was away in Melbourne at the time and couldn't get back quick enough. A few days later, I received a call from Debbie, Dian's sister, that she had passed away.

It was a bleak, grey, miserable dawn when I drove into the city to say my goodbye. Debbie was sitting near the bed gazing at her beloved sister. It was 16 April 2008. My memory of that moment could never be erased—the cold grey dawn gave birth to a cold grey day.

The queen was dead. Her pale, lifeless face showed no pain, no grief, no worry, no joy.

Her tangled, damp, curly hair framing her face, unlike Queen Boadicea, whose flaming locks drove an army to war. She was at peace now. I could visualise her sitting in the corner of the ceiling, looking down on us, wondering what the hell 'it' or life was all about.

After sitting there for a couple of hours with her sister, we cut off some locks of her hair, kissed her cheek, and said goodbye.

Her funeral brought people from far and wide. Her coffin draped with the flags of her beloved organisation—the pink, yellow, and blue logos of Origins. The 'mother-heart' of it was gone, but her warriors remained.

Where to go, and what to do? It was obvious we only had one battle and that was to get a senate inquiry. That would be the legacy Dian would inspire.

The National Portrait Gallery in Canberra was opening an exhibition of *My Favourite Australian*[33] that spotlighted unsung heroes. It was a wonderful opportunity to put Dian up. She was our unsung hero.

The opening of the exhibition was attended by all the Canberra dignities up to the very highest, the prime minister.

The 'portrait' was a short video presentation of Dian's life and work. As one of twenty in her category, it toured the country, sending out her message, even though she was not with us.

*

Once again, the forgotten Australians and child migrants had another senate inquiry, this one to see what recommendations had transpired from the first senate inquiry.[34] The final report and responses were nothing less than expected from the Commonwealth

[33] https://www.portrait.gov.au/exhibitions/my-favourite-australian-2008
[34] https://www.aph.gov.au/Parliamentary_Business/Committees/Senate/ Community_Affairs/Completed_inquiries/2008-10/recs_lost_innocents_ forgotten_aust_rpts/report/index

Government, with most of the recommendations being passed off by the federal government to the states and territories as their responsibility.

On 9 June 2009, Professor Ian Jones made an apology on behalf of the Royal Brisbane Women's Hospital to a small support group. Although they (the hospital) had ample opportunity to give me one before or after a landmark court case, I still had not received one from either the state or the hospital.

I was disgusted that the very hospital where I, and many other mothers like myself had lost their newborns would give a limp apology to only a couple of women.

To further our cause, we set up an online petition for our inquiry and went about lobbying the media. I was asked to appear on *Mornings with Kerri-Anne*, where they gave me a twenty-minute interview. Once again, I took the opportunity to request an inquiry on national television.[35]

Not long after the handing down of the second report, I received a phone call from the Minister of Social Services' office. The committee of Origins was invited to Canberra for a meeting with her staff. We were not quite sure why we were being invited and went along mostly out of curiosity.

Elizabeth Edwards from Victoria, Linda Bryant from Queensland, our mental health researcher Wendy, and I met with three of the minister's policy advisers. At the meeting, we were asked all sorts of questions. The first one though was to do with what we wanted.

We had no hesitation in telling them that we wanted the same as the other groups: a senate inquiry. The day after the meeting, I had a phone call from one of the minister's advisers letting me know that there was to be a national apology to the forgotten Australians, including the child migrants.

---

[35] https://www.youtube.com/watch?v=dkxP1iEWN7Q

Startling was the fact that the federal government was prepared to include mothers who lost children to adoption. If we did accept the offer, no doubt there would be funding and support for Origins.

I was horrified and realised what the meeting was all about: they wanted to tack our issues onto the other two groups' apology. Hardly a word was spoken about our issues in the media, although there were crossover issues with the forgotten Australians. The child migrants were another story. The two groups would be resentful that ours, being a completely separate issue, was thrown into their hard-fought-for apology.

After all, we were still seen as those deadbeat women who willingly gave their children away to strangers. Their offer was firmly rejected. Our mothers deserved the same right as others to tell their stories, and it was not our right to take that away from them.

Apology day for the forgotten Australians and child migrants was a far cry from the Stolen Generation event, with flowers, music, and marquees with hot dinners and desserts on the lawn of Parliament House.

Once again, Prime Minister Kevin Rudd gave an emotional address to those who attended. It was indeed a day to remember. But there was no mention of compensation or redress given at the speech.

We even managed to have a meeting with Tony Abbott whilst in Canberra and put the notion to him of a senate inquiry, and as leader of the opposition, he agreed to support us. Things were starting to happen for us now that the forgotten Australians had their issues met. We were becoming too vocal to ignore.

By that time, Linda and her colleagues in Queensland managed to get the legislation changed to finally get rid of the objection to information that forbade mothers and adoptees to know the names of their birth family—a big win after nearly thirty years of lobbying. However, the objection to contact remained.

Our Origins America colleagues had also done us proud and held their second *Shedding the Light on Adoption* conference in one of the city's universities.

My son Tim accompanied us, despite the dire threats of his adoptive family that they would disown him if he did. Tim was intrigued with New York and the hustle and bustle and went out every night after the conference to mingle with the locals.

One of the biggest highlights of the conference was to meet the Pulitzer Prize winner, Edward Albee. He was also adopted and, in his presentation, told how some of his plays were based around his adoptive mother.

He learned he was adopted at the age of seven, and from that age on, 'the deal was off,' in his words. He said that he felt like he had been bought and sold and commented that he related more to his nanny than he did to his adoptive mother.

We spent a month over there and took in sites that included Niagara Falls, Washington, and many of the states where the civil war was fought.

The last couple of weeks were spent with my first cousin Flo and her husband, Dick. They lived in a beautiful Spanish-style house in Palmdale in the middle of the Mojave Desert.

As soon as we walked through the front door, a large, framed portrait of my grandmother Bridget, Grandfather John, and her brother Patrick greeted us. I immediately pointed to it and asked him if he remembered seeing it in some of the photos I had sent him and he said, yes, he did remember it.

'They are your grandparents, seen by you halfway around the world. These people share that with you. Flo is your second cousin.' I thought that would give him something to think about—his true identity and his truthful history. At point, seeing the distant look on his face, I thought it was all about my wishful thinking rather than his.

*

I was still heavily involved with the NSGA and, on my return, had quite a few projects going with them. One included a 'life's journey' project with a group of Aboriginal elders at a community health centre.

The project focused on creating a scrapbook of their lives, and they were asked to bring in photographs from as far back as they could remember, and we would put them together into a beautiful album.

As we sat together cutting and pasting the photographs and embellishing the pages, the elders would tell me the stories of the people that we were honouring. Lost children, lost families, and stories of removal were told with sad reflection, and each page was a memorial to be handed down to their family.

One of the greatest honours that I had been given was the privilege of being told of things so sad and personal, and the trust that was given to me to treat that with respect.

I had lost contact with most of my family about the time of my son's reunion, but had found another family with aunties, uncles, brothers, and sisters while travelling all over the country with the NSGA. We were like one big family, just like my own.

I became very close to Heather. She was like a sister to me. She was an Aboriginal girl who was removed from the Northern Territory and adopted and brought up in South Australia. Our personalities were quite similar, apart from her talent for art. She also loved to sing. It seemed that nearly everyone who had a traumatic life could put their feelings into song.

Martin was another adoptee taken to South Australia from the Northern Territory. What a lad he was—his big smile and glowing face was like looking at the sun: warm, open, and a joy to be around. He, too, had a beautiful singing voice and, on occasion, would have a singsong after a day's meeting. He was the type of lad that any mother would be truly proud of.

Jim was the Aboriginal co-chair. He was a tall, imposing figure and respectful, as were most of the Aboriginal people I met. He had a gentle but also firm and businesslike manner about him. He was always well-versed in meeting people in high places and knew the best ways to present the issues of the Stolen Generations.

I had been with the Alliance for a few years when I was voted as the non-Aboriginal co-chair. It was a great privilege to be in a position not only for myself but for Origins, who now had two representatives in organisations that sat at a national level in consultation with the federal government. In effect, we had a birds-eye view of what was going on both in funding and the segregating of the two issues.

A few months after the forgotten Australians apology, we were informed that the minister needed more information regarding our claims of unlawful adoption.

The Institute of Family Studies (AIFS) was to make a report on past forced adoption with Origins to provide the Institute with some of our many years of research.[36]

A small group formed as a result of the Queensland apologies and sought apologies from hospitals all over the country, calling themselves the Apology Alliance. The group was headed by one of our ex-committee members. That came as no surprise to us, as most of our mothers were pretty committed activists anyway.

They had a different agenda from ours and were seeking apologies whilst we were seeking accountability for the crimes committed against us. We could not understand how they could accept such menial redress for such a horrid act of the theft of their newborns. The report from the Institute came in after six months,[37] and after reading it, we soundly rejected it. As far as we were concerned, there was to be no 'watering down' of our issues and that was final.

[36] https://aifs.gov.au/publications/archived/77
[37] https://www.dss.gov.au/our-responsibilities/families-and-children/publica-tions-articles/impact-of-past-adoption-practices-summary-of-key-issues-from-australian-research

One evening, I was phoned up by one of the 'apologists' who proudly declared that they had lobbied Senator Rachael Siewert, a West Australian senator, to table a national apology in the senate. I was bloody furious—no one had a right to accept an apology on my behalf.

Dian must have been looking after us from above and along came another mother by the name of Beth, the latest recruit to our cause.

She was tall, slender, blonde, much younger than me, and a brilliant academic—just like Dian—who could peel away the layers of lies like an onion to reveal the truth. She was a person who would be taken seriously, and hopefully, one day, she would take over the leadership of Origins. Knowledgeable and concise to the letter, she knew how to convey our reasons to reject an apology without a senate inquiry with unquestionable accuracy.

It was her arguments for rejecting apologies that always saw Origins have the last say. West Australia was the first state to make an apology. They also acknowledged the illegal practices, and it was music to our ears. Finally, one of the states came clean!

After consulting with Rachael Siewert on the tabling of the national apology, we pleaded with her that if that motion failed that she would put a senate inquiry on the table. She agreed.

In June 2010, the motion in the Senate was voted down, so there was to be no national apology. We were over the moon, but the next part was going to be difficult, and we prayed that she would honour her word and put up the call for an inquiry.

True to her word, Rachael put the motion on the senate table. It sat there for a month until it was time to vote on it.

It was October, and I was travelling with the NSGA for its annual general meeting. We had it in a different state each time so that the Stolen Generations from that state could attend and see what its national body was doing. In the middle of the meeting, I got a call from the senator announcing that the motion for the inquiry was passed in the senate and the inquiry was on!

It was a great celebration that night with my Aboriginal family. This meant that now adopted Aboriginal children would have their say as well.

Now was the time for Origins to hold the whole of government, state and federal, to account.

Chapter 11

It was hell waiting to see the terms of reference that were going to be addressed in the inquiry. Other inquiries could have quite a lot of terms of reference, but ours only had two:

1. *The role, if any, of the Commonwealth Government, its policies and practices in contributing to forced adoptions.*
2. *The potential role of the Commonwealth in developing a national framework to assist states and territories in addressing the consequences for the mothers, their families, and children who were subject to forced adoption policies.*[38]

The gauntlet had been thrown down for us, Origins, to prove that the Commonwealth Government played a part in the forcible adoptions of our children. It was such a simple reference but looked like an impossible task for women who had little or very limited education.

From a legal perspective, the amount of evidence that would be needed surely would be enormous, and how to put it together to prove our claims would be another thing! As with every huge problem, sometimes there is a simple solution, and finding that solution is a matter of choice: we could do things the hard way, or

---

[38] https://www.aph.gov.au/Parliamentary_Business/Committees/Senate/
Community_Affairs/Completed_inquiries/2010-13/commcontribformerforced-
adoption/tor

we could do things the easy way and walk away from the situation and let them define their involvement.

Instead of trying to resolve the problems of the world or explore every avenue of law, I looked at my situation and thought about what a system of governments and institutions had done to me. I was a human being, I was born free, and no chains bound me when I came into the world. I was a citizen of the world and, as such, was entitled to be protected. There were laws and institutions to enact those laws, and they failed people like me.

I decided to open my submission with the following preamble:

I, Lily Josephine Arthur, am a citizen of the Commonwealth of Australia resident in New South Wales.

As a citizen of the Commonwealth of Australia, I have an inalienable right to protection under the Australian Constitution and the common law of this country.

As an Australian citizen, the Commonwealth affords me protection from the unlawful and harmful actions that threaten my right to life, liberty, and justice from those who would deny me these rights, within and without, the borders of Australia.

This preamble was the first thing to establish to the senate committee that regardless of my age, sex, religious beliefs, and anything else that made me a human being, I was entitled to be treated lawfully. From then on, we encouraged every mother, father, and adoptee to put the preamble on their submission, followed by their story.

Having established that we did have legal rights, we now had to find that the Commonwealth Government had played an active part in forced adoption. We knew that the Commonwealth Government had been putting together the framework for a national uniform adoption act from the early 1960s, and it was up to the states to make it relevant to their adoption legislation. But we had to find where the Commonwealth knew of the state's unlawful practices, and that was going to be very difficult.

I remembered reading in the Queensland director's reports to the Queensland Parliament that the state directors of children services met annually with Commonwealth Government representatives to discuss the welfare of children, and that also included prospective uniform adoption legislation.

The new adoption act was meant to provide uniformity in all states and territories and to strengthen the law to prevent practices detrimental to children. These meetings were also attended by representatives from New Zealand and New Guinea.

Having found that information, we went off to the National Archives in Canberra and got the minutes of some of those meetings. It was obvious that in the 1960s, the Commonwealth knew of some of the states' practices and failed to investigate the detrimental practices to mothers and their children by state authorities.

Our allegations in our first submission to the inquiry included that the Commonwealth:

1. *Failed to ensure that unmarried mothers knew of the financial benefits available to them from the Commonwealth government, such as Class B widow's pensions.*
2. *Also neglected to ensure that the financial benefits made available to mothers under the State Grants (Deserted Wives) Act to support their children were distributed in a non-discriminatory and visible manner.*
3. *Failed to adhere to International Human Rights obligations and its commitment to commencing with The Universal Declaration*

of Human Rights (signed 11/12/1948) and many other conventions of human rights it ratified since 1948.[39]

These and more were well-documented in our submission. Our message was loud and clear: that the Commonwealth oversaw the unlawful practices and breaches of the common law of the states of Australia and did nothing about it.

We had submitted sixteen submissions exposing the evolution of adoption in Australia, and the historical timelines that linked back to the 1940s of the federal government introducing overseas social workers into the social services departments following the war. These social workers eventually took control over who was suitable and who was not suitable to raise children.

Beth put together amazing timelines, dating back to the 1800s, of the history of child welfare in Australia. These were done from archival material she found on Trove: a website that had historical media articles.[40] She built a year-by-year account that could not be questioned for its authenticity.

Our committee was knocking its guts out for nearly two years, putting together the submissions. We had sent out over 1,000 flyers to our members announcing the senate inquiry and how to put together a submission.

About that time, it was announced that the Institute of Family Studies was given the task of putting together a full report on the effects of forced adoption. The study was meant to run parallel to the senate inquiry.

In its own words:

---

[39] https://www.aph.gov.au/Parliamentary_Business/Committees/Senate/Community_Affairs/Completed_inquiries/2010-13/commcontribformer-forcedadoption/submissions
[40] https://trove.nla.gov.au/

The key focus of the study is to improve knowledge about the extent and effects of past adoption practices and to strengthen the evidence available to governments to address the current needs of individuals affected by past adoption practices, including information, counselling, search and contact services, and other supports.

A lot was going on, not only putting together our submissions on behalf of Origins, but also our personal submissions. I gathered up every piece of paper documenting what had been done to me as a record of how I had been treated in my fight for justice, knowing full well it would be there hopefully for many years

During the inquiry, Origins provided public venues, including a Facebook® group, where people could connect to discuss the issues and support one another to submit to the inquiry. Thinking we were doing a useful thing, all we did was open a can of worms. Several individuals, due to their emotional problems and ignorance of the trauma associated with forced adoption, made comments that inflamed others. This resulted in conflict between mothers and adoptees, and some of them declared war on us, no doubt due to the pressure of the inquiry. Some responded in a way that provoked or hurt others who were unaware of the extent of the trauma of some group members.

For example, the adoption language being used by newcomers inflamed mothers who believed that their children were kidnapped from them, and that also did not help the situation.

We were still an unfunded organisation, run by volunteers, with very limited resources, and thought we would be a support to submitters. We were wrong.

Not only were we dealing with the trauma of those genuinely looking for answers, but we also became the focus of a group that was determined to undermine and destroy us. It was mostly instigated by adoptees in Australia but also from as far away as Canada. If we were paranoid, we might think they were trying to derail the senate inquiry.

This bullying and intimidation took a heavy toll on the committee, and we eventually closed nearly all public contact with the outside world. As the senate submissions rolled in, it became abundantly clear there were very few submissions from members of other organisations.

After doing a little bit of investigating reading their newsletters, we found out that triad groups that serviced mothers, adoptees, and adoptive parents had not informed their members of the senate inquiry. However, they had informed them of the Institute's survey.

On the twenty-ninth of February 2012, the senate committee chaired by Rachel Siewert, with deputy chair Clair Moore, handed down its report.

We all held our breath in the gallery of Parliament House, waiting to hear if our claims were going to be acknowledged.

Rachel said,

The evidence tells the accounts of mothers and fathers who were pressured into giving up their babies by their families, institu-tions—both state and territory and private institutions—social workers, doctors, nurses and those who they rightly expected to help them. There was evidence of consent not properly taken. There was evidence of coercion. All the pressure, practices and policies have had lifelong impacts on mothers, fathers, adoptees and family members.[41]

To the adoptees, I would like to say: we know that your mothers did not abandon you. You were not thrown away. This is what we have received evidence about as well: the babies who were adopted, who are now adults, felt that they had been abandoned. Mothers have told us that they do not want their now-adult children to feel that. I quote from the report:

---

[41] https://rachel-siewert.greensmps.org.au/articles/rachels-speech-forced-adoptions

'The committee received evidence from hundreds of women
who gave birth in hospitals and other institutions between the
late 1950s and the 1970s.'[42]

'Overwhelmingly, these women alleged that laws were
broken or that there was unethical behaviour on the part of staff
in those institutions. The common failings included applying
pressure to women to sign consents, seeking consent earlier than
permitted by the legislation, failing to get a consent signature
or obtaining it by fraudulent means, and denial of reasonable
requests, particularly for a mother to have access to her child.'[43]

A scream was heard across the gallery and mothers burst into tears, hugging and clapping that the committee finally brought them acknowledgment.

Following recommendation one of the report, Origins was asked to endorse a representative to sit on a committee set up by the federal government to give input into a national framework. We thought that Beth would be a champion for our cause and nominated her to be our representative from the Origins committee. We found out later that she had been heavily involved with the group of abusive adoptees that had given us a hard time throughout the whole of the senate hearings. After a turbulent time with her and her cohorts, we withdrew her right to speak on our behalf, which left Origins with no representation at a national level to have input into the follow on from the inquiry.

The AIFS report was going to influence a national framework that would decide who to fund, a national apology, and service provision. It was important to Origins that we were finally given the resources for our self-empowerment. God knows we had earned it.

---

[42] https://rachel-siewert.greensmps.org.au/articles/rachels-speech-forced-adoptions
[43] https://rachel-siewert.greensmps.org.au/articles/rachels-speech-forced-adoptions

We were later distressed to find out through some accidental leaking of emails that some of the participants of the committee had prior knowledge of the outcomes of the AIFS study that 'supported their cause.'

We were not sure just exactly what their 'cause' was but strongly suspected that it would be the funding of triad adoption support organisations—the very ones that did not inform their members of the inquiry.

Origins had applied for funding through that committee to enable us to provide support whilst the framework and the national apology was being organised.

We were shocked to see on Facebook that a woman in Canada who was not part of Origins was spreading details of our application on the web. The only place that information could be known was from the committee that was sworn to confidentiality.

We were furious that our confidential information found its way across the other side of the world and wrote a detailed report to the committee chair.

*

The second AIFS report was released in August 2012.[44] It was quite an impressive document, but I was shocked and horrified when I realised that section ten was specific to a service provider's survey.

That survey was launched in November 2011. The first phase included sending regular emails to a wide audience of professionals, interest groups, and so forth, informing them of the online survey.

According to the report, we, as service providers, should have been on the service providers list. This was not so—Origins never received any emails or contact from the AIFS to alert us of the survey.

---

[44] https://aifs.gov.au/publications/past-adoption-experiences

As an incorporated association and with DGR (donor gifts recipients) charity status, it was obvious we were not deemed to be a service provider by the AIFS and did not receive the same recognition as other adoption support organisations. The truth was revealed in its final report when it failed to mention us as a service provider.

The published report goes on to say there was limited response to the first phase, so a targeted follow-up was taken whereby they physically phoned organisations to inform them to fill in the survey.

At no time was Origins approached to do this, yet we were approached by the AIFS to send out their individual surveys. Despite having asked for 1,000 surveys, we received only 200 specifically for mothers. That amount did not cover the over-1,000 contacts we had on our database that included not only mothers but fathers and adoptees.

Not only did we put together the information to post it out, but the survey was also on our website and Facebook, reaching an indeterminate number of people.

We were never contacted about the separate survey for service providers and that blew our chances for any funding out of the water, despite us being used not only for our research and promotion of the survey but also for our membership contacts and support.

It is hard to describe the feelings of being sabotaged, used, and exploited for the gain of those professionals who fed off our misery. Later, I met one of the authors at the release of the report and approached him about it. He asked if I was happy with it.

I replied, 'Yes, ninety percent of it was fine, but ten percent was not good.'

He asked what I was unhappy about, and I drew to his attention the fact that we had not even been mentioned as a service provider despite eighteen years of supporting people separated by adoption.

I had no problem in telling him that he had ruined our chances of ever getting funding.

He made all the excuses under the sun, but it was clear that the report gave precedence and acknowledgment to the already funded adoption organisations. In that climate of hostility, it was every man or organisation for themselves. We were seen as a 'radical' group, so it was easy to cast us mothers as 'nutters'—as we were described by the head of one of the other support organisations.

We may have been non-compliant with the mindset of supposed professionals, yet we were the ones who held the largest research library of mental health information on adoption effects and its history. Anyone who wanted information, or to make use of our membership database, came to us.

The national apology had been announced and another committee had been established to write up the actual document. It was contributed to by people from all over the country. Needless to say, the majority of the committee was formed from the participants of the former 'framework committee'.

Of course, we had our say on what it should look like, given that we were the organisation that had long called for a senate inquiry.

The date set for the apology was 21 March 2013, two days after my birthday. A bit ironic—maybe that was to be my birthday present?

Origins applied for and got funding of $25,000 to get as many of our members to attend. We managed to get around 120 with travel and accommodation—far more than any of the other organisations. Surely this would prove to the government that we could effectively handle funding.

I received an email with the final draft of the apology and was asked if it was going to be accepted. I agreed that Origins would not object to it if it stayed unchanged, as the wording stated that the practices were 'illegal'.

The world press was watching this historic event. My grandson Tyson, who was travelling in Germany, was surprised to see me on the news over there. It was such an event no other country had done anything like it.

The big day arrived and the Great Hall in Parliament House was once again filled with the throng of those looking for healing and redemption. Yes, we were those 'fallen women', those not fit enough to raise our own children, scorned by society as an aberration to human nature as women who could willingly give up our newborns to strangers.

This apology was going to cleanse us of our 'sins' of immorality.

SBS Television was filming our arrival. They held us back until everyone was seated. There was a certain air of pomp and ceremony. One could also most envisage the classical tune of 'The Arrival of the Queen of Sheba' as Steve and my family and I went into the hall and sat on the back seats.

It was wonderful to see all my adopted Aboriginal 'family' there. They were as emotional as everyone who was touched by the pain of their separation and loss of their culture. Julia Gillard looked radiant in her white suit trimmed with black, a true vision of a woman of dignity and integrity. She was magnificent in her delivery of the apology. One could see that she meant every word she said. Her words of sincere regret set a lot of mothers free from the shame and guilt they carried for a lifetime. This was her finest moment.

Looking over at Steve and seeing his tears, I knew that I could never take her validation for the fathers away from him. There was a sense of great relief following the emotional event and everyone lined up to place flowers on the stage, a symbol of remembrance to lost ones.

A copy of the apology was handed to everyone as they walked out the door of the hall into the front entrance of the House. Marquees lined the front of Parliament House once again, and the tables were filled with another wonderful feast to celebrate the event; mothers and adoptees were telling their stories to the press.

God only knows what was going on in the backrooms of the parliament that day, but an unexpected announcement saw Julia Gillard dealing with a leadership challenge straight after delivering a national apology from the Australian government. Mothers, adoptees, and their families celebrated their big day, and while some of the affected were in the middle of telling the press their gratitude for the apology, the press heard word from the House that there was to be a leadership spill.

They raced up the hill to get the news, leaving mothers and adoptees in the middle of reliving their trauma and the emotion of the apology, some fainting on the grass.

Julia's historic moment in time had been sabotaged while the world watched the spectacle.

So, this significant day was turned into a circus watched by so many, a historic day awaited for decades and forgotten in a minute.

I should have had an idea that this event was going to be turned into a debacle, not knowing that it would leave our prime minister fighting for her political career and the country in confusion.

Later, finding out that our historic day was held on Harmony Day made me even more cynical. Harmony Day is an Australian Government program that centres on the message that 'Everyone belongs,' reinforcing the importance of inclusiveness to all Australians. Since 1999, thousands of Harmony Day events have been staged in childcare centres, schools, community groups, churches, businesses, and federal, state, and local government agencies across Australia. We certainly had never felt included in society; in fact, we were reviled and ostracised.

So, we had to share our significant day with an event that gets funding and is celebrated by everyone who felt 'left out'—what a joke!

Why hadn't the committee that arranged the apology considered the impact this had on our day of acknowledgment?

Of course, my predictions regarding funding came true. Funding for services was given to Relationships Australia, its description being:

> *Relationships Australia is a leading provider of relationship support services for individuals, families, and communities. We aim to support all people in Australia to achieve positive and respectful relationships.*
>
> *We are a community-based, not-for-profit Australian organisation with no religious affiliations. Our services are for all members of the community, regardless of religious belief, age, gender, sexual orientation, lifestyle choice, cultural background or economic circumstances.*
>
> *We offer services around the country that include counselling, family dispute resolution (mediation) and a range of family and community support and education programs.*[45]

Of course, Relationships Australia knew nothing of our issues, so I had to give them a workshop to inform them what they were dealing with. At a meeting of fifteen social workers, I asked how many of them had read the senate inquiry report and was answered just one. Relationships Australia won the funding for services in every state except Queensland. It was remarkable that the only state-funded adoption triad support organisation got federal funding, despite never having supported our allegations that adoptions were illegal.

Of course, we felt angry. Had our work been in vain just to give the benefits and credit to those who did not support us?

The final straw came when we were approached to become involved in the exhibition for forced adoption that was allocated to the National Archives. Again, we were approached by the archivists for our research and access to our memberships to gain stories

---

[45] https://relationships.org.au/

and input into the exhibition. It took a lot of persuading for me to be convinced that we would get a decent acknowledgment for our contribution of involvement. The archivist spent a great deal of time with me and our committee in other states, pleading with them to the point of tears to become involved. My granddaughters and I spent three days putting together the information to send out through our membership, informing them of the upcoming exhibition—a final opportunity to tell their story or make donations of mementos of their babies.

The *Without Consent* exhibition opened in Canberra in March 2015.

Fulfilling my expectations once again, and despite the amount of effort Origins went to, there was little to no acknowledgement of the Origins contribution. Flags, banners, and all sorts of memorabilia from other organisations graced the walls. Words could not express my disgust at once again being used to promote an agenda of supposedly keeping us involved, only to shut us out in the long run.

I made my feelings heard when I told the archivist that once again, our trust in the senate inquiry recommendations of the efforts to enable our healing was once again sabotaged.

She stood there and told me it was not her decision on the final result of the exhibition, again shrugging off responsibility to a faceless decision-maker.

The last acknowledgment of the gravity of our experience was again watered down to a tale of misery and woe, and the point of exposing the crimes against us was lost.

We should remember that the giving of apologies or exhibitions will never excuse the dodging of laws that should have protected us from the crimes that were committed against us.

Mothers are waking up all over the world. Origins Canada, following the lead of Origins Australia, also obtained a senate inquiry and report.

Although the Canadian government has acknowledged that forced adoption took place in Canada and that lives were irrevocably damaged, they have yet to address the recommendations of the report, which also include an apology, mental health support, and a call for religious and social service institutions to review their role in these practices.

There had been unspeakable crimes committed against us that remained unresolved. It will be carried down through many generations. The future will always carry the remnants of what Dr Rickarby described as the 'single mother's holocaust'.

The Final Word: Lily's Lament

E very miserable night, from the time I lost my firstborn, I spent
thinking that somewhere there would be a time in my life
where I would feel the golden warmth of the sun on my face and the
possibility of peace.

As I lay for hours on end each night wondering what life had in
store for me, the only thing that kept me going was that life must get
better and the hope that one day, I may once again feel what it's like
to be happy.

Was I destined to be un-human, just a lackey for others to scorn
and use?

I had been born with a fighting spirit, the daughter of warriors,
and yet I allowed my kind heart and spirit to be battered by
others ... why?

The judge in my court case described me as being 'embittered'. I
was a child of the state seeking justice and denied it—why wouldn't
I be embittered?

A social worker at Crown Street Hospital that I had only seen
for a few minutes described me as being 'retarded, and possibly on
drugs.' Her comments on my next visit changed that to a description
of me being 'not too bright,' and had my daughter ear-marked
for adoption.

Labels on my records denigrating me to justify the theft of a
second child.

People unknown to me made decisions that altered my life and gave my identity as a mother to a stranger. My child's ancestry was gone, and my firstborn, who was to carry on my family name and lineage, was given over to strangers.

Did my destiny hold for me to be the vessel for others to use and discard?

Was my fight for truth and justice an insult to society and the law that was supposed to protect the vulnerable?

I have questioned myself countless times over why I have lived to fight battles that could never be won and suffered the futility of defeat.

Viewed as a deserting 'no-hoper' to justify my abuse in my court case, it was never acknowledged that my father, who fought for a country that was not his own for nine years, put his life on the line for the freedom of others. He lived with the fact that each day may have been his last, finally dying without his children to mourn him, an end that no human being should suffer.

It took me many years to get over my childish anger for a man that dared to dream and to take his family far away to a strange land for a better life. He was, after all, just flesh and bones, just like me, who also dreamed of a place and time where we could be happy.

Wisdom comes when one is coming to the end of a long journey.

I now understand my father's despair and the madness that came upon him at the end of his life. Somehow it is better to have no memory in the end than to take one's troubles to the grave.

I have often said to those who tell me of their problems an experience I had when I was at my lowest. Seeking peace and out of despair, I went back to church to find comfort. An old priest was giving a sermon on getting one's house in order, and if that could not happen, then it would crumble and fall.

He gently said, 'You have to lose your life to find it.'

Those words have stayed in my mind ever since, and yes, I had to lose my life as I knew it to find that place in the golden sun. My struggle to redeem my son was to find my peace when I let him go. He told me at our reunion that he was going to look for me when both of his adopters had died. It would have meant another twenty year's wait for me. Little did I know that my wait for my son to reconnect with me would take a lifetime and beyond.

Although I expected 'her' (his adoptive mother's) death, it did come out of the blue, posted on Facebook by my son's wife, Mylene.

My first reaction was that a load had finally lifted from my back. No longer was I carrying the burden of a stranger who had lived my life, taking every future generation from me. I was going to get something that reminded me of my freedom, just like the Waterford cross I bought when the nuns paid me some compensation, a physical testament of getting rid of some of my torment.

However, I found nothing that could represent her absence in my life.

His sad comments mourning the loss of his 'Mum' on Facebook reminded me that she would never be truly gone. She would always be there, in the names given to my son, his wife, and my grandchildren to carry on for infinity.

As I write the final words of a book that has taken me over thirty years to write, I come to an extraordinary event that has an ironic twist for me.

Having had an Irish background and being held in a Magdalene Laundry and my newborn taken from me in a state-run hospital, I witnessed on 14 January 2021 the apology by the Irish Government to the mothers and children that were abused and separated by adoption in Irish mother and baby homes. Is this to be another apology with great promises that could never replace the justice so many seek?

To date, no one has ever asked how or why, from the 1950s to the 1970s, a generation of millions of young women across the world supposedly 'willingly' gave up their newborns to strangers en-masse.

In 2021, a quarter of a million mothers in Scotland and England are demanding an apology for the taking of their newborns.[46]

The wheel is going full circle, and mothers across the world are following the lead of the Australian mothers still demanding justice.

In December 2020, Origins requested a meeting with the Queensland Minister of Child Safety through a departmental adviser. The intended meeting was to discuss what response the Queensland government was going to do in respect of the recommendations of the Senate report.

After waiting eight months for a reply, I received an email from the adviser, stating:

> *The Minister will not be meeting with post-adoption stake-holders in regards to the issues that were raised last December, shortly after she came into office.*
>
> *We have been advised by the Minister's Office that she will consult/liaise with relevant groups or individuals on matters of concern should a very specific need arise or in response to legislation/policy changes etc.*

So, once again, our issues are in the 'too hard basket', not only for me but also for the 50,000 Queensland mothers and their taken children.

*

It has now been eight years since the national apology for forced adoption and the stories of the mothers are like dust that settles and gets swept away. It reminds me of the ashes of those who are still waiting for justice, hoping for justice that will never come. Our babies

---

[46] https://www.scotsman.com/news/opinion/columnists/why-forced-adoption-needs-an-apology-dr-gary-clapton-3315550?fbclid=IwAR3rSD39vD-KhHMOWgwTUzlhuE_Ur5zC8p6guFsoRTE6SKpksi6I-aOqssl4

and countless generations are still stolen from us, and the rivers of tears that have been spent can never be dried.

As a mother who has been stripped of her only function in life— to bring forth another human being—only to have it snatched away from her as she lay defenceless and tied down like a wild animal, yes, I have an inalienable right to be 'embittered and angry' as described in my court case judgment.

A place where the sun shines on my face overlooks a hill and lots of trees on the Gold Coast—a place where I can reflect and hopefully find the peace I have longed for.

Steve comes and visits me from time to time and we relive our experience. He is not the handsome young man I fell in love with, but his cheerful and optimistic personality still shines as youthful as it did when we were young.

People have often asked me why I have not moved on in my life and ask why I am not grateful that my son had a wonderful life.

My response is, does one have to be thankful to those who have taken care of a kidnapped child, and I ask, would they have moved on from the time that child was taken? I don't think so.

Like every other mother in my situation, I still bear the scars on my body left by my stolen child, a constant reminder that he lived within me. The scars will stay forever, as will the memory of 'Shane'—a child who never existed beyond his first eight days.

I was brutally informed by a departmental worker, 'He is a dead identity.'

Yes, I took up the poison chalice and drank from it. It has cost me dearly, emotionally, and financially, and lost relationships, and yes, I have learned many things from many people, mostly far worse-off than myself.

And if anything positive came out of my journey, it would be that God (if there is one) has given me the blessing of my husband

Des, my daughter Amanda and her children, and my son and his wife and children.

My utmost gratitude goes to the Aboriginal people I have met in my journey and those I haven't; they are the family that I chose and have taught me humility and patience, tolerance, and most of all, love.

Printed in the USA
CPSIA information can be obtained
at www.ICGtesting.com
LVHW020048290124
770081LV00002BA/199